SKIING
SAFETY II

International Series on Sport Sciences

Series Editors: **Richard C. Nelson and Chauncey A. Morehouse**

The principal focus of this series is on reference works primarily from international congress and symposium proceedings. These should be of particular interest to researchers, clinicians, students, physical educators, and coaches involved in the growing field of sport science. The Series Editors are Professors Richard C. Nelson and Chauncey A. Morehouse of The Pennsylvania State University. The series includes the eight major divisions of sport science: biomechanics, history, medicine, pedagogy, philosophy, physiology, psychology, and sociology.

Each volume in the series is published in English but is written by authors of several countries. The series, therefore, is truly international in scope and because many of the authors normally publish their work in languages other than English, the series volumes are a resource for information often difficult if not impossible to obtain elsewhere. Organizers of international congresses in the sport sciences desiring detailed information concerning the use of this series for publication and distribution of official proceedings are requested to contact the Series Editors. Manuscripts prepared by several authors from various countries consisting of information of international interest will also be considered for publication.

The *International Series on Sport Sciences* serves not only as a valuable source of authoritative up-to-date information but also helps to foster better understanding among sports scientists on an international level. It provides an effective medium through which researchers, teachers, and coaches may develop better communications with individuals in countries throughout the world who have similar professional interests.

International Series on Sport Sciences, Volume 5

SKIING
SAFETY II

Selected publications and reports given at the Second International
Conference on Ski Trauma and Skiing Safety, Granada, Spain

Edited by: **José M. Figueras, M.D.**
Department of Research and Prevention of Ski Accidents
Hospital Cruz Roja
Barcelona, Spain
Series Editors: **Richard C. Nelson, Ph.D.**
and
Chauncey A. Morehouse, Ph.D.
The Pennsylvania State University

University Park Press
Baltimore

UNIVERSITY PARK PRESS
International Publishers in Science and Medicine
233 East Redwood Street
Baltimore, Maryland 21202

Typeset by Action Comp Co., Inc.
Manufactured in the United States of America by
The Maple Press Company

Selected publications and reports given at the Second International Conference
on Ski Trauma and Skiing Safety, held in April 1977, Granada, Spain.

Library of Congress Cataloging in Publication Data

International Conference on Ski Trauma and Skiing
Safety, 2d, Granada, Spain, 1977.
Skiing safety II.

(International series on sport sciences; v. 5)
Bibliography: p.

1. Skis and skiing—Accidents and injuries—Con-
gresses. 2. Skis and skiing—Safety measures—Con-
gresses. 3. Skis and skiing—Physiological aspects—
Congresses. I. Figueras, José M. II. Title.
III. Series. [DNLM: 1. Athletic injuries—Prevention
and control—Congresses. 2. Skiing—Congresses.
W3 IN192H 2d 1976s/QT260 I54 1976s]
RD97.I57   617'.1027   78-4096
ISBN 0-8391-1209-2

Contents

ETIOLOGY AND EPIDEMIOLOGY OF SKI INJURIES

BIOMECHANICAL FACTORS

PHYSIOLOGICAL FACTORS

Contributors

A. **Aigner,** Department of Sport and Kreislaufmedizin, General Hospital, Innsbruck, Austria

C. **Algara,** Department of Research and Prevention of Ski Accidents, Hospital Cruz Roja, Barcelona 25, Spain

E. **Asang,** Technische Universität München, Bealgrad Strasse 5, 8000 München 40, West Germany

B. **Balkfors,** Department of Orthopaedic Surgery, University of Lund, Malmö General Hospital, Malmö, Sweden

W. **Bandi,** Chirurgische Abteilung, Regionalspital, CH-3800 Interlaken, Switzerland

G. **Blümel,** Institute for Experimental Surgery, Technical University Medical School, Ismaninger Strasse 22, D-8000 Munchen 22, West Germany

G. **Bonivento,** Orthopaedic and Traumatology Clinic, University of Trieste, Trieste, Italy

F. **Borrás,** Hospital Cruz Roja, Barcelona 13, Spain

E. **Campailla,** Professor of Orthopaedics, Orthopaedic Clinic, University of Parma, Parma, Italy

K. **Danielsson,** National Swedish Board for Consumer Policies, S-162 10 Vällingby, Sweden

N. **Dekleva,** Department of Traumatology, Clinical Hospital, Zemun, Yugoslavia

J. **Dekleva-Djordjevic,** Department of Physiatry, Clinical Hospital, Zemun, Yugoslavia

J. M. **de Moragas,** Department of Dermatology, Hospital de la Santa Cruz y San Pablo, Autonomous University, Barcelona, Spain

P. **Edwards,** Department of Orthopaedic Surgery, University of Lund, Malmö General Hospital, Malmö, Sweden

A. **Ericksson,** Department of Physiology III, Karolinska Institutet, Stockholm, Sweden

E. **Eriksson,** Section of Trauma, Department of Surgery, Karolinska Hospital, S-104 01 Stockholm, Sweden

C. F. **Ettlinger,** Vermont Ski Safety Equipment Co., Inc., Underhill, Vermont 05489, USA

J. M. **Figueras,** Department of Research and Prevention of Ski Accidents, Hospital Cruz Roja, Barcelona 25, Spain

G. **Flora,** Chirurgische Universitätklinik, Anichstrasse 35, A-6020 Innsbruck, Austria

J. G. **Garrick,** Affiliated Bone & Joint Surgeons, 33 East Virginia— Suite 101, Phoenix, Arizona 85004, USA

B. **Glenne,** Department of Civil Engineering, University of Utah, Salt Lake City, Utah 84112, USA

W. **Gördes,** Orthopädische Universitätklinik, Harlachingerstrasse 51, 8000 München 90, West Germany

C.-M. Grimm, Ländstrasse 5, 8 München 22, West Germany

W. Hauser, Technische Universität München, Balgradstrasse 5, D-8000 München 40, West Germany

J. Heiss, Rechts der Isar, Surgical Clinic, Technical University Medical School, Ismaninger Strasse 22, D-8000 München 80, West Germany

T. Hewell, Rechts der Isar, Surgical Clinic, Technical University Medical School, Ismaninger Strasse 22, D-8000 München 80, West Germany

T. K. Hight, Department of Mechanical Engineering, Stanford University, Stanford, California 94305, USA

F. G. Höflin, Oberalpstrasse 41, CH 4054 Basel, Switzerland

M. L. Hull, Department of Mechanical Engineering, University of California, Davis, California 95616, USA

D. Hummel, Krevzeckstrasse 25, 8132 Tutzing, West Germany

M. Jäger, Orthopädische Universitätklinik, Harlachingerstrasse 51, D-8000 München 90, West Germany

R. J. Johnson, Orthopaedics Department, College of Medicine, University of Vermont, Burlington, Vermont 05401, USA

J. Karlsson, Laboratory for Human Performance, National Defense Research Institute, Stockholm, Sweden

W. Kossyk, Orthopädische Universitätklinik, Harlachingerstrasse 51, D-8000 München 90, West Germany

H. Krexa, Ländstrasse 5, 8 München 22, West Germany

P. Krueger, Rechts der Isar, Surgical Clinic, Technical University Medical School, Ismaninger Strasse 22, D-8000 München 80, West Germany

M. K. Lamont, Private Bag, Auckland 6, New Zealand

J. Lange, Rechts der Isar, Surgical Clinic, Technical University Medical School, Ismaninger Strasse 22, D-8000 München 80, West Germany

M. Llobet, Department of Research and Prevention of Ski Accidents, Hospital Cruz Roja, Barcelona 25, Spain

D. Loo, Massachusetts Institute of Technology, Room 37-207, Cambridge, Massachusetts 02139, USA

P. C. Maurer, Rechts der Isar, Surgical Clinic, Technical University Medical School, Ismaninger Strasse 22, D-8000 München 80, West Germany

J. A. Merino, Department of Research and Prevention of Ski Accidents, Hospital Cruz Roja Barcelona 25, Spain

M. A. Molino, Baquerira-Beret, S.A. Salardu (Lerida), Spain

W. Mong, Rechts der Isar, Surgical Clinic, Technical University Medical School, Ismaninger Strasse 22, D-8000 München 80, West Germany

C. D. Mote, Jr., Department of Mechanical Engineering, University of California, Berkeley, California 94720, USA

D. A. Nagel, Division of Orthopaedic Surgery, Stanford University School of Medicine, Stanford, California 94305, USA

G. K. Neureuther, Bavarian Mountain Rescue Hospital, D-8100 Garmisch-Partenkirchen, West Germany

P. Nilsson, Department of Ear, Nose, and Throat Diseases, Malmö General Hospital, Malmö, Sweden

U. Noelpp, University Clinic, 3000 Bern, Switzerland

E. Nygaard, August Krogh Institute,

University of Copenhagen, Copenhagen, Denmark

S. Pechlaner, Chirurgische Universitätklinik, Anichstrasse 35, A-6020 Innsbruck, Austria

W. Phleps, Chirurgische Universitätklinik, Anichstrasse 35, A-6020 Innsbruck, Austria

G. Philadelphy, Chirurgische Universitätklinik, Anichstrasse 35, A-6020 Innsbruck, Austria

R. L. Piziali, Department of Mechanical Engineering, Stanford University, Stanford, California 94305, USA

M. H. Pope, Orthopaedics Department, College of Medicine, University of Vermont, Burlington, Vermont 05401, USA

F. Prats, Hospital Cruz Roja, Barcelona 13, Spain

G. W. Prokscha, Rechts der Isar, Surgical Clinic, Technical University Medical School, Ismaninger Strasse 22, D-8000 München 80, West Germany

E. Raas, Department of Sport and Kreislaufmedizin, General Hospital, Innsbruck, Austria

J. Rastegar, Department of Mechanical Engineering, Stanford University, Stanford, California 94305, USA

R. K. Requa, Division of Sports Medicine, Department of Orthopaedic Surgery, University of Washington, GB-15, Seattle, Washington 98195, USA

M. Spielberger, Chirurgische Universitätklinik, Anichstrasse 35, A-6020 Innsbruck, Austria

J. J. Stanley, 1181 Burke Road, Kew 3101, Victoria, Australia

P. Tesch, Laboratory for Human Performance, National Defense Research Institute, Stockholm, Sweden

J. Tresserra, Hospital Cruz Roja, Barcelona 13, Spain

E. Ulmrich, Deutscher Skiverband, Elizabethstrasse 25, 8 München 40, West Germany

M. Ungethüm, Orthopädische Universitätklinik, Harlachingerstrasse 51, D-8000 München 90, West Germany

W. van der Linden, Östersunds Sjukhus, S83101, Östersund 1, Sweden

A. Vogel, Chirurgische Abteilung, Regionalspital, CH-3800 Interlaken, Switzerland

B. vonAllmen, 2871 South 2870 East, Salt Lake City, Utah 84109, USA

D. Vujnovic, Department of Physiatry, Clinical Hospital, Zemun, Yugoslavia

T. Wagner, Rechts der Isar, Surgical Clinic, Technical University Medical School, Ismaninger Strasse 22, D-8000 München 80, West Germany

G. Weisman, Orthopaedics Department, College of Medicine, University of Vermont, Burlington, Vermont 05401, USA

N. E. Westlin, Department of Orthopaedic Surgery, University of Lund, Malmö General Hospital, Malmö, Sweden

B. F. White, Orthopaedics Department, College of Medicine, University of Vermont, Burlington, Vermont 05401, USA

P. E. Wiklund, Department of Orthopaedic Surgery, University of Lund, Malmö General Hospital, Malmö, Sweden

G. Wittman, Technischer Uberwachungsverein Bayern, Kaiserstrasse 14, D-8000 München 40, West Germany

L. R. Young, Massachusetts Institute of Technology, Room 37-207, Cambridge, Massachusetts 02139, USA

Conference Organization

Site
> Hotel Melia
> Sierra Nevada
> Granada, Spain

Main Theme
> The program emphasized selected aspects of skiing trauma and safety,
> including etiology and epidemiology of ski injuries, safety measures and
> treatment modalities, and biomechanical and physiological characteristics.

Organizing Committee

Co-Chairmen:
> S. A. R. Alfonso de Barbon, President
> Spanish Ski Federation
> Juan F. Marcos-Becerro, M.D., President
> Spanish Federation of Sports Medicine

Secretary General:
> José M. Figueras, M.D.

Committee Members:
> Manual Peregrina
> Sr. D. Enrique Berruezo
> Sr. D. Martin Gomez Vazquez
> Jorge Manrique
> José L. Navarro
> Tomas Gomez-Quesada
> Enrique Mendoza
> Angel Sanz

Assistant Secretaries:
> José A. Merino, M.D.
> Carlos Algara, M.D.
> Miquel Llobet, M.D.
> Jordi Duixans
> Srta. Joana Mateu

Scientific Committee:
> Ernst Asang, West Germany
> Katarina Danielsson, Sweden
> Ejnar Eriksson, Sweden
> José M. Figueras, Spain
> Gerhard Flora, Austria
> Victor H. Frankel, USA
> Michael Lamont, New Zealand

FOUNDING OF THE
INTERNATIONAL SOCIETY FOR SKIING SAFETY

Plans for the founding of an International Society for Skiing Safety were initiated at the First Conference in Riksgränsen, Sweden, in June, 1974. Under the leadership of Ejnar Eriksson, Chairman of the Interim Board, detailed Articles of Association were formulated. These were presented to the participants of the Second International Conference in Granada, Spain, and accepted with minor modification during the Founding Meeting on Thursday, April 21, 1977. Five members were elected to the Board of Directors at this meeting: Ernst Asang, West Germany; Katarina Danielsson, Sweden; Ejnar Eriksson, Sweden; José Figueras, Spain; and Dan Mote, USA.

Following the Founding Meeting, the Board of Directors met to elect officers and additional members. These were: Gerhard Flora, Austria; Victor Frankel, USA; Michael Lamont, New Zealand; Gerhard Wittman, West Germany; and Laurence Young, USA. Ejnar Eriksson was elected President; Dan Mote, Vice President; Katarina Danielsson, Secretary; and Gerhard Flora, Treasurer.

The purpose of the International Society for Skiing Safety is to stimulate interest at the international level in the prevention of skiing injuries. This is accomplished through the individual efforts of the members and the collective efforts of the Society. Scientific exchange is provided through the international conferences and regional meetings sponsored by the Society. It is anticipated that the ISSS will become an influential body in all areas of skiing safety and trauma prevention. The Founding of this Society at the time of the Second International Conference marks an event of historical significance to the sport of skiing.

Preface

The Second International Conference on Ski Trauma and Skiing Safety, which was held in Sierra Nevada near the beautiful city of Granada in the southern part of Spain, represented a continuation of the task started in Riksgransen, Sweden, in 1974. At that time, a large group of people, including physicians, engineers, ski teachers, and managers of winter resorts, gathered to discuss the epidemiology and biomechanics of ski injuries with emphasis upon their prevention. The main problems encountered in the treatment of ski injuries were discussed, while only certain aspects of physical therapy and rehabilitation programs for injured skiers were analyzed. As a means of extending this area of interest, I accepted the responsibility for organizing the Second International Conference in Granada. It has been my contention for many years that the norm for treating ski injuries does not constitute a separate orthopaedic speciality but is rather a part of the general field of modern orthopaedic surgery. Most orthopaedic surgeons are trained to treat any ski injury, but many are unfamiliar with their etiology and are consequently uninformed about their prevention and control. It was anticipated that the program of the Second International Conference would include important information concerning this problem.

All of us who worked on the organization of the Second International Conference on Ski Trauma and Skiing Safety are very proud of the quality of the scientific contributions and the fact that over 200 people, representing 17 countries, attended.

The organizing committee wishes to thank the following for their help in ensuring the success of the Second International Conference in Granada: The Spanish National Delegation of Physical Education and Sports; the Spanish Ski Federation and the Spanish Sports Medicine Federation, who provided generous support; the University of Granada Medical School; the Municipal Government and Deputation of Granada, who contributed greatly to the scientific and social activities; the Directors of the Winter Station of Sierra Nevada (EETURSA and CIT of Granada) and the Andalusian Ski Federation for their hospitality during our stay in Granada; and the Department of Investigation and Prevention of Ski Accidents of the Red Cross Hospital of Barcelona, who contributed the secretarial support. Finally we wish to acknowledge the direct sponsorship of the International Ski Federation and the International Sport Medicine Federation.

A special event that occurred during the Conference was the official founding of the International Society of Skiing Safety (ISSS). This society has as its primary goal a reduction in the number and severity of injuries that occur in skiing. One of the activities designed for this purpose is the sponsorship of future conferences. The Third International Conference on Ski Safety is scheduled to be held in New Zealand in 1979. It is hoped that this Conference will continue in the tradition established by the first two.

J. M. Figueras

SKIING
SAFETY II

Etiology and Epidemiology of Ski Injuries

Ultraviolet Light Injury in Winter Sports

J. M. de Moragas

Not all ski injuries are related to the physical activity of the skier. Frost-bite is an example of a lesion that may be sustained by expert and novice skiers alike, and by ski lift attendants as well. Sunburn is even more common: on clear days in March and April, it affects all people who are in the sun unprotected longer than 30 minutes, or for even shorter periods at higher altitudes or lower latitudes. This paper furnishes basic know-ledge of ultraviolet light injuries occurring in winter sports to illustrate the rationale of protective measures to avoid unnecessary skin and eye injuries.

EXPOSURE AND ITS EFFECTS

The sun gives off light in a continuous spectrum at the rate of 2 cal/sq cm/min at the outer atmosphere of the earth. Two-thirds of this will reach the earth's surface, but all light under 290 nm wavelength will be blocked out when it filters through the oxygen and ozone contained in the atmosphere's upper layers. Of the sun's radiation, 50% is in the visible range, 40% in the infrared range, and only 10% in the ultra-violet range. The amount of atmosphere the sunlight must go through is the major factor in how much light reaches the earth. Other interrelated factors are latitude, season, time of day, and elevation above sea level.

An all-important factor in the determination of sky light is the re-flection characteristics of the ground surface. Freshly fallen snow reflects 85% of the ultraviolet light (UVL), grass only 2.5%. Every increase in the water, ozone, or aerosol content of the atmosphere will decrease the amount of surface irradiation. A light cloud cover or cloud patches can scatter UVL, causing it to come from different directions and simul-taneously decreasing the infrared irradiation. Depending on its ability

1

to produce erythema on human skin, the UVL reaching the earth is divided into UV-A (400–315 nm wavelength), which does not produce erythema, and UV-B, which does, with a minimal threshold erythema at 279 of 2.5×10^4 micro watt seconds. The amount of energy to produce erythema (minimal erythema dose—MED) may show fivefold variations in normal Caucasians. The erythema appears 4 hours after exposure and does not disappear in less than 24 hours. This amount of UV-B energy is equivalent to 20 minutes' exposure with a high noon midsummer sun at sea level in light skinned people. A black person will require ten times more exposure to effect the same result. The amount of UV-B will increase at higher altitudes by about 30% for each thousand meters above sea level. In Figure 1, the relative intensities of UV-B are given as they occur at noon throughout the year.

Our winter sports fan will show marked variation in his susceptibility to the harmful effects of UVL. Some will tan without a significant unfavorable reaction. Most, however, will show marked erythema response with edema on the exposed area. Few will have an acute sunburn reaction with blisters that will require medical care. To evaluate the reaction of the skin to UVL, eye color is more significant than skin color.

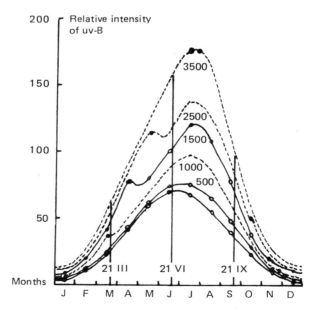

Figure 1.   Relative intensities of UV-B at noon throughout the year at different altitudes.

The skin is self-protecting in parts that are not being desquamated in the basal layer where the genetic code should be kept untouched by the harmful effects of the UV-B photons. To accomplish this, the skin has three main defense mechanisms. The corneal layer, the outermost layer, increases its thickness after UVL exposure. The main absorber of UVL in this layer is urocanid acid which, by undergoing reversible trans ⇌ cis isomerization, gives off the UV-B energy absorbed as heat radiation. In addition, the corneal layer has several molecules that are good absorbers: keratin, the main component of the corneal layer; other proteins; nucleic acids; and the main protector, the dark pigment melanin. About two billion specialized cells known as melanocytes are engaged in the synthesis and transfer of pigment granules of melanin (melanosomes) to the keratinocytes in the innermost layer of the epidermis, or basal cell layer. The melanin located as a "cap" above the nucleus of the keratinocytes absorbs UVL and performs as a "free radical trap" protecting the cell and especially its nucleus from the harmful effects of the UV photons. Lighter melanin in its reduced form is oxidized to its darker shade by UV-A of 365 nm wavelength. Shorter UVL activates in the melanocyte the enzyme tyrosinase 72 hours after the onset of erythema, initiating the synthesis of newly formed melanin. Once the melanin granule or melanosome is completely melanized, the melanocyte transfers the melanosome to the keratinocytes in its vicinity. In dark individuals the melanosomes are given off as single units. In Caucasians the melanosomes appear in units of two to four inside a lysozome membrane with hydrolytic enzymes that take care of the catabolism of the melanosome. From the biological perspective, suntan has nothing to do with good health. It is the result of a number of natural protective mechanisms intended to diminish as much as possible the harmful action of unlimited sun exposure.

Of major significance are the long-range effects of sunlight exposure. The most important are accentuation and acceleration of atrophy (farmer's or sailor's skin) and the development of keratoses, which may progress to either basal or squamous cell carcinomas. Cancer of the skin doubles in incidence with each 10° change of latitude as one approaches the equator. It is more common in light-colored people who sunburn easily because it is induced by UV-B, the same waves that effect the erythemogenic response.

Another organ subject to UVL injuries is the eye. Prolonged exposure to sunlight will cause damage to the structures of the eye, similar to those of the skin in general. The cornea blocks out UVL shorter than 300 nm wavelength. Unprotected exposure will produce intense keratoconjunctivitis with temporary blindness due to superficial necrosis of the corneal epithelium. Of a more serious nature is injury to the macula induced by the visible and infrared irradiation with burns in the coroidal and retinal layers.

PROTECTIVE MEASURES

Various methods have been used to prevent active injury to the skin, the most practical being the topical application of compounds that, because of absorption of light, or opacity, or both, will block out impinging erythemogenic radiation. However, how can we retain the image of the bronzed hero and yet avoid the red, raw, blistered skin that overexposure can produce? Compounds are available that will permit the passing through of UV-A and that convert reduced lighter melanin to oxidized darker melanin and a harmless amount of UV-B to stimulate the synthesis of new melanin. Among several good UV absorbing chemicals, para-aminobenzoic acid may be considered the parent type; it screens out damage yet permits tanning. It does stain fabrics, while its esters do not. It is not removed easily by sweating or swimming nor altered chemically by impinging solar irradiation. The preparations with para-aminobenzoic acid or its esters p-N,N-dimethylaminobenzoate (Escalol 507) are cosmetically acceptable, being invisible and without odor or color on the skin. These compounds (e.g., Presun and Pabanol) are effective at 5–25% solution in ethyl alcohol.

If a more complete sunscreen is desirable, the benzophenones (Uvinals) are total UV absorbers. The action is complete and prevents passage of even harmless skin tanning rays. These are not very popular in the cosmetic market where the pale faced angel has become a vision of the past. However, in extreme conditions, as in high altitude spring skiing, they are the choicest products. They are usually formulated at a 10% concentration in a water-washable base. Uval is one such product.

Skiing Injuries in Children and Adolescents

R. K. Requa and J. G. Garrick

Recently there has been increasing interest in the younger skier; certainly there has been increasing participation on the part of children and adolescents at many ski areas. Authorities have suggested that their injuries may be increasing as well. The young skiers' specific injury problems need careful examination. An adequate study must obtain sufficient numbers of appropriate subjects to describe properly their injury experiences and must avoid biases in sampling as well as in injury identification and classification.

METHOD

During the 1971–1972 and the 1972–1973 skiing seasons, the names of the participants of five major ski schools in the Greater Seattle metropolitan area were obtained, and questionnaires were mailed to each person at the close of the seasons. Two schools were for junior and senior high school students, and three appealed primarily to children. Information was requested concerning various background characteristics, equipment used, amount of skiing experience, and, if an injury had been sustained, information was requested concerning its type and location, time loss involved, and whether it had been reported to a physician or ski patroller. The 82% responding represented 3,534 skiers, of whom 431 reported sustaining injuries that interfered with work or recreational activity for one or more days.

Identification of a group prior to its exposure avoids the difficulties that are involved in drawing a representative control sample at an often busy ski area. It also avoids the reporting bias inherent in utilizing only ski patrol or clinic reported injuries: the cohort selected represents the entire population at risk throughout the skiing season.

Table 1. Sex distribution[a]

| | Age | |
Sex	3–13	14–19
Male	51.4	48.9
Female	48.6	51.1
Total	100.0	100.0

[a]Expressed as percent of total population.

In a survey of this type, an 82% response is considered excellent. No significant demographic variations could be detected between respondents to the first mail questionnaire and those contacted after the third mailing by telephone, suggesting that the nonrespondents are likely to be similar to those responding. Lack of any evidence for differences between those who responded and those who did not supports the validity of the sample.

Skiers returning forms that were illegible or contained inconsistencies were recontacted by telephone, as were a number of those indicating they had sustained injury. Information obtained is considered unbiased, because inconsistencies were primarily the results of innocent mistakes.

RESULTS

The respondents ranged in age from 3–19, although the concentration was highest about the average of 13½ years. The population was almost equally divided between males and females (Table 1). At season's end the 14–19-year-old age group claimed greater expertise than did those

Table 2. Expertise claimed by respondents[a]

| | Age | |
Ability	3–13	14–19
Snowplow	7.0	.7
Stem turn	10.2	2.3
Stem Christie	18.6	8.9
Beginning parallel	26.0	22.3
Parallel	29.4	47.2
Short swing	8.7	18.7

[a]Expressed as percent of age group.

3–13 (Table 2), and, as would be expected, the older group had more skiing experience (Table 3).

The 3,534 skiers collectively skied over 47,000 skier days for an injury rate of 9.1 per 1,000 skier days. The percent of injuries sustained that were reported to a physician declined through the 14–15-year-old age group, then the proportion began to climb once again (Table 4). Proportionally fewer of the injuries were reported to the ski patrol in the 14–15-year-old age group, but here there seemed to be no overall pattern of reporting change with age.

There was an upward trend for the rate of injury with age through the 12–13-year-old age group (Table 5), and males were observed to have lower rates in most cases than females.

Table 3. Skiing experience

Seasons skied	Age group	
	3–13	14–19
1	44.7%	21.3%
2	21.5%	26.0%
3	11.4%	22.6%
4	9.2%	13.5%
5 (or more)	13.2%	16.6%
	100.0%	100.0%

Interestingly enough, the professed ability of the skier at the end of the season did not seem to be related to the overall rate of injury in any dramatic way, nor did this differ by sex (Table 6). Another method of rating ability, asking the skier to rate the difficulty of the slopes generally skied, also failed to show very much difference in injury rate (Table 7).

Comparing the types of injuries sustained by age group, we can see that the younger group had a higher rate of injury for fractures, while

Table 4. Injuries reported by age

Percent reporting to:	Age group					
	≤9	10–11	12–13	14–15	16–17	18–19
Physician	80%	72%	59%	44%	52%	67%
Ski patrol	50%	52%	57%	39%	45%	56%

Table 5. Injury rates by age—number of injuries/1,000 skier days

Age	Males	Females	Average
≤ 9	2.40	3.89	5.75
10–11	4.83	8.09	6.26
12–13	10.21	10.15	10.23
14–15	9.18	11.28	10.22
≥ 16	7.98	10.55	9.24

the older group sustained higher rates of sprains, abrasions, and bruises (Table 8). Sprains were by far the most common type of injury sustained overall.

Knee injuries occurred at a higher rate than did injuries to any other location of the body, followed by ankle and upper extremity injuries. The older groups sustained higher rates of upper extremity, thigh, knee, and ankle injuries, although the greatest difference was seen in the rates of injury occurring at the ankle. Those 13 or younger had higher rates in only one area, the leg (Table 9).

Table 6. Rates by claimed ability—number of injuries/1,000 skier days

Ability	Male	Female
Snowplow	6.27	13.31
Stem turn	10.26	10.52
Stem Christie	9.38	8.55
Beginning parallel	8.91	12.61
Parallel	8.55	9.10
Short swing	6.86	8.99

Considering sprains alone, those 14 or older sustained a higher rate most significantly at the ankle, where the rate was approximately twice as high as it was for those less than 13 years of age (Table 10). For fractures, the situation reversed quite dramatically (Table 11). Here the rates, although quite low in absolute terms, were doubled for the

Table 7. Rate by run difficulty—number of injuries/1,000 skier days

Run	Injuries
Easiest	10.89
More difficult	9.19
Most difficult	8.82

Table 8. Rates by injury type—number of injuries/1,000 skier days

Type of injury	Age group	
	3–13	14–19
Fracture	1.40	0.67
Sprain	4.20	5.48
Dislocation	0.29	0.26
Laceration	0.48	0.48
Abrasion	0.14	0.37
Bruise	1.11	1.90
Other	0.53	0.56

younger skiers for ankle fractures, while for the leg the rate of occurrence for fractures was over five times as high.

Evaluation of the bindings and boots in relation to the type of injury did not seem to indict any one brand of binding or type of boot. Injuries potentially related to binding function—fractures, sprains, and dislocations to the lower extremities—occurred in approximately the same proportions for the most popular brands of bindings, nor did leg fractures seem to congregate in a single type of boot.

DISCUSSION

Because of the absence of reporting bias, this study is not comparable to most others. In a closed population of young adults, Shealy found an injury rate of 8.9 per 1,000 skier days, a rate similar to what was found in this study among the skiers 14 years old and over.

Table 9. Rates by location—number of injuries/1,000 skier days

Location of injury	Age group	
	3–13	14–19
Head/Neck	0.58	0.63
Upper Extremity	1.21	1.42
Thigh	0.19	0.45
Knee	2.66	3.06
Leg	0.82	0.56
Ankle	1.79	2.72
Foot	0.24	0.22
All Other	0.68	0.67

Table 10. Sprains—number of injuries/1,000 skier days

| Sprains | Age group | |
	3–13	14–19
Upper Extremity	0.63	0.78
Knee	2.17	2.46
Ankle	1.16	2.16
All Other	0.24	0.07
All Sprains	4.20	5.47

No support could be found for the concern that children 13 years old and younger outstrip their older compatriots in risk of injury in Alpine skiing; indeed, the rate seemed to decline with the age of the skier. This, of course, although true may still represent an increase over previous years. Several years of study are necessary in order to spot trends over time.

Younger skiers did, however, seem to sustain different kinds of injuries than did those 14 and over. The former were less apt to sustain sprains, particularly of the ankle, while more apt to sustain fractures. In this study the rate of tibial fractures was over five times higher for the younger skiers. This finding agreed with information presented by Dr. Tapper at the American Orthopaedic Society for Sports Medicine's recent meeting in Tamarron, Colorado. He is said to have described very high rates of tibial shaft fractures occurring in young skiers.

At the same time, it is important to keep in perspective that, despite the relative risk for this injury being quite high in this sample, the overall probability of sustaining a tibial fracture is quite low, representing less than 4% of all injuries reported.

Table 11. Fractures—number of injuries/1,000 skier days

| Fracture | Age group | |
	3–13	14–19
Upper Extremity	0.29	0.19
Leg	0.58	0.11
Ankle	0.39	0.19
All Other	0.14	0.19
All Fractures	1.40	0.68

Injuries to the Pelvic Girdle During Participation in Winter Sports

N. Dekleva, D. Vujnovic, and J. Dekleva-Djordjevic

Injuries to the pelvic girdle occurring during participation in winter sports, especially skiing, are often the result of forces caused by sudden linear deceleration and impact. The degree of injury and the amount of deformation occurring are proportional to the acceleration experienced by the skeletal system.

Because these injuries are usually patient-specific, it is difficult to classify them according to their fracture morphology. Furthermore, the dynamic situation involved includes a wide variety of complex movement patterns that makes the development of a mathematical model virtually impossible. If the events leading to the injury could be studied using a static model, the body and body segment parameters necessary for analysis could be obtained. These include the masses, location of center of gravity, moments of inertia, and contact areas of the joint surfaces. This difficulty in parameter determination, combined with the complexity of movement, makes even a loading simulation experiment using a dummy too inexact for any practical use. The types of pelvic fracture incurred as a result of a skiing accident are also very different from those caused in automobile or parachute accidents. In these situations, the pelvic girdle is less dependent on support from the femur, while in a skiing situation, the pelvic girdle and the weight of the body are supported by the femur.

The general functions of the musculo-skeletal system are locomotion and support. Therefore, the system must contain elements to provide both movement and structural stability. In normal, everyday situations, the bones comprising the pelvic girdle must support the weight of the trunk, head, and upper extremities as well as provide a base for the movements of the lower extremities.

The geometry of the pelvic girdle must be taken into account when considering the effect different loadings exert on it. Alterations of the point of application and/or the amplitude of the various stresses and strains may drastically change the multiphasic nature of the biological material. Consideration of fractures of the pelvic girdle occurring during skiing must include the problem of energy absorption, because absorbed energy is proportional to the product of the maximum load and the maximum deformation.

If these traumas are examined in terms of energy transfer, they seem to represent a transfer of energy from a kinetic state to one of strain. In the case of skiing accidents, the resultant force appears to be applied to some point on the pelvic girdle, often causing a fracture in one of its bones.

In the event of a fracture of the pelvic girdle, rehabilitation must begin immediately, except in those cases involving trauma to the urethea, in order to avoid the onset of the hypokinetic syndrome. Since this type of fracture generally results in massive hematoma, the patient must remain under observation for 7-10 days.

Hopefully, this exposé has served to clarify the complexity and severity of skiing-induced fractures of the pelvic girdle, injuries that often pass almost unnoticed and later cause many complications if not treated.

Hazards to the Femoro-Patellar Joint Resulting from Modern Skiing Techniques

A. Vogel and W. Bandi

At the beginning of the current century, people who participated in sports were almost considered outsiders by society. The trend today is in the opposite direction, with continually increasing sports involvement by the masses. However, during the same period that sports awareness has been spread by government institutions, medical confederations, and the school systems, the number of professional people who deal with sports analysis and sports injury has remained disproportionately small.

Skiing accidents in Switzerland last winter caused approximately 80,000 cases that needed medical attention. It therefore seems to be important that the general public be made more aware of the possible hazards involved in their increased participation, and that physicians be informed of the most current information available concerning injury prevention and care.

With sports injury, there is a more direct correlation between movement and the resulting injury than there is in other types of accidents. By considering the conditions under which sports injuries occur, and by identifying the factors causing the accidents, methods can be proposed for the prevention of accidents or for the mitigation of the effects of injury.

The sportsman has some control through his own actions over how hazardous a sport is. Outside influences not under his direct control must also be considered, and are likely to be the causative factors in many accidents. A skier often does not realize, until it is too late, the dangerous speed or body position he has developed.

In skiing, individual aggressive behavior can become a potential danger in terms of uncontrollable high speed or extreme bending positions, as in "hot dog" skiing. While both of these factors may be considered unsportsmanlike and without discipline, they are also harmful to the knee joint of the skier. Damage to the knee in the bending position results from the muscles and joint structure being subjected to forces considerably greater than those incurred in normal motion. The area suffering the most trauma is the femoro-patellar joint in front of the knuckle cartilage, as can be explained by the mechanics of the joint.

The pressure exerted by the patella against the femoral condyles in the bending position is six times greater in skiing than in the normal position, because the moment arms effective to the thigh and leg are considerably longer in the bending position. The intensity and the direction of this trauma produce a tear of the tangential tissues of the patellar cartilage, damage to the chrondrocytos, and afterwards a secondary dissociation of the cartilage, with a resulting chondromalacia, and, finally, arthrosis of the femoro-patellar joint and global gonarthrosis, because, as is already known, a destroyed cartilage cannot be recovered and, at best, can be replaced by a fibrous tissular cartilage. Lesions caused by these indirect forces have to be treated as soon as possible in order to end a progressive destruction and to prevent an early arthrosis. Damage to the cartilage is of importance because it is very difficult to diagnose, and the long-term functioning of the joint depends to a great degree on the early prognosis.

With reference to training, it can be said that muscular efficiency is increased in opposition to the efficiency of the cartilage on the dorsal face of the knuckle, so that the well trained skier is still susceptible to injury. Injuries of the type described here are common, and efforts should be made to discourage uncontrolled movements, as might be found in "hot dog" skiing. Skiing associations, skiing schools, institutions where the skiers often ask for information, and physicians should make skiers aware of the dangers involved.

As therapy for the lesion described we suggest the following: protection of the injured joint (eventual plaster); shed puncture (to eliminate enzymes, and simultaneously to apply substances to blockade enzymes); the offer of tonic elements and the stimulation of the formation of proteoglucanes (proteins, hyaluronic acid); and operation only in case of traumatic dislocation of a complete piece of cartilage or at the beginning of an arthrosis.

Knee Injuries in Skiing

R. J. Johnson, M. H. Pope, C. F. Ettlinger, G. Weisman, and
B. F. White

During the 1972–1973, 1973–1974, 1974–1975 and 1975–1976 ski seasons, 1,052 individuals sustained 1,141 ski injuries severe enough to
report to the Ski Injury Clinic in the base lodge of a large northern
Vermont ski area. All of the skiers were prospectively evaluated by
obtaining information immediately following their accidents concerning
their skiing habits, experience, ability, causes of their accidents,
mechanism of their injuries, and their bindings' previous performance
and maintenance. The extent of the patients' injuries was ascertained
by orthopaedic surgeons who were present in the clinic throughout the
skiing season. The equipment of the injured skiers was evaluated to
determine the release torques in unweighted and in combined loading
configurations that simulated slow twisting falls. Eight hundred and
twenty-seven randomly selected uninjured skiers were similarly evaluated
to compare to the injured population. Lower extremity injuries accounted for 60.3% of the total, and 72.5% of these probably resulted
from failure of the binding to release properly. Twenty-six and eight-
tenths percent of all ski injuries involved the knee region; while 21.6%
involved knee ligaments. Eighty-six and two-tenths percent of knee
ligamentous injuries occurred to the medial collateral ligament.

The results presented hereafter deal only with the 195 medial
collateral ligament injuries that probably occurred due to the failure of
the binding to release properly. Many of these were associated with
damage to the anterior cruciate and, occasionally, to other structures
about the knee.

The injuries were divided into three severity categories (Table 1).
Grade I injuries produced microscopic trauma and no clinical evidence
of ligamentous laxity. Grade II injuries resulted in a partial tear of the
ligament with mild clinical laxity present. Sprains associated with com-

---

Supported by NIH Grant #18499.

Table 1. Medial collateral ligament sprains

Severity	Number	Percent
Grade I	133	68.2
Grade II	35	18.0
Grade III	27	13.8
	195	100.0

plete disruption of the ligament and marked ligamentous instability were termed Grade III injuries.

Females sustained a higher proportion of Grade I medial collateral sprains than males, but suffered the more severe sprains at a similar rate. Individuals who were less experienced and considered themselves less skilled, and those who were smaller and younger, sustained a higher incidence of Grade I medial collateral sprains. Skiers sustaining complete tears of the medial collateral ligament were no less skilled or experienced than the control population, nor were they smaller or younger.

Good edging conditions increased the frequency of medial collateral injuries relative to non-lower extremity injuries. The kinetic energy available to the injury was greater for the individuals who sustained medial collateral ligament sprains than for those 80 individuals who suffered tibial fractures during the four seasons of this study. Medial collateral ligament injuries are produced by external rotation and/or valgus forces, yet only 68.6% recalled correctly that their tibias had been placed in this configuration during their accidents.

It was demonstrated by vector analysis that a pure rotational torque applied to the leg of a skier would result in a release of a conventional, properly set binding before an injury would be sustained by the medial collateral ligament. This was previously unknown, for all binding settings are based on the breaking strength of the tibia and not on ligamentous strength.

The majority (in this study, approximately 80%) of conventional bindings release only in side-to-side twist at the toe and in forward lean in the heel. The analysis of a hypothetical loading of the knee in pure valgus indicates that roll or shear from the top of the ski would be necessary to protect the leg. Frame-by-frame evaluation of a movie film in which a skier sustained a severe medial collateral sprain clearly demonstrated that a twist release at the heel of the binding is also necessary to prevent knee ligament injury. The relative incidence of knee ligamentous injury has remained at approximately 20% of all skiing injuries during the past forty years, while ankle sprains, ankle fractures and, in the most recent years, tibial fractures have decreased.

It is possible that no reduction in the relative incidence of medial collateral ligament sprains will occur until a large proportion of the skiing population use bindings that release in roll, shear, and twist at the heel, along with the conventionally present release in twist at the toe and forward lean at the heel.

Fatal and Severe Skiing Accidents

J. Lange, W. Mong, T. Hewell, and P. C. Maurer

Every winter the Surgical Clinic "Rechts der Isar" in Munich treats skiers with severe injuries. The increase of very severe, atypical, and fatal skiing accidents caused the clinic to investigate their origins more clearly to prevent further ones or, at least, to reduce their numbers.

Three thousand years ago, skis were used only as a means of locomotion in snow. Grandma and grandpa still regarded skiing as a pleasant leisure time sport. Because of the rapid developments of the last few years, from a wooden ski to a plastic ski and from laced boots to buckled boots, and because of improvements in ski outfits, speeds that were not dreamed of in the past can be reached today.

The times of a few enthusiasts using the slope as a playground are long past. Today's modern mass transportation carries thousands upon thousands to the mountains, making collisions like those in dense road traffic unavoidable. The introduction of safety bindings has reduced the number of typical ski injuries, but there has been an increasing number of severe and fatal skiing accidents. It has been concluded that the essential reasons for severe and fatal skiing injuries are aggressive skiing or excessive speed.

Accident causes are:

1. A fall on the open track
2. A fall with sliding and injury by bouncing
3. Bouncing against obstacles, such as rocks, trees or fences
4. One's own or another person's skiing equipment
5. Collisions with other skiers

This study dealt with 31 fatal ski accidents that occurred during the years 1959—1976. The average age of the victims was 24 years. Ten sportsmen lost their lives during races or training. Another five accidents were the consequences of uncontrolled racing; that means 50% of the injuries took place at excessive speed. Table 1 shows an analysis

Table 1. 91 Lethal ski accidents (avalanche victims excluded)

Accident	Literature	Observation	Number	Percent
1. Fall on free slope	6		6	7
2. Fall and slipping	11	8	19	21
3. Collision with obstacles	27	12	39	43
4. Injuries by ski equipment	12	7	19	21
5. Collision with other skiers	4	4	8	9
Totals	60	31	91	101[a]

[a]The 101 percent figure is attributable to rounding.

of accident causes in the 31 ski deaths, together with 60 fatal Alpine ski injuries found in the literature, excluding avalanche victims.

Table 1 shows the percent of the fatal ski accidents that occurred by falls on the open track; the causes were skiing mistakes as well as excessive speed. In 21% of the cases, the skier slid after the fall and had a fatal bounce or crash.

Figure 1 shows a 19-year-old skier who slid down over a 200-m ice slope. In accidents like this, ice-covered slopes that are not properly groomed and low friction synthetic suits certainly play an essential role. Forty-three percent of all fatal skiing accidents occurred through bouncing against obstacles such as trees, rocks, fences, etc.

Figure 2 shows a ruptured liver due to a fall against a tree; the 24-year-old skier bled to death. Twenty-one percent of the fatal injuries are caused by the skier's own or other skier's skiing equipment. Even minor falls may cause a fatal perforation by the ski pole or critical cut wounds from the steel edge.

Figure 3 (a and b) shows a deterrent case. The ski pole penetrated the eye and entered the brain of this 28-year-old male.

It is hoped that the introduction of a ski brake will reduce injuries caused by the ski flailing at the end of the safety strap.

Bonnet reported seeing a collision accident fatal for the two persons involved in St. Anton as early as in 1948. The extension of skiing to a mass sport has necessarily led to an increase of these accidents. Nine percent of the fatal injuries analyzed in Table 1 were due to collisions of this type. In most cases, aggressive, uncontrolled skiing was involved.

Figure 4 shows a fractured jaw after a collision.

In the 31 fatal skiing injuries observed, several causes of death were found.

Table 2 shows that two-thirds of the skiers died of skull-brain trauma. This corresponds to the data given in the literature.

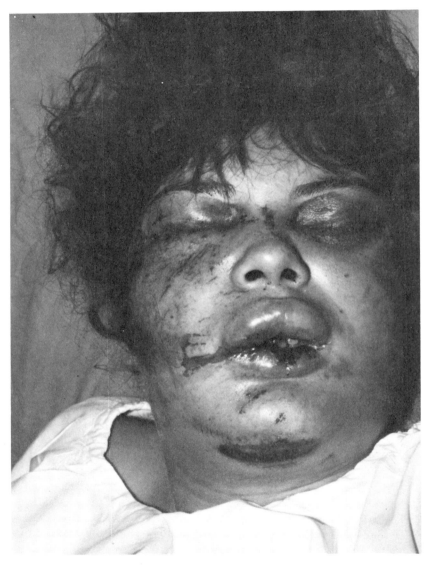

Figure 1.   Accident victim who slid down a slope.

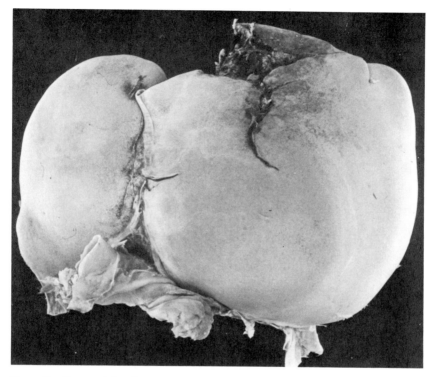

Figure 2.   Ruptured liver from collision with a tree.

Figure 5 shows a crush fracture of the skull caused by a fall over a precipice.

The remaining third of the causes of death were injuries to the abdomen, spine, thorax, etc. To summarize:

—50% of the fatal skiing accidents occurred at excessive speed or in races
—43% were caused by bouncing against obstacles
—In 21% of the fatal accidents, injury was due to sliding down or into the skiing equipment
—Two-thirds of the fatal injuries were skull-brain traumas

In order to avoid such severe or fatal ski accidents, the following suggestions are made:

1.   All skiers should be informed and educated about self-controlled, defensive skiing. Everyone should know and observe the rules of conduct in skiing developed by the International Ski Association.

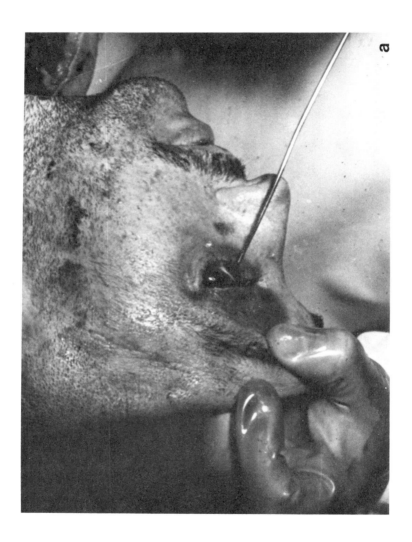

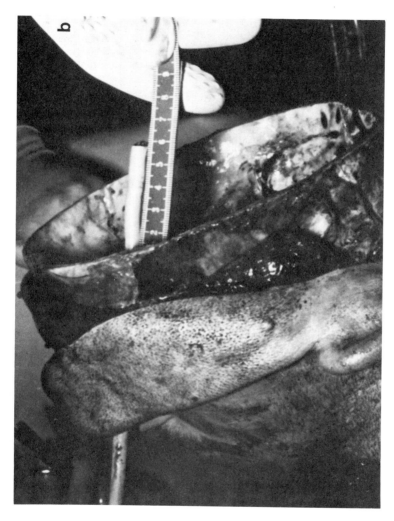

Figure 3.   Injury from a ski pole.

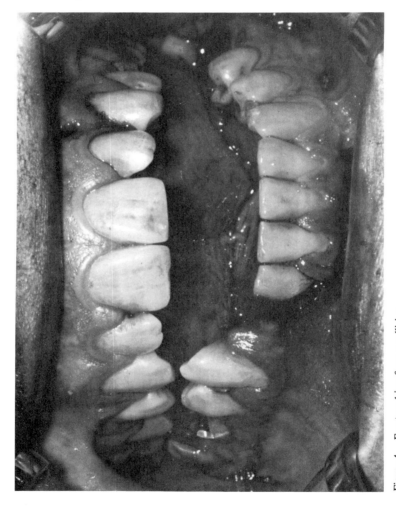

Figure 4. Fractured jaw from a collision.

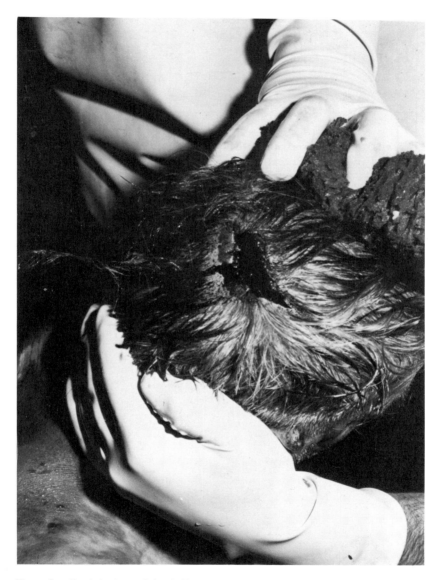

Figure 5.   Crush fracture of the skull caused by a fall over a cliff.

Table 2. Kinds of lethal ski injuries

Injury	Number
Brain injury	20
Polytrauma	3
Spine injury	2
Thoracic injury	1
Abdominal injury	2
Unclear	2
Overall	30

2.   Trails, well marked and sufficiently spacious to allow for falls, should be provided. Permanent safety devices, such as plants, nets, etc., should be placed where falls would be dangerous. Obstacles should be removed or at least well marked and secured by adequate protective devices. The laying-out of the slope should be done in such a way that the speed will be reduced.

3.   The rescue service should, wherever possible, be improved. For example, air rescue by helicopter could be developed.

4.   For slopes through woods as well as stony and rocky slopes, the wearing of crash helmets should be considered, especially for children.

5.   Good, safe skiing equipment should always be used.

6.   Last, but not least, optimal preparation includes fitness training.

Injury Statistics from Two Winter Olympic Games in Innsbruck

E. Raas and A. Aigner

The common aim of all the personnel involved in medical care at the Innsbruck Olympics was to prevent health problems from developing and to provide quick assistance or therapeutic measures in the case of injury or illness. This applied in the same degree to competitors, officials, and visitors, and meant that suitable personnel, premises, and amenities were required.

For this reason, the necessary organization and facilities are first described. The different injuries and accidents are enumerated and divided by type of sport and event. The nature of the injury (slight or serious) and the number of first aid cases and transports carried out are also categorized. Finally, the treatment of injured persons at the surgical department is described. Concluding the injury survey of the 1976 Winter Games is a comparison with the injury survey of the 1964 Winter Olympics.

Table 1 is a summary of personnel with access to Olympic Medical Service in 1976, grouped according to their function and the number of overnight stays. These figures do not include small groups of people to whom the medical service was also available, e.g., members of the various committees of international associations, official guests of the municipality of Innsbruck, etc.

The number of competitors was smaller this time (1,960) than in 1964 (2,122), the number of officials living in the Olympic Village (3,600) was about the same (3,262), and the number of spectators (1,500,000) had increased by about one-third (1,073,000). The medical center was situated on the first floor of the centrally placed building in the village enclosure. The six specialist outpatient departments included accident surgery and general surgery, a central x ray department, and a physiotherapy section.

Table 1. Personnel with access to Olympic Medical Services, 1976 Winter Olympics

	Total number	Overnight stays	Average stay in village (days)
Village enclosure athletes and team staff	1,960	32,343	16.5
Open village officials	3,600	71,807	19.9
Press officially accredited	1,750	26,460	15.1
ORF	1,500	27,280	18.2
Total personnel	8,810	157,890	17.9
Spectators	1,500,000		

First aid posts at the finishing areas of the peripheral sites were either fitted into permanent buildings or in transportable containers adapted for the purpose. These posts were staffed during the official training and competition periods, whereas the medical services in the Olympic Village, the press center, and the ORF were available around the clock.

By increasing the number of days on which they were on duty (Table 2), it was possible to employ fewer doctors this time (78) than in 1964 (120). The number of voluntary helpers from the mountain rescue and mountain watch services, the army, and the Red Cross was 464 as compared to 380 in 1964. The number of nurses cannot be compared because certain changes in the organization in 1976 meant that only 18

Table 2. Medical personnel

	Number	Man-days on duty
Doctors		
Village enclosure	21	340
Open village and press	4	60
Peripheral sites	38	435
Doping tests	11	
Sex checks	1	
ORF	3	62
Total	78	
Students	12	296
Nurses	18	305
Medical assistants	20	
Mountain rescue / Mountain watch	89	
Army	75	
Red Cross	280	1,395
Total	572	

Knights of Malta nurses carried out duties. The fact that the total number of medical staff employed in 1976 (572) was lower than in 1964 (730) is mainly attributable to the bobsled and luge events being held on one combined race course in 1976.

Twelve doctors and 89 men from the Innsbruck mountain rescue, Seefeld mountain rescue, and Innsbruck mountain watch services, 20 doctors and 55 medical officers, medical soldiers, and drivers from the army, and about 280 members of the Tyrolean branch of the Red Cross were employed mainly to attend to and transport the injured. The army ran 19 vehicles, some of them of the newest type, while the Red Cross ran about 23 medical vehicles. The army also supplied the five rescue helicopters required to transport the injured and acute cases quickly. Each of these helicopters was staffed by an experienced doctor and equipped with special first aid materials of all kinds (oxygen machine, resuscitation kit, drainage, intubation and respiration machines, etc.).

Of the total 4,041 medical consultations, examinations, and cases of treatment registered (Table 3), only a relatively small proportion were due to accidents and injuries, with by far the greater number being internal diseases, particularly febrile infections.

Of the 1,309 cases treated in the medical center at the village enclosures, 90 were slight injuries that were attended to on the spot. There was no case that had to be transferred to the relevant clinic, nor was it necessary for any case to receive inpatient treatment in the medical center ward as a result of injury.

Of the 565 physiotherapeutic applications given in the Village physiotherapy section (Table 4), 127 were for contusions, 162 for distortions, 80 for cases of acute lumbago, and others for cases such as myalgia, periarthrosis humeroscapularis, torticollis spastica, etc. The medical section in the open village had to treat only a few traumatic cases. These were minor cuts, excoriations, contusions, and two frac-

Table 3. Number of services and transports

Olympic Village enclosure	1,309
Open village	424
Press	422
ORF	732
Alpine events	36
Nordic events	109
Ice stadium	150
Ice hockey injuries	100
Bobsled and luge events	321
Red Cross	438
Total	4,041

Table 4. Physical therapy in the Olympic Village

Diagnosis	Massage	Micro-short-wave	Neo-dynator	Hot air	Diapulse	Ultra-sonics	Infra-red	Mobili-zation	Total
Contusions	19	17	47	6	18	20			127
Distortions	22	25	87		12	3		13	162
Myalgia	36	23	8	6	6				79
Lumbago	44	12	6	18					80
Cervical vertebral column syn.	9	3							12
Sciatica	4	4			8				16
Periarthrosis hum.		18							18
Torticollis spastica	6	6							12
After fractures		6			3		5		14
Sinusitis, otitis	8	18		4		10			40
Contractures					5				5
Total	148	132	148	34	52	33	5	13	565

Table 5. Ice hockey injuries

Contusions	66
Distortions	9
Cuts	9
Traumatic hemorrhages of the gingiva	3
Traumatic epistaxis	3
Hematoma	2
Fractures	1
Subluxations	2
Concussion	3
Traumatic acute dyspnea	2
	100

tures (ankle and radius). Of the 422 people who received treatment in the press center, none had injuries of a serious nature. The same applied to the ORF first aid post, where there were 732 consultations in all. The medical area heads at the Patscherkofel and Axamer Lizum finishing areas attended to 36 people, nine of whom had slight injuries.

Members of the mountain rescue and mountain watch services carried out 22 transports with mountain stretchers; 18 of these cases were spectators and four were racers. None of these was seriously injured. Nine cases of injury or illness were attended to in the area of the Nordic competitions; two of these were fractures to the upper extremities. Table 5 is a survey of the 100 ice hockey injuries registered during training and during the Games; in 42 cases the cause of the

Table 6. First aid and transport operations

	First aid		
	Slight injuries and illnesses	Injuries and illnesses of more serious nature	Total
Competitors	36	10	46
Spectators	200	38	238
No. of army members assisting	36	1	37
Total	272	49	321
	Transport operations		
	Rescue helicopters	Medical vehicles	Total
Competitors	3	6	9
Spectators	2	22	24
No. of army members assisting	—	1	1
Total	5	29	34

accident was a blow with a hockey stick, in 24 cases it was body checking, and in 20 cases it was the puck.

Members of the army gave first aid assistance in 321 cases and carried out 34 transport operations. Table 6 supplies more detailed information.

The army was on duty at the jumping in Seefeld, for the air rescue service in the area of all Alpine and Nordic events, and, partially, at the ice stadium, the trade fair site, and both large Bergisel events. The medical side of all the bobsled and luge events was attended to solely by the army. Table 7 presents a survey of the number and type of injuries.

Members of the Red Cross gave first aid in 438 cases to 389 spectators, 29 competitors and 20 officials (Table 8).

In 1,099 cases, assistance was given to spectators (Table 9).

The accident surgery department of the surgical clinic registered 132 injuries (and one death) in all (Table 10). One hundred and twenty-five of the injured were treated as outpatients, seven being admitted for treatment. Of the 125 outpatient cases, 23 were athletes,

Table 7. Bobsled and luge events, injuries, illnesses, and transports

| | Slight | | More serious | | Transport | |
	Injury	Illness	Injury	Illness	Med. vehicles	Heli-copters
Competitors (C)	26	1	4	0	6	0
Spectators (S)	50	25	14	2	15	2
Army members (AR)	5	16	0	1	1	0

	Spectators and officials	Competitors	Total
Total injuries	69	30	99
Total transports	18	6	24

Diagnosis "Injuries and illnesses of more serious nature":

C / contusion and hematoma, left hand
C / deep lacerated and contused wound, left knee
C / shoulder luxation, right
C / muscular rupture, right thigh
S / concussion
S / torn quadriceps
S / shoulder luxation and fracture of radius
S / concussion
S / torn Achilles tendon
S / fracture of radius
S / fracture of nasal bone
S / fracture of left forearm
S / fracture of upper arm
S / spinal injury and shock
S / fracture of right forearm
S / fracture of right upper arm
S / fractured ankle, right
S / concussion
S / essential paroxysmal tachycardia
S / renal colic
AR / influenzal infection

Table 8. Number of calls and transports

Events (Date)	Competitors	Officials	Spectators	Total calls	Total transports
Opening Ceremony (4/2/1976)			33	33	15
Jumping Events Bergisel (9/2–15/2)	2	2	23	27	14
Alpine Events Patscherkofel (31/1–5/2)			35	35	15
Alpine Events Axamer Lizum (1/2–14/2)	4		104	108	20
Ice Hockey Events ice stadium (31/1–14/2)	2		25	27	9
Ice Hockey Events trade fair site (28/1–13/2)	2	1	7	10	4
Speed Skating Events ice stadium (5/2–14/2)	1	4	29	34	1
Figure Skating Events ice stadium (28/1–14/2)	3	8	27	38	6
Figure Skating Events trade fair site (28/1–15/2)	2	3	6	11	1
Cross Country—Biathlon Seefeld (1/2–14/2)	12	2	99	113	7
Exhibition, Closing Ceremony ice stadium (15/2/1976)	1		1	2	1
Total	29	20	389	438	93

Table 9. Assistance given to spectators, totalling 1,099 instances

I. Aid	
Alpine events: Patscherkofel	11
Axamer Lizum	25
Nordic events	109
Skating events	130
Army	238
Surgical department of clinic	62
Red Cross	389
Total	964
II. Transport	
Mountain Rescue and Mt. Watch Service	18
Army	24
Red Cross	93
Total	135

43 were officials and employees, and 59 were spectators. Of the seven inpatients, four were athletes and three were spectators. No complicated serious injuries were observed. One member of the army suffered such serious cranium trauma while skiing when not on duty that he died of his injuries.

When these figures are compared with those compiled by Haid (1965) (the special representative of the medical faculty of Innsbruck University) for the 1964 Winter Olympic Games, it is seen that the total number of injuries remained more or less the same; however, the differences within the various events were great. Whereas in 1964 the total number of injuries at the bobsled and luge run was 66, this figure was 99 in 1976. It is striking, however, that, of the 66 injuries in 1964, 48 cases were competitors, while in 1976 the number of competitors injured was only 30 and the number of injured spectators was 69, more than three times greater than in 1964. The combined run thus proved to be far less prone to accidents than both 1964 runs together, but more spectators suffered slight or somewhat more serious injuries in 1976—

Table 10. Clinical treatment

Athletes	23 outpatients	
	4 inpatients	27 total
Officials, employees,	43 outpatients	
and army	1 death	44 total
Spectators and	59 outpatients	
others	3 inpatients	62 total

The total injured were: 125 outpatients and 7 inpatients.

probably due to inadequately gritted paths—than in the winter of 1964 with its scant snow. Whereas at the 1964 Alpine events there were 29 injuries, there were only seven in 1976. The relatively large number of injuries (100) suffered by ice hockey players in 1976 as compared to 1964 (41) can probably be explained by the fact that in 1976 all ice hockey injuries were registered for statistical purposes, whether or not they were attended to by Organizing Committee doctors and helpers; the majority of ice hockey injuries are attended to by the team doctors from the various nations.

In conclusion, it can be said that big sporting events like Olympic Games require considerable material and personnel in the medical sector, too. As in 1964, all requirements for proper care, attention, and transports were available in 1976. The injuries were less this time than in 1964, and there were no really dangerous injuries immediately connected with the organization and running of the Games.

REFERENCES

Haid, B. 1965. Arstliche Betreuung bei den IX. Olympischen Winterspiele 1964 in Innsbruck (Medical Attendants at the 9th Olympic Winter Games 1964 in Innsbruck.) In: Abschlubbericht uber die IX. Olympischen Winterspiele 1964 in Innsbruck, Innsbruck Organizing Committee, pp. 240–246.

Raas, E. 1976. Die Organisation des Sanifatseinsatzes im Rahmen der XII. Olympischen Winterspiele 1976 in Innsbruck. (The organization of individual health care in the structure of the 12th Olympic Winter Games 1976 in Innsbruck.) In: Mitteilung der Osterreichischen Sanitatsverwaltung 76, 1.

Skier Falls and Injuries: Video Tape and Survey Study of Mechanisms

L. R. Young and D. Loo

A video tape study of naturally occurring falls was carried out during the 1975-77 seasons at Waterville Valley, New Hampshire. Binding release torques were also measured. Falls were analyzed as to potential danger and the principal mode of torque exerted on the binding: pure twist (PT), forward twist (FT), backward twist (BT), forward bend (FB), backward bend (BB), or roll (R). Finer subdivisions were made according to the American Society of Testing and Materials (ASTM) binding test procedures and according to a set of 18 fall category sketches. Differences in speed, fall type, and binding release were evident between skiers of different abilities. Results were compared with a simultaneous survey of fall types incurred by injured skiers studied by means of a nationwide questionnaire. The frequency of fall types in injury was far different from those in the noninjured cases or in the innocent falls. In particular, whereas the FT fall accounted for the largest portion of beginner to advanced injuries and FB the largest portion of expert injuries, BB accounted for the largest percentage of innocent falls among the video tape cases. The report showed not only the frequency of certain modes of falling, but the potential danger for leg injuries and other injuries resulting from such falls.

The team of students recorded 271 falls at Waterville Valley. Skiers were interviewed about ability, experience, height, weight, and age, and their unweighted toe and heel release torques were measured with a Look release tester; the results are preliminary, awaiting the taping of further cases. The tapes were reviewed by at least four observers and the falls were classified as either dangerous or nondangerous. (A dangerous fall is one in which it is deemed desirable to have the binding release.) They were also categorized according to the ASTM test configuration and according to the drawings in the MIT injured skier questionnaire shown in Figure 1. It was necessary to add another category (R) to account for pure roll without any ski entrapment. Because of the small number in each category, the fall types were collapsed into six groups. Finally, each skier's speed was estimated. The video tape population was as follows: 271 falls, 8% beginners, 35% intermediates, 36% advanced, 21% expert. The injured skier data from our questionnaire involved 191 responses; 11% beginners, 20% lower intermediates, 31% intermediates, 25% advanced, 12% experts.

The overall distribution of fall types for the skiers videotaped, none of whom was injured, is shown in Table 1, along with the number considered dangerous in each category. BB and FT were the most common types of falls observed. Although a large percentage of the FT falls were considered dangerous, especially category F (twist while falling down and forward with ski trapped at tip), the situation was different for BB. Of the large number of BB falls recorded at all ability levels, nearly all were quite harmless. Only seven of the 103 BB falls were assessed as potentially dangerous. Similarly, the falls involving pure roll were, as expected, all without danger. On the other hand, the PT falls, which normally involved a trapped ski, were considered highly dangerous (Category A) as were the sudden deceleration FB falls (Category M). A further breakdown of the video tape population is given in Table 1. It can be seen that FB falls became more frequent and relatively more important to the dangerous fall category as ability increased. While BB was less common for the expert than other falls, it was still relatively frequent, although normally not dangerous. In all ability levels, the weighted forward leaning twist is apparently the fall to be most concerned about in terms of both frequency and probability of danger.

Finally, the video tape data are being analyzed in terms of the correlation between different types of skier ability, speed, the binding release adjustment setting, and the probability of the binding releasing in a dangerous fall. Preliminary data from a small number of cases is also shown in Table 1. In general, it may be seen that the bindings tended to function best in PT and FB, reasonably well in FT except Category D (combination shear and twist), and worst in BB. Detailed studies of the relationship between generic binding types and their function in these falls and for the injured skier are underway.

Turning now to the study of fall types indicated in the questionnaires sent back by injured skiers, it is possible to apply similar types of analyses. Related studies of fall types in injury were performed by Ellison et al. (1962), Bally (personal communication), and Eriksson and

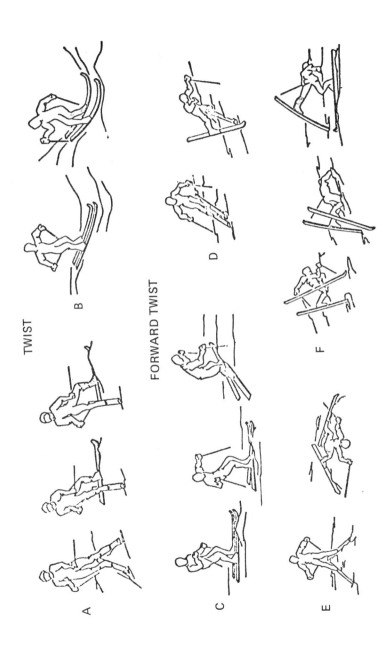

TWIST

FORWARD TWIST

Figure 1.   Legend on next page.

Figure 1. Fall category sketches from injured skier questionnaire. TWIST A. Pure twist, ski unweighted. B. Pure twist, ski flexed downward, as in valley between moguls. FORWARD TWIST C. Twist (internal rotation) while falling forward, ski is trapped. D. Twist while ski is pushed sideways, ski trapped in front. E. Twist (external rotation) combined with forward pressure, ski trapped. F. Twist while falling down and forward, ski trapped at the tip. BACKWARD TWIST G. Twist combined with backward pressure, ski trapped in front. H. Twist while falling backward, weight on tails. I. Twist with ski pulled down, away from boot, bending leg backward. J. Twist while falling down and backwards, ski trapped at tail, bending leg forward. FORWARD BENDING K. Pure forward bending, no deceleration, tails of skis trapped (as if by another skier). L. Forward bending, upward pressure on tips and deceleration. M. Pure forward bending, sudden deceleration, forward fall. N. Forward bending, weight forward, combined with twist. O. Forward bending, combined with slight twist. BACKWARD BENDING P. Pure backward bending, no acceleration, shovels of skis trapped (as if by another skier). Q. Backward bending, with weight on tails, skis accelerating.

Table 1. Video analysis data[a]

	PT		FT				BT						FB			BB		R
	A	B	C	D	E	F	G	H	I	J	K	L	M	N	O	P	Q	R
Total falls	8	4	24	32	12	9	3	25	8	6	4	4	6	1	4	8	94	19
Dangerous	6	0	10	17	8	9	1	5	6	6	2	1	5	0	3	1	6	0
Beginner	0	0	1	3	0	0	0	3	1	0	1	1	0	0	0	3	7	2
Dangerous	0	0	0	2	0	0	0	0	0	0	0	0	0	0	0	0	0	0
Intermediate	1	2	5	15	7	2	1	3	3	1	2	2	1	1	2	5	37	4
Dangerous	1	0	2	7	5	2	0	0	3	1	2	1	1	0	1	1	3	0
Advanced	5	1	10	9	4	5	1	8	3	4	1	0	1	0	1	0	35	10
Dangerous	3	0	4	6	3	5	0	2	2	4	1	0	0	1	0	0	1	0
Expert	2	1	8	5	1	2	1	12	1	1	0	1	4	0	1	0	15	3
Dangerous	2	0	4	2	0	2	1	3	1	1	0	0	4	0	1	0	2	0
Binding release in dangerous falls (all abilities)	4	0	7	6	5	5	1	1	2	2	2	0	3	0	2	1	3	0

[a]PT = Pure twist; FT = forward twists; BT = backward twist; FB = forward bending; BB = backward bending; R = roll. Letters A-Q indicate the appropriate illustration in Figure 1.

Danielsson (1977). Table 2 shows, for each ability level, the percentage of falls in each category; thus, 61% of the beginner injuries reported were the results of FT and only 8% of the beginner injuries reported were the results of BT. It is clear that the FT was the major injury mechanism for most skiers, but that it decreased in relative importance as ability increased. Conversely, the injuries resulting from FB assumed increasing importance as skier ability increased, reaching fully one-third of the expert injuries. (Care should be taken in interpreting the expert injury data because the number reported was so small.)

The overall incidence of injuries separated into fall type is given in Table 3, along with the number that occurred at the hip or below ("leg injuries") and might reasonably be attributed to binding function or malfunction. Note that nearly all of the PT injuries were leg injuries while a large number of the FB, R, and BB injuries were to other parts of the body. Many of these were thumb, arm, shoulder, or head injuries resulting from being thrown to the snow with or without a binding release, but unrelated to any direct torque on the leg.

The speed at which the skier takes a given type of fall has clear implications both for the danger potential and for the required binding release function. The number of leg injuries is also shown as a function of slow, moderate, and fast speeds in Table 3. The FT fall contributed injuries at all speeds, whereas FB appeared to be much less of a problem at slow speeds than at moderate or fast speeds. On the other hand, BB became less of a contributor to leg injuries at high speeds than at slower speeds. This analysis of fall type versus speed for injured skiers was in general conformity with the analysis of the danger of falls from the video data, where it was concluded that PTs were for the most part considerably more dangerous at higher speeds than at lower speeds, FTs were most dangerous at higher speeds, as were FBs, BT falls contributed a high danger potential at any speed, but BB falls became much less dangerous as speeds increased. None of the R falls analyzed was considered dangerous.

On the basis of the video data, the potential for injury for any

Table 2. Injured skiers: percentage of fall type by ability

	PT	FT	BT	FB	BB	R
Beginners, $N = 13$	8	61	8	15	8	0
Lower intermediates, $N = 22$	14	50	14	14	9	0
Intermediates, $N = 41$	10	41	19	24	5	0
Advanced, $N = 33$	18	42	12	21	6	0
Expert, $N = 15$	20	20	7	33	20	0

given fall was computed by taking the product of the possibility of that fall type occurring times the probability that such a fall would be dangerous. On this basis, falls with the highest danger potential were FT (14% probability of any fall being dangerous), followed closely by BT (13%), dropping to 6% for FB, 4% for PT, and 3% for BB. This low danger index for BB, for example, results from the fact that, although the fall occurs frequently, the probability of it being dangerous is quite low.

The video analysis and injured skier survey data are compared in Figure 2. The data from the survey in general bore out the video analysis. In cases such as FT, for example, the analysis of the video data showed that the percentage of all falls that were dangerous and in this category (52%) was considerably higher than the percentage of all falls, dangerous or not, that fell in this category (28%). This was borne out by the injured skier data, which showed a much higher percentage of injuries in this category (40%) than determined by the percentage of all falls. Similar comments apply to the PT and FB categories as the categories that were identified as dangerous from the video analysis and borne out as such by the injury data. Further confirmation was seen in the case of BB, where the video analysis indicated a relatively small percentage of the BB falls as dangerous, and, in fact, a quite small percentage of the injured skiers indicated BB falls as the cause of their injuries.

The analysis of binding tension measured for those skiers whose falls were recorded on video tape as well as those indicated on the questionnaires is still being carried out. On the basis of a preliminary analysis of the video tape cases, it was found that most of the skiers had their bindings set well above Lipe recommendations (Johnson, Pope, and Ettlinger, 1974; Shealy, 1973; Matter, Muller, and Ott, 1976). All of the beginners tested had either lateral or upward releases set too tight; 84% of the intermediates and 77% of the experts also had tight bindings. As the ability level increased, the binding adjustment errors seemed to shift from toe or lateral release settings to heel or

Table 3. Injured skiers: leg injuries by fall type and speed (complete returns)

	PT	FT	BT	FB	BB	R
Injuries	12	38	11	31	9	4
Leg injuries	10	29	7	13	4	0
Slow speed	2	6	1	1	1	0
Moderate speed	6	15	5	7	2	0
Fast speed	2	8	1	5	1	0

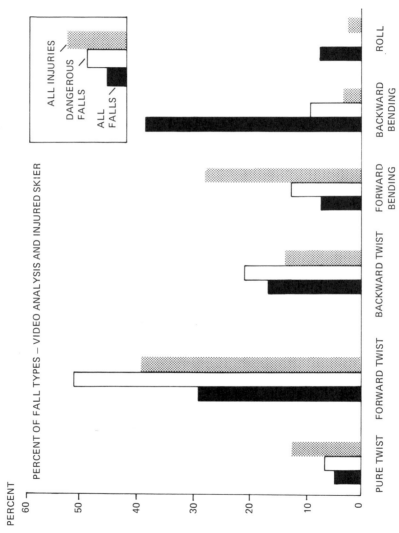

Figure 2.   Comparison of video and injury populations.

upward release settings. The relationship between probability of release in a dangerous fall and binding settings will be reported in a later publication.

This analysis of 271 falls led to several preliminary conclusions. Both the video tape data of injured skiers in naturally occurring falls and the results of an injured skier questionnaire indicated that the FT fall remained the principal source of ski injury danger, but that FB falls achieved increasing seriousness with higher speeds and among more advanced skiers. BB falls seemed to be of more concern at slow speeds, and to beginners, than at high speeds. Backward weighted twisting falls were a source of concern for all abilities at all speeds. Further research on binding release characteristics and fall types is required to establish guides for optimal protection of the skier in a fall.

ACKNOWLEDGMENTS

This project was carried out as an Independent Activities Period Project at the Massachusetts Institute of Technology by a group of undergraduate students. We are grateful for the technical support furnished by G. Delouche and C. Gantet of the Salomon Company, and for the support and encouragement of Henry Crane, M.D., and the Waterville Valley Ski Area Management.

REFERENCES

Ellison, A. E., Carroll, R. E., Haddon, W., and Wolf, M. 1962. Clinical study. Public Health Reports 77(11):985.

Eriksson, E., and Danielsson, K. 1977. Ski injuries in Sweden—The value of a national survey. Proceedings of the First Scandinavian Conference in Sports Medicine. Syntex Therapy 2:135–141. Strømmen, Norway.

Johnson, R. J., Pope, M. H., and Ettlinger, C. 1974. The interrelationship between ski accidents, the resultant injury, the skier's characteristics, and the ski-binding-boot system. J. Sports Med. 2:299–307.

Matter, P., Muller, D., and Ott, Ch. 1976. Frequency of ski injuries in the Davos region. In: Orthopedic Clincs of North America, pp. 31–36. Vol. 7. W. B. Saunders, Philadelphia.

Shealy, J. R. 1973. Ski release bindings: comparison of static settings and accident rates in a closed population. In: Proceedings of the Human Factors Society, pp. 445–456.

A National Ski Injury Survey

E. Eriksson and K. Danielsson

In all countries of the world where downhill skiing is possible, it has been one of the most rapidly increasing participant sports. Parallel with this, an increase in the ski injury rate has been noted. It is reasonable to believe that some 500,000 people are sustaining severe injuries each year while skiing. Many attempts to reduce the ski injury rate have been made around the world. In Germany, the IAS organization has developed guidelines for proper adjustment of release bindings (Asang, 1972). In Switzerland, a similar organization, BFU, has also done comparable work. In Sweden, we took the initiative to form the International Society for Skiing Safety. In 1974, the first truly International Conference on Ski Trauma and Skiing Safety was organized in Riksgransen, Sweden. Its proceedings were published in the January, 1976, issue of Orthopedic Clinics of North America. At that meeting the results of a 1973–1974 national survey were reported (Eriksson, 1976).

This study was repeated during Winter 1975–1976; herewith are the results from that study. In both the 1973–1974 and the 1975–1976 studies, questionnaires were sent to all Swedish general surgeons and orthopaedic surgeons and to the local doctors in all ski areas. They were paid a sum of money for filling in a form when a ski injury was treated. The injured skiers were asked a series of questions about their equipment, training, ability, how the injury occurred, state of the slope, binding release, direction of fall, if they had noticed propaganda about ski safety, etc. In addition, a control group of Swedish skiers who had either gone to the Swedish mountains or travelled to the Alps by

This study was supported by a grant from the National Swedish Board for Consumer Policies.

charter flights were asked to answer the same questions. Also included were 73,395 skiers from a number of Swedish ski slopes in different parts of Sweden at different intervals during the day and at different periods during the winter. Each of these skiers was asked to report his/her age and sex. In this way, a second set of control data was obtained that permitted a comparison between expected and obtained frequency of ski injuries in different ages and between males and females.

Since the snow conditions varied considerably from year to year, the ski injury frequency and the number of skiers on the slopes were monitored in a control area in the north of Sweden (Västerbotten) where the skiing conditions have been good even in years with minimal snowfall.

INJURY DATA

During the 1973-1974 study, 1,199 questionnaires were returned, while the 1975-1976 season yielded 2,444 returned forms. The number of injuries in different types of skiing is shown in Figure 1. These figures seem to indicate an increase in the skiing injury rate; however, the larger number of skiing injuries actually reflects the fact that, during the 1973-1974 season, skiing was possible only in the northern part of Sweden, while, in 1975-1976, it was possible to ski all over Sweden because the snowfall was so plentiful. The Swedish National Board for Consumer Policies surveyed the number of Swedes who devote themselves to skiing and tried to pinpoint the number of people devoting themselves to cross-country skiing and downhill skiing. About three million Swedes devoted themselves to cross-country or mountain touring; the number of injuries in these types of skiing was about 0.2 per thousand. The number of downhill skiers was about 300,000, and their injury rate was about six per thousand.

A special problem of the 1975-1976 season was the so called mini- or toy skis. These are small plastic skis, more toys than real skis (Figure 2). Because they are very short, the skier has problems with balance. They do not have any type of release binding: the boot is tied to the ski with bands. By January of 1976, a considerable number of mini-ski injuries had already occurred. The press, radio, and TV were therefore contacted, and a campaign was started against the use of mini-skis on the slopes. This led to a considerable decrease in the rate of mini-ski injuries (Danielsson, Eriksson, and Strand, 1976).

During the 1973-1974 investigation, a great number of children were injured, with the greatest frequency of injury occurring around 13-14 years of age. The same tendency was found in the later investiga-

DOWNHILL 1974 = 885
1976 = 1804

MOUNTAIN TOURING 1974 = 98
1976 = 215

CROSS COUNTRY 1974 = 140
1976 = 381

SKI JUMP 1974 = 22
1976 = 44

Figure 1. Number of skiers injured in different types of skiing during the two seasons investigated.

tion, as can be seen from Figure 3. When, however, the number of obtained ski injuries is compared with the number of expected ski injuries calculated from the age groups of the 73,000 skiers counted on different ski slopes, it is evident that the high frequency with which young skiers are injured is dependent on the fact that so many youngsters go skiing. In fact, as can be seen from Figure 3, the obtained frequency of ski injuries was not higher than expected. For young girls, it was even lower than the expected frequency. The older age groups, however, had a considerably higher frequency of injury. As can be seen from Figure 4, ladies over 50 years of age had a frequency of injuries about 240% higher than expected. Thus, it is evidently not the children that are the highest risk group on the slopes but rather the middle-aged female skiers.

Figure 2.   A skier with so called mini-skis. These are made of plastic material and since they are very short they are difficult to ski with on ordinary slopes. The skier easily loses his balance and falls.

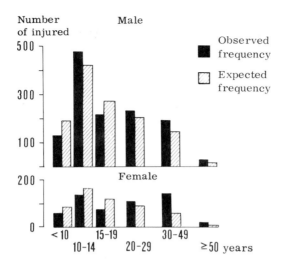

Figure 3.   Age distribution of the injured skiers, 1975–1976. The large number of in-jured boys and girls depends on the large number of youngsters on the slopes. The num-ber of injured are here compared with the expected number of injured calculated from the age distribution of 73,395 skiers on different Swedish slopes.

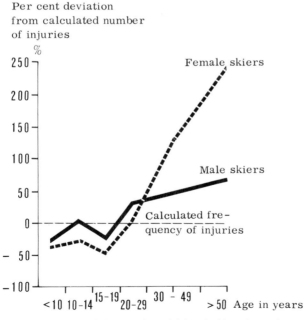

Figure 4.   Percent deviation of the number of injured skiers from the number of cal-culated injuries is seen in this diagram. It is not the children that constitute the problem group; it is the parents—especially the women over 50 years of age.

Table 1. Mechanism of injury

	1973-1974	1975-1976
Fall sideways	473 = 42%	725 = 42%
Fall forwards	523 = 47%	801 = 46%
Fall backwards	119 = 11%	201 = 12%

USE AND TESTING OF RELEASE BINDINGS

Of the downhill skiers, 86% used release bindings, but only half of them had recently tested the bindings with test instruments. It is not surprising that 47% of the injuries occurred among skiers whose release bindings had not released. This is, however, a somewhat better result than the 1973-1974 study revealed, when 57% of the bindings of those injured had not released. As can be seen from Table 1, about 12% of the injuries in both the 1973-1974 and 1975-1976 studies occurred from falling backwards. This further stresses the need for bindings with a toe up release.

Table 2 shows that the frequency of complaints about bad slope grooming diminished. It is interesting to note that the injured skiers reported a higher frequency of complaints than did the control group.

The types of injuries in the 1973-1974 and 1975-1976 seasons can be seen in Figure 5. A shift to somewhat more injuries to the upper extremities and somewhat less to the lower limbs is evident. This may be attributed to the fact that more skiers have released from their bindings and have then fallen against their outstretched arms. In the 1975-1976 investigation, 255 so-called ski thumb injuries were noted. These injuries, with ruptures of the ulnar collateral ligament of the thumb, were hardly reported in the 1973-1974 investigation. The explanation for this is not a steep increase in this type of injury, but the fact that, in 1973-1974, the questionnaires were not sent to the departments of hand surgery in Sweden. Evidently, these patients do not report to the ski slope attendent or their local doctor but go directly to a hand surgical department. A frequency of about 10% ski thumb injuries is, however, surprisingly high and means that there might be a need for a warning to avoid extending the thumb when falling. Young and Loo (see page 42) also found an increase in ski thumb injuries.

Table 2. Complaints about bad slope grooming

Injured 1973-1974	50%
Injured 1975-1976	38%
Controls 1975-1976	9%

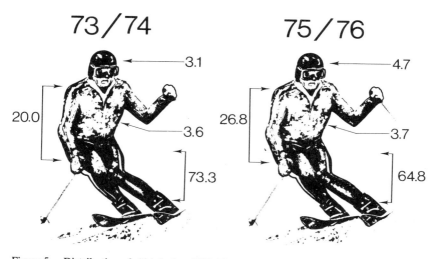

73/74

20.0

←————3.1

←————3.6

73.3

75/76

26.8

←————4.7

←————3.7

64.8

Figure 5. Distribution of ski injuries, 1973–74 and 1975–76 seasons, expressed as percent of total for each year. As can be seen, an increase in the number of injuries of the upper extremities has taken place.

After the Riksgransen conference of 1974, a considerable amount of propaganda for increased skiing safety was started in Sweden. Swedish television reporters attended the conference and made an excellent program about skiing safety. Swedish newspapers and radio have repeatedly stressed the importance of testing release bindings, of grooming slopes, of going to ski school, etc. It is therefore somewhat disappointing that twice as many ski injuries were registered in 1975–1976 as in 1973–1974. The third control investigation in the north of Sweden was, however, more comforting. As can be seen from Figure 6, the frequency of ski injuries in the area of Västerbotten decreased considerably after the introduction of propaganda for safer skiing. During the 1975–1976 season, every person who was injured in Västerbotten was contacted personally on the telephone by one of the examiners and asked on which slope the injury took place. In this way the reports from the ski slope attendants in Västerbotten could be carefully controlled. A very good correlation of over 95% was obtained, so the reports from this area can be relied upon. As indicated in Figure 6, despite an increased number of skiers during 1975–1976, a continued decrease of ski injuries was observed in this control area where the skiing conditions have been about the same during all the tested years. It is therefore evident that the propaganda has had some effect.

It is, however, obvious that there is still a need for more propaganda about proper adjustments of release bindings. Table 3 shows that TV, radio, and press are better channels for information than the

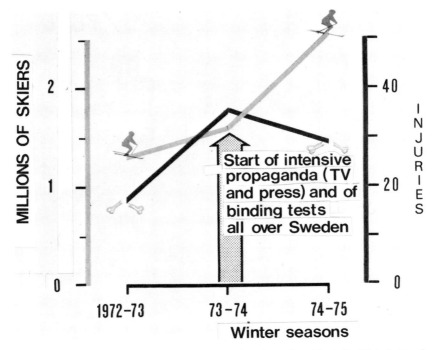

Figure 6. Numbers of skiers on the slopes and registered accidents in Västerbotten in the north of Sweden, 1972-1976. As can be seen, the propaganda for testing of release bindings, for grooming of slopes, etc., has led to a decrease in the number of accidents despite the increase in the number of skiers on the slopes.

different associations that have involved themselves in propaganda. It should, however, be noted that the Consumer Policies Board, the Association for Outdoor Life, and the authors initiated much of the TV and press propaganda.

It is interesting that, in this study, although there were many injured children and adolescents, it is not this group that is the problem group, but rather the skier over the age of 40. It should be remembered, however, that ladies over the age of 50 may have a higher injury rate than younger individuals because of the increasing frequency of osteoporosis in women after menopause. It should also be noted that the reason for the great number of ski injuries in children is simply that children are in the majority on the ski slopes.

In a study reported elsewhere in this volume (Nygaard, Ericksson, and Nilsson, pp. 273-278), muscle biopsies were taken during downhill skiing. Muscle fatigue was implicated as a cause of ski injuries. In this study it was found that one day of downhill skiing empties the muscles of their glycogen to the same extent as a major sports event like the 55

Table 3. Effectiveness of propaganda

	Injured (2,057)	Controls (1,004)
Noticed propaganda of all	66%	68%
Consumer board propaganda	8%	12%
Associated outdoor activities	16%	24%
Mass media (TV and radio)	76%	63%

mile Vasa cross-country ski race. One more conclusion from this study was that downhill skiing used mostly the so called Type 1 (red) muscle fibers; this means that the same type of fiber used for downhill skiing is used for cross country skiing. Physical conditioning and training before going to the mountains may therefore be another way of preventing injuries. It was also found that a proper diet is necessary. It is essential to eat somewhat more carbohydrates than normal before engaging in downhill skiing.

There are probably few other sports where it is so easy to prevent injuries as in downhill skiing, in which it is mostly a question of information and propaganda. A short 16 mm movie about the importance of ski binding adjustment is now available. At the end of this movie, the famous Swedish slalom skier Ingmar Stenmark says, "I think it is very importent to adjust your release bindings properly." If all skiers did that, many ski injuries could be prevented.

REFERENCES

Asang, E. 1972. Verletzungsschutz beim Skisport (Prevention of injuries in the ski sport). Sportartz Sportmedicine 8:209–222.

Danielsson, K., Eriksson, E., and Strand, O. 1976. Skador fororsakade av mini-skidor (Injuries caused by mini-skis). Lakartidningen 73:1216–1217.

Eriksson, E. 1976. Ski injuries in Sweden: a one year survey. Orth. Clin. North Am. 7:3–9.

New Zealand Ski Injury Statistics

M. K. Lamont

During the Winter of 1975 (June through October), statistics were gathered from one isolated ski area in the North Island of New Zealand—Mt. Ruapehu. It is interesting to note that Mt. Ruapehu is almost the antipode of Granada, Spain, differing by only 2° latitude and 1° longitude.

The mountain is a volcanic peak of over 9,000 feet, and provides the main ski facilities for the more northern of the two main islands of New Zealand. Mt. Ruapehu is 220 miles from the major cities of Wellington and Auckland and is in the central part of a national park. Its geographic isolation offers unique features for the study of the injury patterns of the visitors to the ski areas.

While the general aim of this study was to reduce the incidence of ski injuries, the more specific objectives were to delineate the causative factors and at the same time determine the economic cost of ski injuries to New Zealand. All persons who suffered an injury that brought them into contact with a ski patrolman had an injury report form duly completed. At the end of the season, a two-page questionnaire was mailed to each of them and they were asked to complete and return it. There was a 64% response to this questionnaire. At the same time recordings were made of the number of visitors and weather and snow conditions (including temperature, texture, and wind speeds and directions).

Because of the isolation of the ski area, most accident victims who required hospital treatment were referred to the nearest hospital, 1 hour's drive away. At the hospital, further statistical information was obtained that included the confirmed diagnosis, the treatment given, and the cost to the hospital. All statistics were collated and a social sciences statistical computer package from the University of California at Davis was used to do the analysis.

RESULTS

In strictly analytical terms and using the 286 returned victim question-naires, 56.5% of the subjects were males and 43.5% were females. Ages ranged from 4 to 66 years, with a median of 19.2 years and a mode of 18 years (Young et al., 1976). Interestingly, the job category of the injured was highest on Scale 4 (56.6%), Scale 5 (14.0%), and Scale 6 (11.9%) of the Congalton–Havighurst Scale of status rating occupations in New Zealand; that is, the greatest number of injuries were among the semi-professionals, the small business operators, the farmers, and the skilled manual workers, while the second high injury group included the office and sales people and some light manual workers, and the third category represented the semi-skilled manual worker group.

In terms of skier experience, 45.6% considered themselves beginners, 37.9% intermediates, and only 14.7% advanced skiers. It was therefore not surprising to find that 58.4% were members of holiday tour parties visiting the ski area or day visitors, while 38.5% were regular skiers who belonged to a ski club that had accommodation facilities on the mountain. This finding endorses early studies (Young et al., 1976). Not unexpectedly, 44.4% of the victims had rented their equipment, while 43.7% had used their own. Concern must therefore be felt for the beginner or single-day visitor who arrives at the ski area and rents equipment. This is the skier at risk. The rented equipment came from two main rental facilities and, not surprisingly, the injury ratio was lower on the equipment that was fitted with the multidirectional release Spademan binding system.

The release binding system appears to be misnamed 'safety binding' when it is found that 41.6% of victims stated that their bindings did not release in their fall and when 45.1% indicated that their injuries resulted from a combination of speed and/or loss of control while speeding. The times of day the accidents occurred, the type of injury, and the injured parts of the body are shown in Tables 1–3.

There is a high correlation between the years 1974 and 1975.

Table 1. Time of day of skiing accidents

		1975	1974
9 a.m.–noon	3 hr	31.8%	31%
noon–2 p.m.	2 hr	31.8%	37%
2 p.m.–5 p.m.	3 hr	33.24%	31%
5 p.m.–9 a.m.		3.16%	1%

Table 2. Skiing injury types

Injury	1975
Exposure	5
Fractures	59
Suspected fractures	48
Sprains	132
Dislocations	22
Concussion	13
Cuts	119
Sickness	19
Other	27
Total	444

Table 3. Proportions of injuries to specific body parts

Body Part	1975	1974	1973
Head	14.21%	12%	18%
Arms	13.72%	5%	9%
Hands	9.73%	14%	16%
Legs	24.44%	18%	25%
Feet and ankles	8.98%	17%	9%
Abdomen	2.00%	4%	11%
Knee	20.45%	30%	12%
Exposure and other	6.48%		

Other investigators have recorded lower incidences of head injuries (Eriksson, 1976); however the high percentages that are consistently recorded may result from the difficult terrain on which this ski area is situated.

Some definition of the problem was obtained, and the statistics were not significantly different in basic terms. Further statistical analysis was necessary, and a binary multiple regression model was used to calculate the known variables that may have led to an accident against the ratio of victims to population. This equation was used:

$$LN(F/(1-F)) = BO \times B1 \times X1 + B2 \times X2 X \ldots$$

where F = Frequency that dependent and variable accident = 1.

The normalized variable may be expressed as Variable − Mean/ Standard deviation.

Actual visitors totalled 205,603 during the ski season: 265 accident cases were analyzed. Table 4 contains plots of the known variables as a basis for calculation. By driving the variables into the equation and selecting the seven highest chi-squared values, Table 5 was generated.

Surprisingly, the variables with the highest chi-squared values were:

> Overcast skies
> Skiable level
> Snowing
> Cloudy weather
> Monday
> Icy snow conditions
> Wet snow conditions

Table 4. Variables in skiing accidents

Variable	Mean	Standard deviation
Day of week		
Sunday	0.3071	0.4613
Monday	0.0768	0.2663
Tuesday	0.0768	0.2663
Wednesday	0.0761	0.2652
Thursday	0.0768	0.2663
Friday	0.0750	0.2634
Saturday	0.3113	0.4630
Snow level	4550.5946	520.8348
Skiable level	5348.8242	209.1036
Snow conditions		
Firm	0.0231	0.1503
Wet	0.5033	0.5000
Icy	0.1911	0.3932
Weather		
Cloudy	0.2748	0.4464
Overcast	0.3893	0.4876
Misty	0.0143	0.1186
Precipitation		
Rain	0.1433	0.3504
Snow	0.4385	0.4962
Sleet	0.0680	0.2518
Wind direction		
Sin direction	-0.3494	0.5626
Cos direction	-0.4426	0.4753
Wind speed	16.0399	16.5208
Population	3406.5173	1570.1375

Table 5. Regression coefficients and standardized partial regression coefficients for the seven most important conditions associated with injury

Variable	Coefficient	Normalized coefficient	Chi-square to remove
Constant	4.6602	− 6.799	8728.1
Overcast	− 1.0645	− 0.519	39.7
Skiable level	− 0.0022	− 0.452	9.1
Snow	0.6560	0.326	19.4
Cloudy	− 0.5047	− 0.225	10.0
Monday	0.6276	0.167	9.6
Icy	0.6098	0.240	9.6
Wet	0.3844	0.192	6.0

The probability of having a reportable accident under the high risk variables is as follows:

Snowing	1.93 times greater
Monday	1.87 times greater
Icy snow conditions	1.84 times greater
Wet snow conditions	1.47 times greater
High skiable level	.9978 times greater
Cloudy weather	.60 times greater
Overcast weather	.3449 times greater

DISCUSSION

The ski area injury population statistics have been presented. Their pattern does not differ widely from epidemiological studies conducted by other researchers. Continual concern must be expressed about the incidence of injuries to younger people. The occupation scales of the injured citizens would lend some support to the theory that the more physically untrained skier is more likely to be hurt.

The cost to New Zealand is as yet undetermined; however, initial first aid treatment at Mt. Ruapehu costs approximately $10,000 to $12,000 per winter. Initial treatment costs at the nearest hospital add another $14,000, while the overall cost in terms of loss of production and loss of wages has not been determined.

Beginners and tour members remain the highest at-risk population, and publicity campaigns must be undertaken: to encourage increased physical fitness of the skier; to encourage the beginner to have ski lessons; and to encourage rental facilities to use good release bindings that are specifically adjusted at each rental.

While such variables as snow and slope conditions—as well as slope population densities—would seem to mitigate toward injury, the surprising variable of Monday has been statistically verified. This relates to a recently published report from the Accident Compensation Commission in New Zealand that states that Monday is the worst day for injuries in industry. In a report by Nygaard, Eriksson, and Nilsson it was shown that muscle glycogen levels dropped from 81 to 52 mM/kg between Days 1 and 5 during recreational downhill skiing. Extra carbohydrate intake can increase muscle glycogen by 50%; however, alcohol consumption can prevent the absorption of carbohydrates to a significant degree. To hypothesize further, it is not unusual for skiers at Mt. Ruapehu to eat very little food during skiing because of the poor on-slope facilities. They also drink very little during skiing and this leads to dehydration. At the completion of the day's skiing, alcoholic beverages are taken prior to eating. Morning glycogen levels may well be reduced and would not be replaced during the day. On the third day (Monday), glycogen levels would be very low and thus the propensity to injury would be high. Further physiological studies to prove this hypothesis would be worth undertaking.

REFERENCES

Eriksson, E. 1976. Ski injuries in Sweden: A one year survey. Symposium on Ski Trauma and Skiing Safety. Ortho. Clinics Nor. Amer. 7:3–9.
Young, L., C. M. Oman, H. Crane, A. Emerton, and R. Heide. 1976. Etiology of ski injuries: An eight year study of the skier and his equipment. Symposium on Ski Trauma and Skiing Safety. Ortho. Clinics Nor. Amer. 7:13–29.

Treatment
of Injuries

Incidence and Treatment of Ligament Injuries in the Lower Extremities due to Ski Accidents

G. W. Prokscha, J. Heiss, and T. Wagner

In conjunction with the increase in the number of skiers in the last 20 years, the frequency of injuries due to ski accidents has also increased considerably. In any one season, 3.5% of all the skiers in Germany have accidents. Injuries involved in downhill skiing are more numerous than those caused by other kinds of winter sports such as cross-country skiing, skating, tobaggoning, and ice-hockey.

A result of this impetus is that injuries are found in the lower extremities, where about 90% of all fractures due to skiing are localized. The distribution of ligament injuries is similar.

Based on cases of two years (1975 and 1976), ligament injuries were analyzed in the lower extremities with regard to localization and method of treatment. At the hip joint, ligament lesions could not be demonstrated. One case of luxation and five cases of fractures at the neck of the femur and of the pertrochanteric region were found. All cases of ligament lesions were found at the knee and at the ankle. The minor joints of the feet seem to be protected by the ski boots so well that ligament lesions are rare.

The diagnosis of a ligament lesion usually consisted of a case history, clinical examination of the injured joint, and x-rays (eventually stressed x-rays). In some cases, an unambiguous diagnosis was not possible. Acute pain, hemarthrosis, or extensive hydrarthrosis did not allow examination of the ligaments. After splint fixation, abatement of swelling, and arthrocentesis (after 48 hours), the diagnosis could be made exactly.

The classification of ligament lesions was as follows:

1. Tearing of ligament
2. Stretching of ligament
3. Partial rupture
4. Total rupture
5. Tear out of the bone (dislocated or not dislocated)

From this classification system, the method of treatment was derived.

In total, the ligaments of the knee had been affected in 127 cases. Between males and females the distribution was approximately the same. No tendency toward one side of the body was found.

Localization and treatment of 127 ligament lesions of the knee are shown in the following list:

	conservative	operative
tib. col. lig.	86	6
fib. col. lig.	13	3
ant. cruc. lig.	15	2
post. cruc. lig.	2	
Total	116	11

Simple tearing of the collateral ligaments without loss of joint stability demands only an elastic bandage.

Major distortions and stretching of ligaments as well as partial ruptures and unessential dislocated tear-outs of the bone demand immobilization of the knee joint with a cast. The femur plaster splint with fixation of the knee joint in 170° is the most suitable dressing. The time of immobilization was usually 2-6 weeks.

Operative treatment is indicated only in case of total rupture of the collateral ligaments and cruciate ligaments in the ligamentous part and in cases of considerable dislocated tear-outs of the bone. In some cases, a recent rupture of a ligament can be sutured. Older ruptures and extensive lacerations demand a ligament plasty. In case of the tibial collateral ligament, the suture with strengthening by the tendon of the semitendinosus has proved to be very effective. For the tibial collateral ligament, plasty fascia lata is used.

Ruptures of the cruciate ligaments were sutured with Supramid or wire (Figures 1-3), reinserting them into the femur or the tibia by drilling through the bone or replacing them totally by a flapped fascia lata strip. Tear-outs of the bone of the Emimentiae intercondylicae were fixated with bone screws.

If the indication for operative treatment of the tibial collateral ligament was not clear, the knee joint was first immobilized for 6 weeks

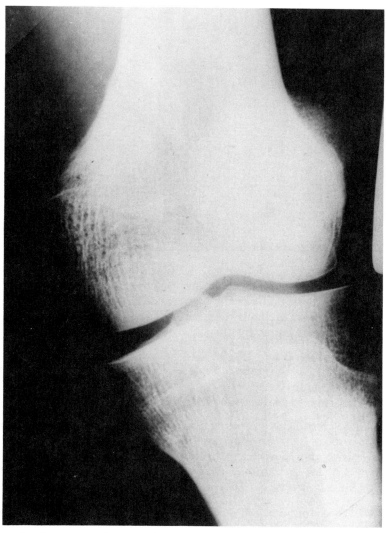

Figure 1.   Stress x-ray of a case with ruptures of the tibial collateral and the anterior cruciate ligament.

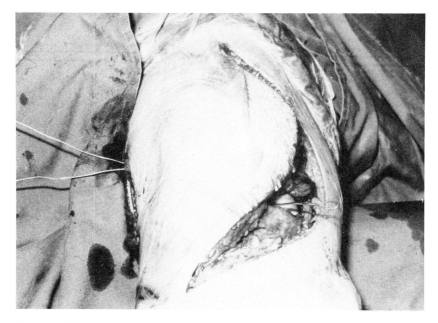

Figure 2.   Wire fixation of the anterior cruciate ligament through the femur.

with a cast. If the interarticular space of the tibial joint could still be extended, an operation was then performed.

The operative methods for reconstruction of ligaments of the knee joint are summed up as follows:

1.   Suture of ligament
2.   Ligament plasty (fascia lata plasty, tendon plasty with insertion of the semitendinosus muscle)
3.   Reinsertion (osteosynthesis, wire fixation)

Of 132 ligament injuries at the ankle, 106 cases were distorsions, partial ruptures, or tear-outs at the bone (80%). The treatment was conservative and consisted of fixation with lower leg plaster splint for 4-6 weeks. In 26 cases of ligament lesions at the ankle, operative treatment was necessary. They were distributed as follows:

Deltoid ligament (isolated)	1
Deltoid ligament (combined with fractures of the ankle)	11
Distal tibio-fibular syndesmois (combined with fractures of the ankle)	14

In most cases, the total rupture of the deltoid ligament at the ankle can be sutured. The majority of ruptures of the deltoid ligament are combined with fractures of the ankle (Figures 4 and 5). Ruptures of

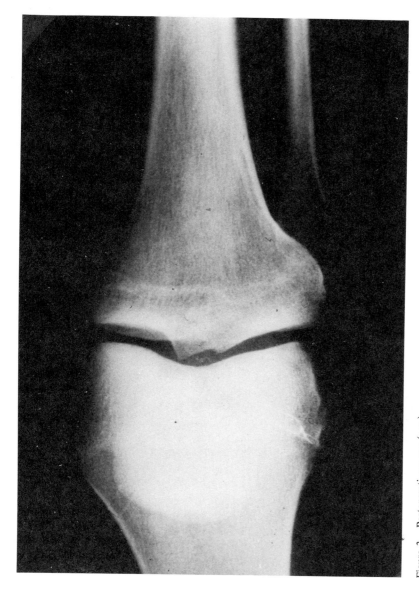

Figure 3.   Postoperative x-ray (a.p.).

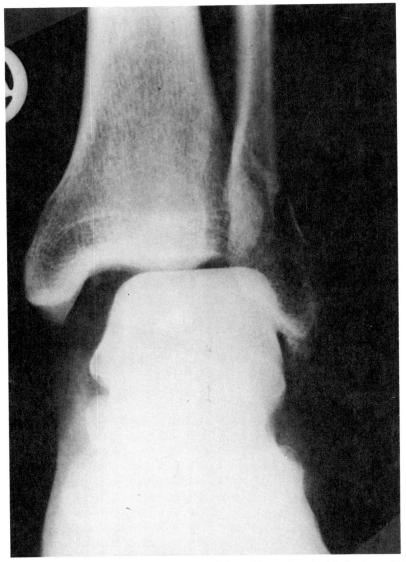

Figure 4.   Rupture of the deltoid ligament of the ankle combined with fracture of the lateral malleolus (x-ray a.p.).

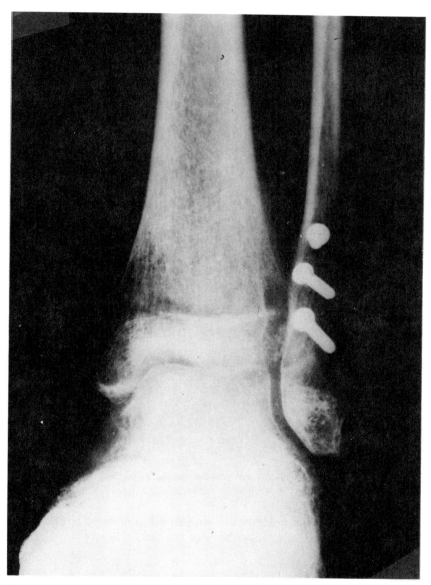

Figure 5.   Postoperative x-ray.

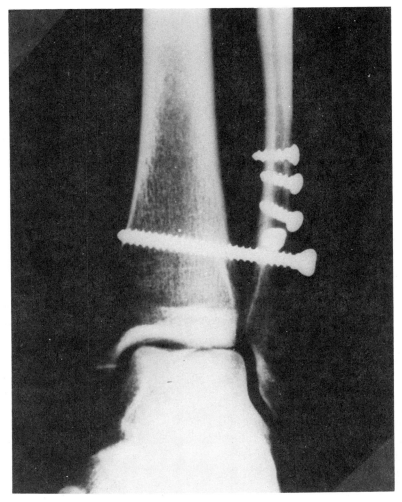

Figure 6.   Positional screw fixation and osteosynthesis after rupture of the tibiofibular syndesmosis and the fracture of the lateral malleolus.

the distal tibio-fibular syndesmosis are sutured or fixated with a positional screw during the osteosynthesis of the ankle (Figure 6).

CONCLUSIONS

The following results were obtained in this study:
—Ligament lesions due to ski accidents are the most frequent injuries next to fractures. More than 90% concern the lower extremities,

with the ligaments of the knee joint and ankle almost exclusively the injured sites.

—The increase in the height of the ski boots causes a much higher incidence of lesions in the knee region.

—At the ankle, the deltoid ligament and the distal tibio-fibular syndesmosis show the highest rate of injuries.

—In 8.7%, we operated on ligament lesions of the knee, while 19.7% of ligament injuries of the ankle were surgically tested.

—According to the conservative treatment, an immobilization of the injured joint with plaster or light cast was necessary for 6–10 weeks, while trivial lesions and slight distorsions are not treated in this way.

—Together with the gymnastic exercises, ligament injuries show by conservative treatment as well as by operative treatment a longer period of rehabilitation than fractures.

The Diagnostic Value of Examination of Joint Stability Under General Anesthesia in Knee Injuries

B. Balkfors, P. Edwards, and N. E. Westlin

The difficulties involved in examination of joint stability after knee injury are well known. These difficulties are probably most obvious in athletes with good muscle defenses. The objective of this chapter is to evaluate the diagnostic value of examination of the knee joint under general anesthesia after knee injury.

MATERIAL AND METHODS

During 2½ years, about 3,000 knee injuries were seen in the emergency room of the Orthopedic Department in Malmo. Initial examination included stability tests with the knee in straight and slightly bent positions, the drawer sign test, and a modified McMurray test for meniscus lesions. When hemarthrosis was suspected, a puncture was performed. In most instances a standard radiogram was also obtained.

Of these patients, 360 were selected for further stability tests on the grounds that they were suspected to have unstable knee joints or that the examination, because of pain and muscle tension, could not be correctly performed.

Financial support was obtained from the Swedish Sport Research Council and the Swedish Medical Research Council (Project No. B 76-17X-2737-08A).

RESULTS

The age and sex distribution of these patients is demonstrated in Figure 1. Fifty-four percent of all injuries were caused by sports activities (Table 1). The patients were brought to the operating room within the first few days after the injury to be examined by an experienced trauma surgeon. First, the stability test was repeated without anesthesia. In 41 cases ligamental rupture and other serious injuries were excluded; however, two of these were later operated on because of semilunar cartilage ruptures. The distribution of patients between the various steps of the diagnostic procedure is demonstrated in Figure 2.

Three hundred and nineteen were examined under general anesthesia. Of these, 193 were judged stable but 14 were nevertheless operated on because there were other pathological signs and symptoms. The findings at these operations are listed in Table 2. Of the stable joints, an additional 11 joints were operated on after an average of ten months (Table 3).

Of the 126 unstable cases, two had histories of old injuries and were operated on later, whereas 124 were operated on immediately. In these cases, complete rupture of either cruciate or collateral ligaments

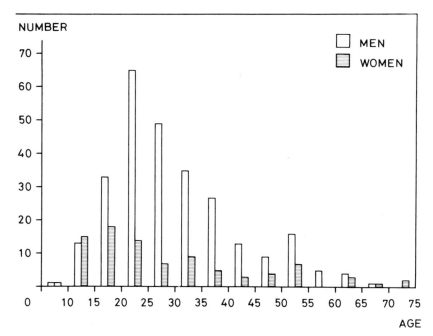

Figure 1.   Age and sex distribution.

Table 1. Distribution of injuries between various sports activities

Sports	Percent
Soccer	63
Skiing	14
Handball	4
Badminton	3
Wrestling	3
Other	13

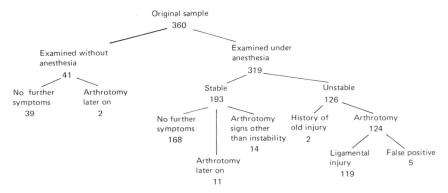

Figure 2.   Patient flow through the various diagnostic steps.

or both were found in all but five cases. No reason was found for the joint instability detected under anesthesia in these cases.

Twenty-five cases (compare Figure 2) were operated on in spite of a stable joint under anesthesia, 14 cases because of signs other than instability and 11 cases because of persistent symptoms. Complete anterior cruciate ligament ruptures were found in ten instances.

Table 2. Immediate operation on 14 stable joints

Joint injury	Number[a]
Partial med. collat. lig. rupture	5 (1)
Partial ant. cruc. lig. rupture	1
Complete ant. cruc. lig. rupture	4 (2)
Complete old ant. cruc. lig. rupture	2 (1)
Semilunar cartilage rupture	2

[a]Parentheses indicate cases combined with semilunar cartilage rupture.

Table 3. Later operation on 11 stable joints after 1–24 months

Diagnosis after arthrotomy	Number [a]
Partial ant. cruc. lig. rupture	3 (2)
Complete ant. cruc. lig. rupture	4 (3)
Semilunar cartilage rupture	4

[a]Parentheses indicate cases combined with semilunar cartilage rupture.

DISCUSSION

Table 4 presents the relationship between the diagnosis arrived at from a stability test before general anesthesia and the diagnosis when the stability test was performed under anesthesia. All patients who were judged to be stable without doubt before anesthesia remained stable under anesthesia, and, likewise, all patients who were considered unstable before remained unstable after. This indicates that patients who can be properly examined and are stable need no further examination. Similarly, the patients with a clear instability do not benefit from further examination; it serves only to confirm an already established diagnosis. The interesting group are the 229 cases in whom the diagnosis could not be properly established in the initial stability test. Forty-nine of these cases were found to be unstable when examined under anesthesia. This number is sufficient to justify the procedure if the aim of the diagnosis is an early repair of the torn ligament.

There were 4% false positive cases that could not be explained when the joint was surgically explored. There was, however, an incidence of about 5% of false negatives in the series, as far as can be judged, from that subset of the patients (25) who were operated on. In addition, there is no way of knowing whether there are any hidden ligamental ruptures among the 168 (compare Figure 2) patients who

Table 4. Comparison of results of stability tests with and without anesthesia

Diagnosis	Without anesthesia			With anesthesia		
	Stable	Unstable	Total	Stable	Unstable	Total
Clear	13	77	90	13	77	90
Obscure	(?)	(?)	229	180	49	229
Total			319	193	126	319

were free of symptoms. It appears that an isolated rupture of the anterior cruciate ligament is compatible with full joint stability even under general anesthesia. It is suggested that patients with hemarthrosis caused by an indirect or obscure trauma to the knee joint should be examined for joint stability under general anesthesia if the initial examination is inconclusive, because one-fourth or more of these patients have complete ligamentous ruptures. Since some isolated anterior cruciate ligament ruptures may not cause instability of the knee, these injuries, which are almost always followed by hemarthrosis, can be detected only by arthroscopy or arthrotomy.

CONCLUSION

Examination of knee joint stability under general anesthesia is a valuable tool to reveal ligamental injuries in those cases that are inconclusive or difficult to evaluate with standard methods. In such cases, instability is found in more than one-fourth, and is usually a sign of a complete ligamental rupture. However, not all ligamental ruptures can be disclosed by this method; isolated ruptures of the anterior cruciate ligament are particularly difficult to diagnose.

Hemarthrosis in Knee Injuries

N. E. Westlin and P. E. Wiklund

There is a tendency today to perform more active surgery and reconstruction in acute ligamentous injuries in the knee joint. The clinical
investigation prior to surgery is of utmost importance, and hemarthrosis
is a common clinical sign. The aim of the present study was to evaluate
the diagnostic value of hemarthrosis in knee injuries.

MATERIAL AND METHODS

Included in the study were 276 consecutive patients with acute knee
injuries examined at the emergency room of the Orthopaedic Department of Malmö General Hospital during the three month period from
February to April of 1976. The Orthopaedic Department provides the
only emergency service for orthopaedic trauma in the city of Malmö
with its population of 265,000. The knees were routinely examined
according to clinical signs of injury. In cases with signs of effusion, the
joint was aspirated and the hemarthrosis evacuated. The examination
was then continued with standard radiogram, and, in cases where
instability could not be ruled out, with examination under general
anaesthesia and arthrotomy. In follow-up examinations after one year,
it was established whether or not the patients, after the initial diagnostic procedures, had developed signs or symptoms of knee injury that
had led to diagnosis and/or treatment.

Financial support was obtained from the Swedish Sport Research Council and the
Swedish Medical Research Council (Project No. B 76-17X-2737-08A).

RESULTS

Sports contributed 37% of the patients, with soccer and skiing the dominant causes. Hemarthrosis was found in 106 of the 276 patients. The age and sex distributions of patients with and without hemarthrosis is demonstrated in Figure 1.

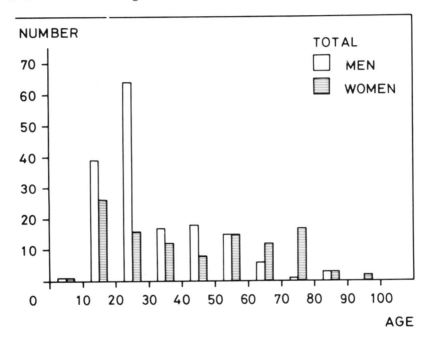

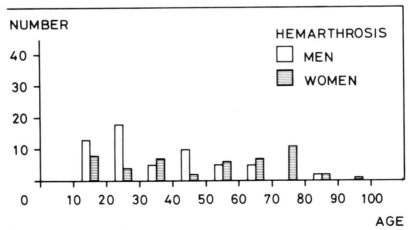

Figure 1.   Age and sex distribution.

The diagnoses in patients with and without hemarthrosis are listed in Table 1. Almost all serious injuries, such as fractures, patellar dislocations, and complete ligamentous ruptures, involved hemarthrosis. Only one complete ligamentous rupture was found in the group with no hemarthrosis. This rupture included only the extra-articular tibial attachment of the medial collateral ligament, and had not caused bleeding into the joint. Most injuries were diagnosed as sprains or contusions in the group without hemarthrosis. In the one-year follow-ups, it was discovered that diagnoses of meniscus lesions had been made subsequently and verified by surgery in five additional cases—one in the group of hemarthrosis and four in the group without.

The diagnosis in relation to the type of trauma is demonstrated in Table 2, where only patients with hemarthrosis are included. Most fractures were found to be caused by direct trauma, but others were caused by distortion or by some more obscure incident. None of the patients with patellar dislocation could properly define the trauma. When all the fracture cases that are easily diagnosed after the roentgen examination and the cases with obvious direct violence are excluded, there remains a group of injuries, one-eighth of the original 276 knee injuries, in which further diagnostic efforts are indicated.

Table 1. Diagnosis in patients with and without hemarthrosis[a].

Diagnosis	Hemarthrosis	No hemarthrosis
Fracture	40	0
Patellar dislocation	5	1
Complete ligamentous rupture	17	1
Ruptured semilunar cartilage	1 (2)	2 (6)
Sprain or contusion	43 (42)	166 (162)
Total	106	170

[a] Numbers in brackets represent the one-year follow-up findings.

Table 2. Diagnosis in patients with hemarthrosis in relation to type of trauma[a]

Diagnosis	Direct blow	Distorsion	Unknown
Fracture	29	3	8
Patellar dislocation	0	0	5
Complete ligamentous rupture	0	14	3
Ruptured semilunar cartilage	0	2	0
Sprain	0	12	3
Contusion	26	0	1
Total	55	31	20

[a] Framed area represents subset in which diagnostic efforts should be invested.

CONCLUSION

Hemarthrosis in the knee joint is a reliable diagnostic sign of serious intra-articular injury. After indirect (distortion) trauma, more serious injuries such as total ligamentous ruptures should always be suspected and additional diagnostic efforts initiated. Injuries without hemarthrosis are rarely serious.

SUMMARY

In 276 consecutive knee injuries, hemarthrosis was confirmed by aspiration in 106. In this latter group, all fractures and most of the serious soft tissue injuries were found, whereas, in patients without hemarthrosis, the only diagnosis of importance was the rupture of semilunar cartilages. If cases in which the injuries are caused by direct trauma and cases with radiographic evidence of fracture are culled from the hemarthrosis group, a subset remains that constitutes less than one-eighth of the original sample and in which efforts should be made to diagnose ligamentous ruptures or other intra-articular injuries.

First Aid Measures for General Hypothermia

G. K. Neureuther

SCENE OF ACCIDENT

Conscious Victim

If the victim is conscious, the core temperature is above 30°C.

Mountain Rescue Guard Member Position the victim cautiously, but do not move him; later, share your body heat by close contact. Apply the heat package as described by Hibler:

Make up the heat packs, put a 5x folded cloth, moistened with hot water from a thermos flask, at the inside on top of the ear and under breast and abdomen. Do not put it on uncovered skin. Cover the victim with a pullover and jacket and then wrap aluminum foil around the body only, leaving the extremities unwrapped. Cover the entire body including the extremities in several covers. Close contact of the covers at the neck is important. If a sleeping bag is available, it should be employed.

Administer hot drinks with sugar, especially after long exposure to the cold. No alcohol! Do not allow the victim to walk, even when the hypothermic believes he can, because the cold blood of the periphery could become mixed with warm core blood, causing "after-drop."

Mountain Rescue Guard Physician The principle is to bring warmth to the core first. Administer hyperthermic intravenous infusions (circa 43°C) of glucose and, eventually, isotonic natriumbicarbonate (1.5%), since slight acidosis will be present. The amount of acidosis need not be determined initially. Infuse slowly! For example, an infusion at 40°C will warm the 2 liters of core blood from 30 up to 33°C. No drugs and

and especially no digitalis should be given because of the possibility of arrhythmia of fibrillation in hypercalemia. Application of cortisone is controversial, because physiologists emphasize that, in prolonged swimming tests of rats, exhaustion of the adrenals could not be proven. Be especially cautious of subcutaneous or intramuscular injections; the drug will be trapped in the periphery and, after effective warming up, will reach circulation in an uncontrolled dose or rate.

Unconscious Victim

If the victim is unconscious, the core temperature is below 30°C.

Mountain Rescue Guard Member   For cardiac arrest, use cardiac massage; for respiratory standstill, use mouth-to-mouth ventilation. Employ no technical devices, no "Ambu," because it would bring cold air into the core. Use warm packages. During transport, careful observation of heart action or respiration is essential at repeated intervals. A mountain rescue member should be checking the pulse of the victim almost continuously. Eventually cardiac massage and mouth-to-mouth ventilation are used.

Mountain Rescue Guard Physician   Follow the same procedures used in treating conscious victims.

MOUNTAIN CABIN SITUATION

Mountain Rescue Guard Member

Transport the victim into a room with a temperature of 20–25°C. Heat package the victim. If a bathtub is available, a warm bath may be administered ("reasonable rewarming") at a temperature of about 30°C. During the next half hour, warm the bath to 40°C, keeping the extremities outside the bathtub. This treatment, however, will be more useful in ocean emergency rescue; in mountain emergencies, bathtubs or large amounts of warm water will not be available. The heat package will therefore remain the treatment of choice. For unconscious victims, renew heat package every 1–2 hours and intensify by wet, hot packings at the back. Cardiac massage and mouth-to-mouth ventilation may eventually be necessary.

Mountain Rescue Guard Physician

The victim will be treated at the scene of the accident more intensively. A stomach pump with warm water and the inhaling of warm oxygen will be rejected because they are disagreeable and inconvenient; a heat package will bring more heat to the core. For pain because of possible injuries (fractures), give analgesics intravenously. Use antiarrhythmic medication for extrasystole or arrhythmia.

HOSPITAL TREATMENT

The following treatments are recommended:

1. Regular heartbeat: heat package, blood gas check, EKG (ideally by monitor), potassium. Slow correction of acidosis by isotonic $NaHCO_3$ solution. In extreme cases, treat with peritoneal dialysis or extracorporeal circulation using hyperthermic solutions.

2. Cardiac fibrillation: cardiac massage, intracardiac injections of Na-Bic, defibrillation.

3. Asystole: Isoproteronol, external pacemaker. If this is not successful, alkalize by using maximal 250 ml of 8.5% $NaHCO_3$ solution. Ultimate treatment may require cardiopulmonary bypass with heat exchanger for the extracorporeal part of circulation; if this is unsuccessful, thoracotomy and cardiac massage and application of warm saline to the heart should be used.

Modern First Aid Equipment for Use in Winter Sports Injuries

G. Flora, M. Spielberger, and W. Phleps

Winter sport tourism in the Alpine countries is increasing continuously. On fine weekends, cable cars and ski tows are crowded by thousands of ski fans stressed by everyday life who want to make full use of their expensive tickets, going up and down hill until they drop of weariness ... or break their legs. Telephones on the ski slopes needed to report accidents to the ski slope patrol are not yet installed in every place. Cautious people, like Ejnar Eriksson, carry their own radio sets in their rucksacks or have the sets drawn after them in the akia (Figure 1).

Every cable car and ski tow company in Austria must keep a permanent telephone connection and standard first aid equipment, including a sled, in order to cope with the bulk of weekend skiers. Because of the increasing number of winter sport guests, modern life-saving equipment and first aid equipment for winter sport injuries should be provided.

However, other measures should be taken in addition to the training and equipping of the ski patrol. Every single skiing and mountaineering doctor should have a minimum medical outfit in his ski bag for emergency use at the scene of the accident. Each should also be able to prepare an extension splint for the lower leg with primitive means—e.g., two ski poles, a few straps and strings (Figures 2-3). Along with bandages and dressing material, each doctor should also keep an emergency injection set with analgesics and sedatives as well as cortisone in his ski bag (Figure 4).

With the growing number of skiers, the increasing downhill speed, and the widespread use of safety bindings, the distribution of winter sport injuries has changed in regard to the body regions involved. In

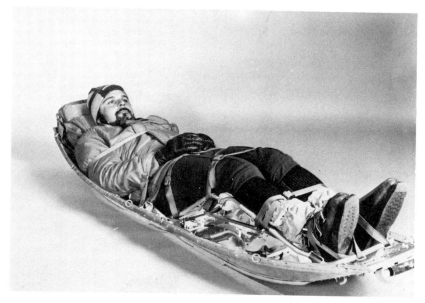

Figure 1.   The akia, the standard means of transportation for winter sport accident victims in almost any Alpine country.

the older statistics of Baumgartner (1960) and Neureuther (1963), more than 75% of all the winter sport injuries involved the osseus system and the ligamentous apparatus of the lower extremities. Now, increasingly serious and even deadly ski accidents are occurring, with injuries dominating in the area of the thoracic girdle and with contusion traumata to thorax and abdomen. Vertebral fractures can also be observed quite frequently.

The sled is still the standard means of transportation for winter sport accident victims in almost all Alpine countries. The sled comes from Lapland and was originally used only for transporting goods drawn by reindeer. In the last years of World War II, 1944-1945, it was adapted in Tyrol as a lifesaving device in winter. It can be carried in pieces on the back and can be provided with a wheel for snowless ground. Double knee support and a blanket for protection against exposure complete the standard equipment.

The ideal positioning in the sled for immobilizing an injured extremity is attained by the vacuum mattress. It consists of a hermetically sealed sack filled two-thirds full with numerous extremely tiny polystyrol globules. In a manner similar to vacuum packing, the mattress can be formed to the shape of the body and cause fixation of a body part by sucking the air off the sack through a valve. The vacuum

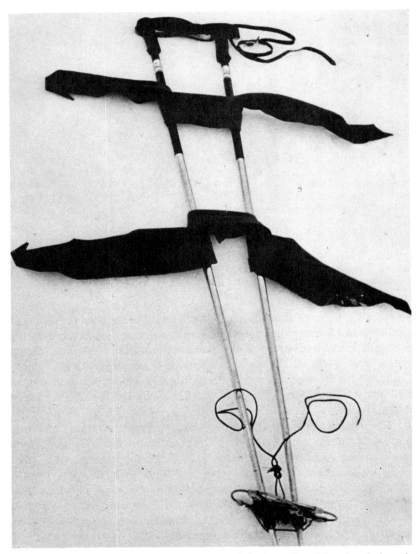

Figure 2. Emergency bandaging of a fracture of the lower leg with a few devices that every skier should have at hand: two ski poles and a few straps and strings.

Figure 3.   A fracture of the right lower leg fixed with two ski poles.

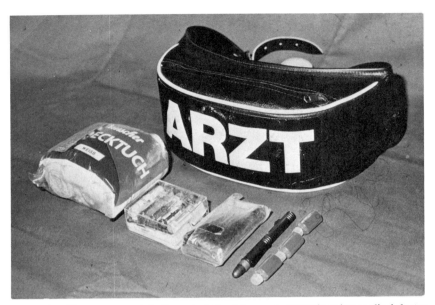

Figure 4.   The emergency injection set of the skiing and mountaineering medical doctor with emergency bandaging material.

cushion is not as bulky and is easier to handle. In Tyrol it has performed well in recent years in the fixation and transportation of the injured by sled and helicopter. It can also be used to fixate all injuries in the area of the thoracic girdle and the arms and all bone and ligament lesions of the lower extremities, and to immobilize fractures of the vertebrae or the pelvis.

In evacuating a victim of a winter sport injury from the high mountain region down to the valley, it is most advantageous that, with increasing exterior air pressure, the vacuum cushion becomes harder and harder and thus also more stable—quite contrary to the way in which the aircushion splints used up to now behaved. In addition, it is possible to make x-rays of the injured extremity through the vacuum cushion at the clinic. In comparison to the former methods of fixing injuries of the extremities with the Kramer–splint, Bofors–splint, extension splint, or aircushion splint, vacuum immobilization proves to be a secure and extremely careful method of fixation and can also be used for traumata to the pelvis and the spine.

The modern equipment of the ski slope patrol includes the indispensable radio set, an instant hot pack, and a rescue blanket to treat hypothermia of a victim in shock when the evacuation takes a long time. A complete life-restoring outfit with Ambu-bag and Ambu-suction pump should also be included (Figure 5). At the beginning of the season, the staff should attend an intensive course of instruction in first aid treatment of injuries of the extremities, shock treatment by nonprofessional helpers, cardiac circulatory revival with artificial respiration by mouth, and external cardiac massage.

Every winter sport resort already has its own avalanche commission which—if necessary—gives out the daily avalanche bulletins and can close ski slopes exposed to this danger. In a special avalanche center, the appropriate equipment, such as avalanche sound detectors, spades, technical searchers, lamps, electric emergency generating set, radio sets, megaphone, etc. is stored for the search crew. In any case, a medical emergency set must be included for use with every serious ski injury and avalanche accident. Beside the life-restoring equipment, the emergency set also contains an infusion set for shock treatment, an electrocardiograph, and other special equipment for cases of cardiac arrest. Only when all these are available will it be possible for the doctor of the mountain patrol or any doctor who happens to be in the avalanche area to give medical first aid at the scene of the accident. Every skier with serious injuries, especially to the skull, the spine, or the blood vessels, or contusion traumata to thorax and abdomen, and every person saved from an avalanche should be brought to the closest

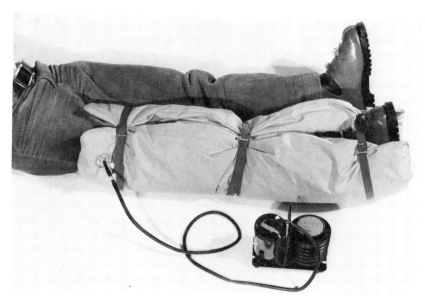

Figure 5. First dressing of a fracture of the right lower leg by vacuum cushion held together by three straps (evacuation performed by means of Ambu-suction pump).

central hospital—if the weather allows it—by helicopter with medical escort.

REFERENCES

Baumgartner, W. 1960. Die Sicherheit der Schiabfahrt. (Safety on ski slopes.) Munch. med. Wschr. 43, 2220.

Flora, G. 1977. Rettungswesen im Wintersport. (Rescue service of winter sports.) Arztl. Praxis 29:228–237.

Margreiter, D. 1971. Erstversorgung von Schiunfällen auf der Piste und im hochalpinen Gelande. (First aid of ski accidents on ski slopes and in Alpine regions.) Zschr. F. Allgemeinmedizin 47:1439–1440.

Neureuther, G. 1963. Bergwacht-Statistik: Ski-Unfälle 1962 (Mountain watch statistics: Ski accidents 1962.) Bayr. Rotes Kreuz, Munchen.

Phleps, W., and Flora, G. 1976. Das Vakuumkissen und seine Anwendung bei alpinen Unfällen. (The vacuum cushion and its use in Alpine accidents.) Notfallmedizin 2:499–502.

Alpine Air Rescue Service for Winter Sports Accidents

M. Spielberger and G. Flora

For quite some time, air rescue has been the preferred means of transport for patients injured in serious accidents in Alpine regions. In Innsbruck, the air rescue service is now in a position to talk about 20 years of experience in air rescue.

On March 14, 1956, the first transport of an injured skier by air was accomplished. Since that day, more than 5,000 injured patients have been transported to the hospital by the air rescue service in Tyrol. In the earliest days, the missions were flown in "Piper" type airplanes, but, after 1964, the aircraft used almost exclusively was the helicopter. The original "Bell 47" was later replaced by the more powerful "Jet Ranger." In accordance with the structure of tourism in the Tyrol area, 70% of those rescued were foreigners, and only 30% were Austrians. During the last 5 years, a remarkable increase in the number of rescue operations has been observed—an annual average of 500 patients were rescued by air. The seasonal distribution of the air rescue operations showed most distinctly that winter sport accidents by far outweigh other mountaineering accidents. Two-thirds of all patients rescued were injured skiers. In 1974, for instance, a total of 471 patients were rescued by helicopter, 301 (64%) of them during the winter.

Of course, the total number of people injured in winter sports accidents in the area serviced by Innsbruck University Surgical Hospital is much higher. Of the 26,147 patients treated in the surgical emergency ward in 1974, 2,042 were injured skiers. The overwhelming majority, however, had been transported by akia and taken to the hospital by ambulance. Helicopters were called only in cases of serious or critical trauma, or to areas from which surface transportation would have been

Figure 1.   Evacuation of a seriously injured skier by plane in 1956.

long and difficult. In these cases the air rescue service offered valuable help not only for the injured skier but also for the rescue team.

In presenting a complete view, however, it should be mentioned that, despite all its advantages, transport by helicopter is not without

Figure 2.   A helicopter, "Jet Ranger" type, in action at the scene of a skiing accident.

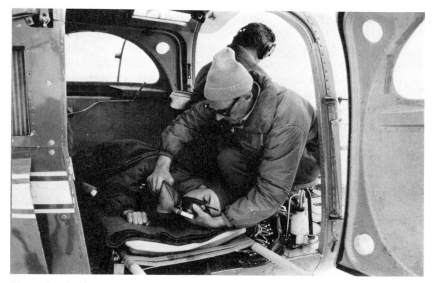

Figure 3.   Artificial respiration for an avalanche victim in the rescue helicopter.

problems. The possibilities of control and treatment during the flight are limited by the lack of room available and by the noise of the aircraft. There also exist some dangers, though minor, for the patient during the flight: kinetic influences due to strong wind gusts, vibrations, and the noise of the aircraft may cause nausea and vomiting, especially in cases of brain injury. These dangers, however, can be minimized by a smooth flight and by proper medical treatment.

Compared with the advantages offered by a quick and smooth helicopter flight, however, these problems appear minor. Even more than the almost painless transport of the seriously injured patient, it is the speed with which help can be brought that makes air rescue superior to conventional methods of rescue. The average time the Tyrol rescue service needs to evacuate an injured patient is only 14 minutes. In cases of emergency, the helicopter uses a special landing point directly in front of the surgical department of the hospital. There, the doctors of the intensive care ward, who have been alerted by radio, receive the patient for further treatment. The central geographic position of both the hospital and the air rescue center helps in achieving these short transport times. Of the operations carried out by this air rescue service, 80% are flown within a radius of 40 km.

With adequate planning and coordination, it is also possible to fly the necessary specialists to the accident scene in the same short time. In this air rescue center, one medically trained person from the mountain patrol and, in winter, one avalanche dog with its master are on permanent duty.

In 1971, Dr. Flora put forward an initiative to establish an emergency service of doctors from Innsbruck University Surgical Hospital for the Alpine air rescue center. At present, this service includes 25 doctors. Three are on duty every day, and this duty is on a voluntary and unpaid basis. The doctors can be called at any time because they carry radio receivers. They can be ready for a flight within minutes because they keep mountaineering equipment in their private cars. Thus, in case a serious mountaineering or skiing accident occurs, one of these doctors can be flown immediately to the injured patient.

The statistics of the Innsbruck air rescue service show that there has been a considerable increase in the number of missions that include doctors. While in 1971 only 11 missions had a doctor on board, 36 each had one in 1973, and, in 1976, 71 flights were accompanied by doctors. The reasons for this increase are that more people know about the service and that there have been more serious winter sports accidents.

Although helicopter flights offer enormous advantages, as indicated previously, there are other considerations, mainly economical, that determine whether the case justifies the use of the expensive aircraft. The decisive arguments may be medical or technical. An urgent medical indication for an air transport exists in cases of brain injury, thoracic and abdominal injuries, bleeding from major vessels, avalanche accident, shock, and general hypothermia, which often accompanies skiing accidents, but can also occur on its own. Technical reasons that justify air transport present themselves when flight is both easier and safer than conventional methods of rescue, or when the accident has happened in an out-of-the-way area, such as a glacial region, from which surface transport would be long and difficult for the rescue team and therefore painful and dangerous for the patient.

In view of the increasing number of serious skiing accidents, the following guidelines for the rescue services of major winter sports areas are suggested:

1. There should be the option of rescuing seriously injured patients by helicopter.
2. The air rescue center should be close to a major hospital and situated in a central geographic position with a radius of action not in excess of 40 km.
3. An air rescue team, including specially trained personnel from the mountain patrol and doctors, should be on permanent duty. Only then will it be possible to make full use of the enormous advantages offered by air rescue.

REFERENCES

Ahnfeld, F. W. 1969. Moglichkeiten und Grenzen des Transportes von Notfall-patienten mit Hubschraubern. (Prospects and limits of helicopter transportation for emergency patients.) Arbeitsgem. der Rettungsärzte Mitteilung 1:16.

Flora, G. 1972. Der bergrettungsarztliche Flugbereitschaftsdienst im Einsatz. (The doctors-stand-by service for Alpine air rescue operations in action.) Ärztl. Praxis 24:397.

Flora, G. 1977. Rettungswesen im Wintersport. (Rescue service for winter sports.) Ärztl. Praxis 29:228-237.

Gutman, J., Weisbuch, J., and Wolf, M. 1974. Ski injuries in 1972-1973. JAMA 230:1423-1425.

Jenny, E. 1971 Ärztliche Probleme beim Hubschraubertransport von Schwerver-letzten. (Medical problems connected with helicopter transportation of seri-ously injured patients.) Österr. Ärztezeitung 26:581-584.

Margreiter, R., and Flora, G. 1974. 3 Jahre im permanenten bergrettungsärzt-lichen Flugbereitschaftsdienst. (Three years of permanent stand-by service of doctors for Alpine air rescue operations.) Österr. Journal fur Sportmedizin 4:3.

Evaluation and Treatment of Lesions of Collateral Ligaments of the Knee

E. Campailla and G. Bonivento

The incidence of lesions of collateral ligaments of the knee has been increased by use of new ski boots. In fact, with almost half of the lower leg closed in the boot, every rotation trauma directly involves the articulation of the knee, inducing an abnormal solicitation of the capsule and ligaments, and particularly damaging to the medial collateral ligament.

Unfortunately, clinical examination is not always made accurately; consequently, proper diagnosis is often not made. Lesions of the medial collateral ligament are of differing severities. Only adequate evaluation can give the exact indication as to the proper treatment. When a severe rupture is suspected, a "dynamic" x-ray examination is indispensable. This is done under general anesthesia, the only method that will evaluate exactly the entity of the rupture. A different surgical technique is necessary in cases of distal or proximal ruptures and disinsertions of the ligament.

This method has been described by Vigliani; a summary follows.

DETACHMENT FROM THE TIBIA

1. A hole is made in the compact bone with a straight awl into which a screw 4–5 cm in length is introduced to a depth of about 1.5 cm, with a slight upward slope towards the head of the fibula.
2. A square segment of cortex about 12 mm wide is cut out around this screw with a thin oscillating electric saw.
3. The segment of bone delineated in this way is extracted by applying

leverage to the screw and placing stress on one side. A small hole is then made in the underlying spongy bone and its distal margin undermined with a Volkmann spoon.

4. The cortical bone of the tibia is then perforated with an awl obliquely from below upwards, about a centimeter lower down, and from the lateral to the medial side in such a way that the curved point of the awl reaches the bottom of the hole, already made in Step 3.

5. Now firmly fix a loop of strong thread to the free end of the ligament with a cross-stitch.

6. The loop, mounted on a curved needle or a Deschamps' needle, is passed into the hole and brought out again through the underlying tunnel.

7. The tibia is placed in maximum varus and external rotation, with a sandbag under the lateral malleolus. Progressive traction is exerted on the stitch so as to drag the free end of the ligament into the tibial tunnel until it is under tension. Care is therefore necessary in selecting the level at which the thread is fixed to the ligament, so that the latter is not too long.

8. The detached square of cortical bone is replaced in its original position and screwed to the underlying spongy bone. At the last turns of the screw, this will grip the substance of the ligament and fix it more firmly to the bone, at the same time increasing its tension. The action in this respect is like the tension screws that tighten the strings of a violin.

Ideal conditions are attained when the segment of bone can be screwed down to just below the level of the surrounding cortex. Care must be taken to keep the ligament and anchoring thread exactly in line with the upper edge of the "window" and the tunnel below it; otherwise, sufficient tension will not be obtained.

DETACHMENT FROM THE FEMUR

1. The upper end of the ligament is isolated, carefully preserving any fibrous bands that branch upward from it after detaching them as closely as possible to their connections with neighboring structures.

2. The ligament, including these bands, valuable because they increase the already inadequate length of the ligament, is then firmly transfixed with a "St. Andrew's cross" stitch by a length of strong thread.

3. On the femoral condyle (or just below it, if the ruptured end of the ligament is short), make a transverse slot, about 10 mm long, 3 mm wide, and 15 mm deep, with a small osteotome.

4. Starting from about 2 cm higher, a narrow tunnel is gouged out to join the base of this slot.
5. Both threads of the cross-stitch are passed through the tunnel from below upwards and the ligament dragged into the slot in the bone. If the measurements have been correct, the ligament will engage under tension. This maneuver is carried out with the knee in slight flexion, maximum adduction, and external rotation, with a large sandbag placed under the lateral malleolus.
6. In order to anchor the ligament firmly and increase its tension, a wedge of compact bone, trapezoidal in shape and marginally larger than the slot, is cut from the anteromedial surface of the tibia with an oscillating electric saw. It is taken from the area between the anterior tuberosity and the lower half of the tibial collateral ligament. This wedge is driven into the femoral condyle with a hammer and beater. As it enters more deeply, the ligament is gripped firmly and the tension increased like strings of a violin.

In both methods, a plaster cast is applied for 40 days, with the knee in 15 degrees flexion.

Surgical treatment of ruptures of the collateral ligaments gives excellent results. Exact diagnosis is very important in all cases, but expecially in ski trauma in which clinical and radiographical confirmation of the lesion give imperative indication for surgical treatment.

Safety
Measures

Injury Thresholds of the Leg: Ten Years of Research on Safety in Skiing

E. Asang

Individual injury thresholds of the human leg were established by different loading experiments on the tibia using static and dynamic situations. These corresponded to the lower tolerance limits of the elasticity thresholds during slow loading, bending forward and backward, and twisting with additional bending loads. As a result, it was possible to determine loading forces, moments, torques, deformations, and energy, and to calculate the moments of inertia, material strength, and their dispersions, depending on loading directions, and the individual cross-sectional shape and dimensions at the fracture site. The frontal diameter of the head of the tibia was found to give an indication of the individual bone dimensions that are easy to measure in vivo. This is fundamental for an individual prognosis of leg injury thresholds under typical skiing trauma and allows an individual safe release adjustment. Nevertheless, it is necessary to have release bindings that can operate in correspondence to the biomechanical properties of the human leg established in this study covering 10 years of research.

FALLS AND INJURIES

Since 1950, a drastic increase in skiing-related injuries has been observed in one clinic (Asang, 1961, 1964, 1966, and 1967; Diem, 1962; Pachl, 1963). This situation was intolerable and so Internationaler Arbeitskreis

Sicherheit beim Skilauf (International Association for Safety in Skiing, or IAS) was founded in 1967 to develop ways to protect skiers.

Naturally, the best protection against injury is to avoid an accident. In skiing, the typical accident is a fall, and there are many ways to reduce falls. However, there will never be skiing without falls; therefore, the decision was made to concentrate on the problem of falls during skiing. The skier is in a dangerous situation when the bones and joints of his leg are subjected to stresses and torques without adequate muscular protection. In a fall it is necessary to release the coupling between the ski and the boot. This is one of the tasks of release bindings. In order to gather necessary information regarding these bindings, the individual injury thresholds of the leg must be determined as well as the force necessary to prevent the binding from opening inadvertently. Another problem that was confronted involved the definition of the characteristics of the bindings to correspond to the biomechanical properties of the human leg.

PROCEDURES

In 1965, mechanical examinations of the loading limits of the tibia during bending and twisting were initiated (Asang, Posch and Engelbrecht, 1969). The dynamic impact resistance and hardness of specimens were measured on 120 bones (Ter Welp, 1971). The fractures produced in these experiments were identical to those experienced in genuine skiing accidents, i.e., single spiral fractures, torsional fractures with "butterfly fragments," and transverse fractures at various locations of the shaft. Only fractures of the lower spongy portion of the tibia near the ankle joint ("boot fractures") have not been examined. These are the subject of an as yet incomplete research program.

All experimental imitations of trauma produced under various loadings in more than 500 human tibias were recorded and analyzed. The soft tissue was removed, leaving the periosteum intact. The bones were then packed inside a plastic bag and frozen because it has been found that freezing has no detrimental effect on bone strength. Before these bones were tested, they were treated with Ringer's solution. Control tests with fresh human shin bones produced the same results.

Each bone was thoroughly documented. The information included individual dimensions, photos, and radiograms recorded before the tests, and photographs of moving fractures taken during the various loading procedures.

Modern technical equipment commonly used for testing materials was specially modified for each series of experiments. Electronic measuring systems and data processing were used.

FINDINGS

Some results were found to be common for all experimental loadings of the tibias:

—There is a definite relationship between the loading limits and the individual dimensions of the bone in healthy adults, teenagers, or children. However, this relationship did not hold for bones from subjects over 70 years of age. In this group, the loading limits were found to be approximately one-half of those for 20 year olds with the same dimensions.

—There are no specific characteristics of the tibia that differentiate between the sexes. Differences in the frequency of the types of skiing traumas affecting the lower extremity were attributed to differences in the male and female anatomy, physiology, statics and dynamics, and were not due to the properties of the tibia itself.

—When the tibia was subjected to torsion, experimental fractures always occurred in the region having the smallest cross-sectional area. This weak zone was generally located approximately two-thirds of the way down the diaphysis.

—During bending, fractures in this area of the shaft occurred at lowest loads. The bending limits of the tibial shaft increased from here both proximally and distally because of the larger cross-sections located in these directions.

—Torsional fractures with "butterfly fragments" arbitrarily produced by eccentric twisting did not require different torques. They occurred during slow as well as faster loading rates.

Slow Bending

Watzinger (1977) extensively tested the slow bending behavior of 96 tibias in both directions in the sagittal plane by loading them between two supports ("three point loading"). The bending forces were measured using an electronic force-transducer, the bending deformations by an inductive way-transducer. Bending force versus bending deformation graphs were plotted during a constant loading velocity ($v = 1$ mm/sec). After the loading tests, the compacta was also measured at three constant points on the fracture site, and proximal and distal ground sections of bone were prepared by cutting bone fragments. The original cross-sectional configuration of the center of each fracture was electronically calculated from these two ground sections (Wittmann, 1973).

The loading diagrams of slow bending clearly demonstrate the dependence of loading limit on the cross-sectional area of the individual bone (Figure 1). Diagrams of ventral bending—the imitation of a forward fall in skiing—differ characteristically from those of dorsal bending

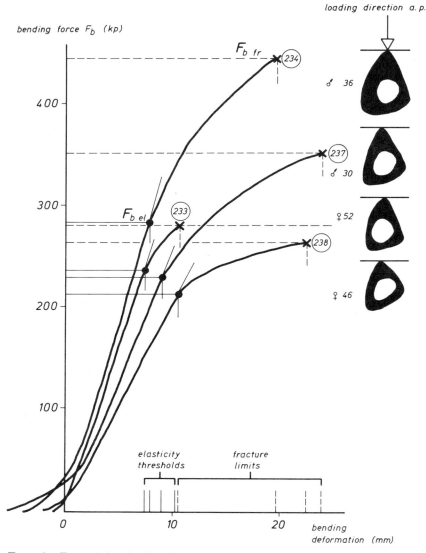

Figure 1. Forward slow bending diagrams at the two-thirds level and respective cross-sections at the fracture sites.

(backward fall) because of the specific cross-sectional shape of the shaft of the tibia. In forward bending, the fracture occurs suddenly at the point of maximal loading ($F_{b\,fr}$). In backward bending (Figure 2), the fracture occurs after the point of maximal loading. Beginning at the

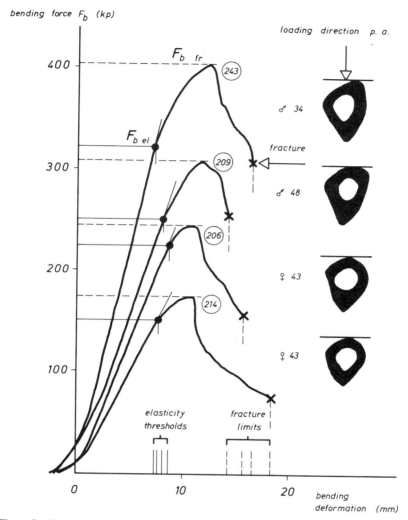

Figure 2. Backward slow bending diagrams at the two-thirds level.

loading maximum, the deformation of bone continues even though load decreases until the gross fracture appears. The total area of deformation is smaller than during forward bending. The loading maxima and the deformation properties of the human tibia depend on the different compressive and tensile loading behaviors of bone tissue (see Table 1).

From the bending forces (F_b), the bending moments (M_b) are calculated (Table 2).

Table 1. Mean deflective deformation during bending

	Mean (mm)	Standard Deviation
Ventral		
Up to the elasticity threshold	8.2	± 17.3%
Up to fracture	26.8	± 18.4%
Dorsal		
Up to the elasticity threshold	7.7	± 14.4%
Up to fracture	27.6	± 18.2%

Slow Twisting

Höpp (1976) tested the torsional loading of 132 tibias. Both tibial epiphyses were fixed (a, e) in the torsion apparatus (Figure 3), which was modified by a supplementary cardan joint (g) in order to avoid immeasurable complementary forces. While the bone was rotated at a constant velocity ($6°$/sec), the torque and the angular deformation were measured using an electronic force-transducer (q) and an inductive way-transducer (r).

Analysis of a torsional loading diagram (Figure 4) demonstrates the biomechanical properties of the whole tibia. The initial linear behavior of the loading line characterizes the elastic behavior of the bone (Hookian line). The subsequent departure from the Hookian line up the point of fracture is caused by the plastic deformation of the bone. During this time, the structure of the bone tissue is being destroyed. Most important to considerations of safety is the energy absorption during elastic deformation up until the point at which elasticity threshold is reached ($E_{t\,el}$ = mean 84.0 kp cm). This energy absorption averages one-third of that of the entire loading mechanism up to fracture ($E_{t\,fr}$ = mean 251.6 kp cm).

Surprisingly, in all loading procedures, the deformation of the tibia varies very little until the elasticity threshold has been reached, despite various values of individual parameters, including the dimensions of the bones. The plastic deformation, to the contrary, is always subject

Table 2. Bending moments

Direction	Moment Elastic (cmkp)	Standard Deviation	Moment Fracture (cmkp)	Standard Deviation
Ventral	2641	± 24.9%	2206	± 22.6%
Dorsal	1515	± 18.0%	1914	± 24.4%

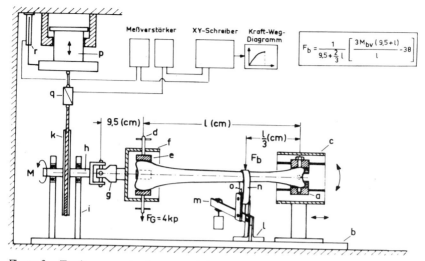

$$F_b = \frac{1}{9,5 + \frac{2}{3} l} \left[\frac{3 M_{bv} (9,5 + l)}{l} - 38 \right]$$

Figure 3.   Torsion apparatus for pure twisting and twisting with additional bending loads.

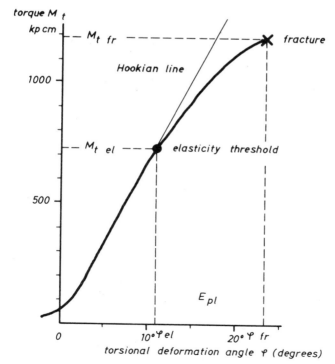

Figure 4.   Analysis of the typical slow twisting diagram.

to a larger individual dispersion. Significant differences between internal and external rotation were not found. The results of torsional loading can be seen in Table 3.

Combined Loading

A combined loading of the leg is the most frequent and most dangerous cause of injury to skiers using the modern downhill style. Being firmly attached to the ski, the lower extremity is unable to accommodate the combined movement of the falling body in both forward and rotatory directions. With simultaneous bending and twisting of the leg, a torsional fracture occurs at the weakest zone of the tibia (Höpp, 1976) because the bending capacity is much higher than the twisting capacity.

A single lever mechanism (m) on our torsion apparatus (Figure 3) enabled us to load the shaft of the tibia with an additional bending load (Figure 5). Bending loads were applied at a joint one-third of the

Figure 5.   Slow twisting with additional bending load.

Table 3. Effects of torsional loading

	Mean Fracture (cm)	S.D.	Length	S.D.	Angular Deformation (degrees)	S.D.	Torque (cmkp)	S.D.	Energy Absorption (kpcm)	S.D.
Elastic threshold	—	—	—	—	12.8	±11%	732.0	±15%	54.0	±26%
Fracture	6.7	±24%	—	—	22.8	±18%	106.6	±16%	251.6	±36%

way from the distal end of the bone because this location offers the lowest loading limits. Different constant bending loads in the anterior direction up to the statistically calculated individual ultimate limit (y_b = 1.0) were tested in twisting experiments (Figure 6); the result was always a typical single spiral fracture without additional fragments, averaging about 5.7 cm in length (S. D. ± 32%), that is, 1 cm or 15% less than in pure twisting.

The influence of additional bending on torsional loading was investigated, and it was found that even maximal bending loads diminish the torque at the elasticity threshold ($M_{t\ el}$) by an average of 110 cmkp or 13%, and the ultimate torque ($M_{t\ fr}$) by an average of 130 cmkp, or 16%. Addition of up to one-half of the ultimate bending load (y_b = 0.5) produced the same torques as those observed during pure twisting. This represents another important finding for skiing safety.

Additional bending load during twisting over y_b = 0.5 and up to 1.0, produces the angular deformations, torques, and energy absorptions shown in Table 4.

Dynamic Loadings

Using a specially constructed ram striking apparatus with an electronic double control system, Kuhlicke (1974) tested 47 bending fractures

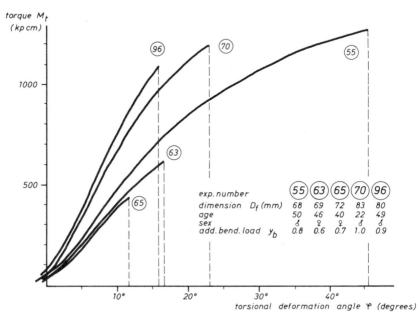

Figure 6.   Combined loading diagrams.

Table 4. Effects of bending loads

	Angular Deformation (degrees)	S.D.	Torque (cmkp)	S.D.	Energy Absorption (kpcm)	S.D.
Elastic threshold	11.8	±11%	613.6	±17%	63.2	±27%
Fracture	21.2	±28%	898.9	±22%	201.6	±53%

(in anterior direction) with a constant impact velocity of approximately 200 mm/sec. Electronic force tranducers at the striking ram as well as at the proximal and distal supports of the bone recorded force as a function of direction and force as a function of time. The ultimate load is the average of the data measured at the two supports.

The forces, which until the elasticity threshold was reached and until failure during 0.1 sec differ only slightly (maximum increase of measuring data about 5%) from those observed during slow bending (v = 1 mm/sec). Fracture types and loading diagrams show the same behavior of the bone.

Dynamic bending loads during 0.01 sec with an impact velocity of approximately 4000 mm/sec were examined with a pendulum device on 41 tibias (Kuhlicke, 1974). Again, fracture types and loading lines did not characteristically differ from those occurring during slow bending tests. Multifragmentary "explosions" of the bone were never observed. However, results increased by approximately 20% when compared to results of similar tibias during slow bending.

The results of dynamic torsional impacts occurring in 0.1 and 0.01 sec (Hauser, 1977) were similar to those that occurred during dynamic bending even though many experimental difficulties were encountered during the 0.01 sec intervals (Table 5). Other investigators have also found this increase in torque during dynamic loading (McElhaney and Vyars, 1965; Burstein and Frankel, 1968; Sammarco, Burstein, Davis and Frankel, 1971; Burstein, Currey, Frankel, and Reilly, 1972).

There is no doubt that an impact between 0.01 sec can occur in Alpine skiing without a fall. This was observed during field measurements; however, in most actual situations, an impact interval of 0.10 sec is the lower limit.

Age Properties

During the various loading series described, it has been established that no characteristic differences in the properties of the bone have been found in tibias ranging in age from 18 to 60 years. In order to determine loading behavior in relation to age, two series of tests were conducted. The tibias of 94 children and adolescents were tested during bending

Table 5. Dynamic torsional impact results

Impact Interval (seconds)	Torque (cmkp)	S.D.
1.00	2206	100%
0.10	2242	102%
0.01	2604	118%

(Lange, 1976). Tibias of 86 people over 60 years of age were tested during twisting (Guttenberger, 1974). Tibal dimensions of people over 60 years of age are very similar to the same dimensions in people between 20 and 60 years of age. However, the tibial dimensions of children who are still growing are much smaller than the dimensions measured in the 20–60-year-old and over-60 age groups. In addition, properties and loading limits of children's tibias are not similar to those of the other age groups.

Guttenberger established a considerable reduction in bone loading properties in people over 60 years of age. These experimental fracture types do not differ from those found in the 20–60-year-old group. However, the deformation angles are smaller than those found in the 20–60-year-olds; loading capacity also decreases (Table 6). The older the person is over 60, the larger is the dispersion of the bone qualities. It seems that this is caused by the differences of a training effect due to activity level.

DISCUSSION

The basic consideration for any statistical evaluation of these loading results was to find an indicator of the individual loading limits for the individual tibial dimensions. Proximally, the distance between the medial and lateral condyles, i.e., the frontal diameter of the tibiahead (D_f) proposed by Outwater (1967), was selected. The lower tolerance limits, especially regarding the elasticity threshold (Figure 7) are far more important in skiing safety than under the regression or confidence limits.

To ascertain the suitability of the head of the tibia, the moments of inertia of the whole tibia were determined from the cross-sectional area

Table 6. Effects of age

Characteristic	Elastic threshold	Fracture
Length (cm)	—	6.7
S.D.	—	± 17.7%
Angular deformation (degrees)	11.1	19.3
S.D.	± 21%	± 27%
Moment (cmkp)	579	830
S.D.	± 37	± 38
Energy absorption (kpcm)	58.5	173.3
S.D.	± 53	± 58
Decrease in loading capacity 60-69 years	− 18%	− 17%
Decrease in loading capacity over 70	− 33%	− 35%

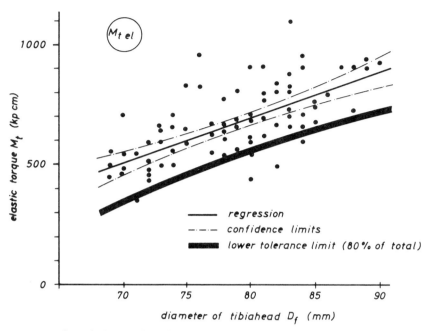

Statistical evaluation of slow twisting: elastic torques ($M_{t\,el}$) versus tibia head

at the fracture site (Figure 8) using EDP (Wittmann, 1973) as proposed by Leitz (1970). The deformation behavior of whole bone is characterized by its cross-sectional area. The anterior position (v) of the human tibia resembles a triangular configuration and the posterior, a curved surface. When bent forward, the tibia was fractured over a rim, and when bent backward, over a circular profile. Since compressive stress values exceed those of tensile stress, the moments of inertia were determined from the distances of the axes of inertia (v and w) to the surface of the tibia. Using the equation $\eta = M_{b\,fr}/M_{b\,el}$ Burstein (1972) found η to be 1.65 in bovine bone specimens. Wittmann found mean values of $\eta = 1.26$ during posterior bending, $\eta = 1.35$ during anterior bending, and $\eta = 1.47$ during twisting of the whole tibia.

The calculated moments of inertia during anterior bending exceeded those during posterior bending. Those observed during lateral bending exceeded those observed during medial bending (Table 7).

Figures 9A and 9B show the moments of inertia during torsion (W_t) and during anterior bending (W_{v2}) versus the frontal diameter of head of the tibia (D_f). The ratio of the moments of inertia in posterior versus anterior bending was found to be 0.92; the ratio of the posterior bending moments versus anterior bending moments was also found to be 0.92.

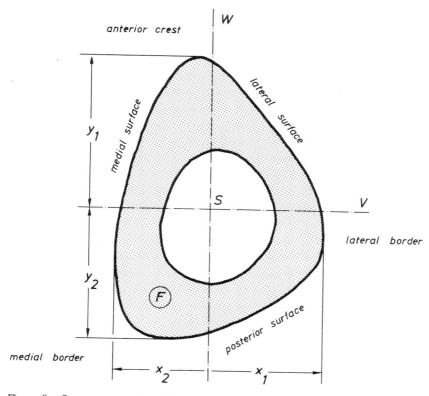

Figure 8. Square cross-section of the tibia at fracture site, the basis calculating the moments of inertia.

A comparison of the diameters of the head of the tibia (D_f) and the moments of inertia (W_{v2}) with the bending moments $M_{b\ el}$ (Figures 10A and 10B) and $M_{b\ fr}$ in the anterior direction demonstrates how well qualified the head of tibia is to be regarded as an indicator of the dimensions of tibia. The comparison of tibia head (D_f) to the bending moments of the posterior direction to the torques, at both elasticity thresholds and failure limits, bring similarly reliable results.

Table 7. Moments of inertia

	Posterior W_{v1}	Anterior W_{v2}	Medial W_{v1}	Lateral W_{v2}	Torsion W_1
Moment of inertia (mm^3)	998	1084	702	895	1449
S.D.	21.7%	23.7%	20.2%	22.4%	21.1%

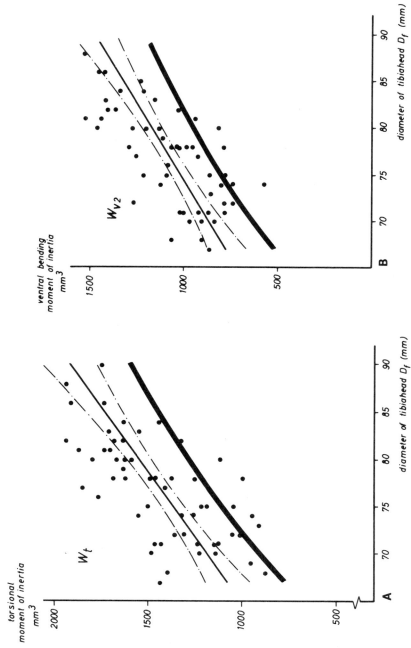

Figure 9.   A (*left*): Torsional moments of inertia (W_t); B: forward bending moments of inertia (W_{v2}) of the human tibia.

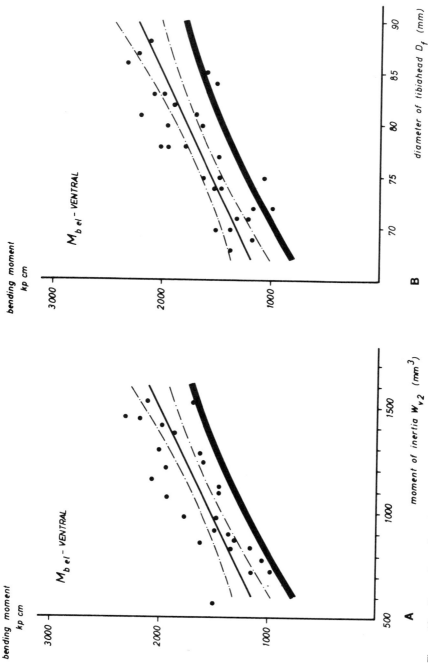

Figure 10. Comparison of statistical dispersions at the elasticity threshold ($M_{b\ el}$-ventral) A: Moments of inertia at the elasticity threshold ($M_{b\ el}$-ventral) A: Moments of inertia in forward bending (W_{v2}); B: Frontal diameters of tibia head (D_f).

The dispersion of values in Figures 9 and 10 exhibits the biological dispersion of strength in organic materials; in other words, it explains the error in estimating the bending moments and torques as if material strengths were constant.

The material strength values of the loading experiments with the tibia were calculated using the equation $\sigma_b = M_b/W_b$. Results can be seen in Table 8.

Medial and lateral bending moments were determined using the determined moments of inertia and a value of $\sigma = 1550$ kp/cm^2 for the mean strength:

$$\text{medial } M_{b\,el} = 1100 \text{ cmkp}$$
$$\text{lateral } M_{b\,el} = 1400 \text{ cmkp}$$

Curiously, the dispersions of the material strength of the tibia of the moments of inertia do not equal the total. On the contrary, the total dispersion of the loading moments is significantly lower. Both the moments of inertia (w) and the bending moments (M) depend on the dimensions of the bone, represented here by the head of the tibia (D_f). Therefore, the standard deviations around the regression lines of W and M must be taken into account rather than the mean total dispersion values (Table 9).

If the material strength (σ) and the moment of inertia (W) were independent of each other, the calculated dispersion for $M_{b\,fr}$ around the regression line would be a value of $\pm 16.1\%$. Because the dispersion of $M_{b\,fr}$ around the regression line was found to the $\pm 12.8\%$, σ and W cannot be completely independent of each other. A comparison of W can be made by eliminating the dependence of the moments of inertia (W) on the bone dimensions (D_f) when calculating the ratio of $W_{v2}/W_{v2\text{-}mean}$ regression. Then the moments of inertia are only related to age (Figure 11A).

It can be assumed from this examination that the value of the moment of inertia tends to increase (Figure 11A) and measures of material strength do decrease with aging (Figure 11B). These relationships indicate age-related altering processes in the anatomical structure of the tibia.

Table 8. Material strength

	Mean (kp/cm^2)	S.D.
Dorsal $\sigma_{b\,el}$	1579	+ 16.9%
Dorsal $\sigma_{b\,fr}$	1988	+ 18.8%
Ventral $\sigma_{b\,el}$	1520	+ 19.3%
Ventral $\sigma_{b\,fr}$	2030	+ 14.9%
Torsion τ_{max}	510	

Table 9. Anterior dispersion

	Strength σ_b	Moment of inertia W_b	Bending moment M_b
Elastic threshold	19.3%	17.3%	14.9%
Fracture	14.9%	17.3%	12.8%

Indeed, repeated control with hundreds of ground sections of the tibia shaft confirm these facts: the external shape of the tibia alters with age, assuming a more triangular shape; and the size of the compacta increases with age. The shape of the tibial head also changes with age. Its cross-sectional area and the diameter increase; in experiments, the average diameter in the 18–60-year-old group was 78.5 mm, while the average diameter in people over 60 was 79.7 mm. These gradual alterations influence the moments of inertia of the shaft to produce a more favorable loading capacity. They compensate for the loss of material strength in the aging bone substance. It is only in old age that this loss of material strength cannot be compensated for by the progressive anatomical alteration of the tibia.

Obysow (1972) conducted tests on human femurs and found that compression strength decreases with age. For 30–40-year-olds, it was 1500 kp/cm^2; in the 75–82-year-old group, it had decreased to 1000 kp/cm^2; and in the over 83 group, it decreased to 600 kp/cm^2. Ter Welp (1970) established a similar state of impact resistance and hardness in specimens of the aged human tibias.

The frontal diameter of the tibial head, which was found to give an excellent indication of the individual dimensions of the tibia, also offers a possibility for in vivo measurement. In vivo prognosis for the individual injury thresholds during different loadings for soft tissues has been added to the dimensions of the bone (Figure 12).

Because of the high frequency of combinations of bending and torsional loading in typical skiing injuries, combined loading results were reported. The loading limits are specified only for adults of 18 to 60 years of age. For people over 60, their diminished loading capacity must be considered. The growing bones of children are subject to other factors during loading which have been described by Lange.

Protecting the leg from typical skiing injuries requires knowledge of two basic facts: 1) the data characterizing individual injury thresholds during different loading processes; and 2) an objective in vivo measurement to estimate individual prognosis for these injury thresholds.

In each fall the leg must be freed from the ski by the release bindings. These force–limiting instruments are only able to work correctly when

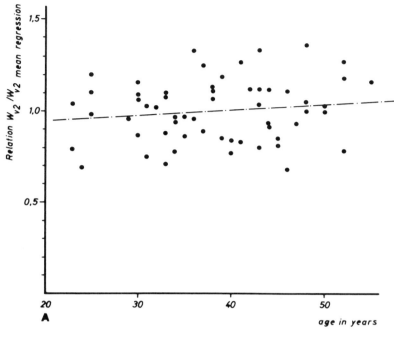

A

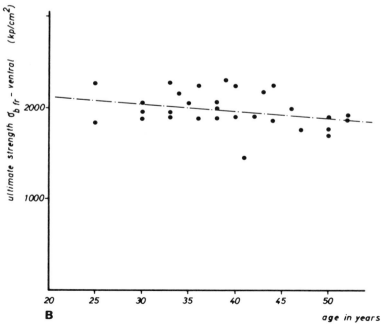

B

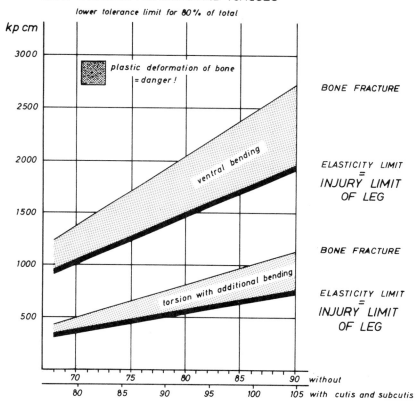

SLOW BENDING MOMENTS AND TORQUES

lower tolerance limit for 80% of total

kp cm

3000

plastic deformation of bone
= danger !

BONE FRACTURE

2500

2000

ventral bending

ELASTICITY LIMIT
=
INJURY LIMIT
OF LEG

1500

BONE FRACTURE

1000

torsion with additional bending

ELASTICITY LIMIT
=
INJURY LIMIT
OF LEG

500

70   75   80   85   90 without
80   85   90   95   100   105 with cutis and subcutis

diameter of tibiahead D_f (mm)

Figure 12.   Injury thresholds of the human tibia in forward bending and in combined twisting.

the release mechanism is adjusted for the individual. Their technical properties must correspond to the biomechanical properties of the leg because they also attach the ski to the leg during skiing when unwanted release must be averted.

This paper presents research on the passive properties of the weakest link in the chain of forces transmitted from the body to the skis—the tibia. Other field and laboratory examinations were made concerning the activities of the leg and of the active and passive forces occurring at

Figure 11.   A: Related moments of inertia in forward bending (dimensions eliminated by calculation of W_{v2}/W_{v2} mean regression); B: Ultimate strength values ($\sigma_{b\,fr}$) in forward bending in terms of ages.

the binding during skiing (Grimm, 1973; Krexa,1973; Sarcletti,; Scherm, 1975; Schipek, 1975; Wittmann, 1973).

In 1967 and 1976, the International Association for Safety in Skiing published the "IAS—Adjustment Table for Ski Bindings"; in 1969 and 1974, the "IAS—Specification No. 100 for Adults—Ski Release Bindings, Requirements and Tests"; and, in 1974, the "IAS—Specification No. 101 for Children and Youths." The effects of these endeavors to protect skiers were controlled consecutively by Walker (1970), Holzinger (1971), Pulkowski (1972), Kolb (1973), Weidenthaler (1973), Olzowy (1974), Mathoul (1974), Uhl (1974), Meynen (1975), and Hauser, Marz, and Asang (1976). A decrease in the number of severe skiing injuries was consistently found by all investigators.

CONCLUSIONS

The human tibia is most vulnerable during slow loading. The dynamic loading capacity of the tibia up to 0.01 sec was found to increase by 20%. Therefore, the tibia's behavior during slow loading can be the basis for preventing injuries of the lower extremity during Alpine skiing.

Elastic deformation and behavior vary more in terms of dispersion than in ultimate properties. Without any doubt, the elasticity threshold characterizes the injury threshold of the human tibia and of the whole leg in skiing, if the protective function of muscles on bones and joints breaks down. The contribution of the fibula is negligible in stabilization.

ACKNOWLEDGMENTS

The author would like to thank all collaborators and the "Technischer Überwachungsverein Bayern, e.V., München" (an organization testing materials under governmental order) for permission to use its technical equipment and EDP. Research costs were borne by the "Deutsche Forschungsgemeinschaft" (German Science Foundation) under the program "Eigenschaften des menschlichen Beins" (Properties of the Human Leg). In addition, further subsidies were granted by the "Internationaler Arbeitskreis Sicherheit beim Skilauf—IAS" (International Association for Safety in Skiing), and by the "Bayerisches Staatsministerium fur Arbeit und Sozialordnung" (Bavarian State Ministry for Labor and Social Affairs).

IAS-Adjustment Table for Ski Bindings

measure → here

Measurement should be made in the sitting position with knee-joint bent. The soft tissues above the tibia head should not be pressed with the sliding caliper.

Instructions on how to use the table

1. The diameter of the lower leg at the tibia head is measured with a sliding caliper. Touch the head of the tibia at the front side just below the knee and measure immediately above that point (see illustration alongside).

2. The values recommended for adjustment are then to be taken from the table corresponding to the measured diameter. The unit N indicated in the table is the new power unit Newton. 10 N = 1 daN ≈ 1 kp.

   Example: Adult up to 50 years:
   Measured diameter: 8,5 cm
   Lateral force: 16 daN
   Release torque: 4,5 daNm
   Heel force: 16 daN
   Release bending moment: 16 daNm
   Adjustment value: **4 . . . 5**
   These values are to be set within a range of accuracy of ± 5 percent.

3. **Adults over 50 years** should deduct 0,5 cm to 1,0 cm from the measured diameter before setting the values.

   Example: Adult over 50 years:
   Measured diameter: 9,5 cm
   Lateral force: 16 . . . 18 daN
   Release torque: 4,5 . . . 5,5 daNm
   Heel force: 60 . . . 70 daN
   Release bending moment: 16 . . . 20 daNm
   Adjustment value: **4 . . . 5**

4. **Adults under 50 years**, well-trained and expert skiers may add 0,5 cm to maximum 1 cm to the measured diameter setting the values.

5. In the case of bindings in which the turning point is more than 4 cm from the toe (e.g. swivel plate ore plate bindings), release moments indicated in the table have to be used. Release forces may then be calculated according to the following equation:

   $$\text{Release force} = \frac{\text{release torque daNm}}{\text{effective lever m}} \text{ daN}$$

6. **Adults over 60 years** and people with extremely small lower leg diameter should use shorter skis.

7. Only reliable testing equipment should be used and should be checked from time to time for accuracy. Since friction between boot and binding elements often effects the binding system, contact surfaces should be moistened or greased before adjustments are made. In addition, there must be a sliding strip or some other anti-friction device on the ski.

8. Adjustment values substantially higher than those indicated, are to be avoided. They are dangerous! Should they nevertheless be needed, this would generally indicate a poor or faultily mounted binding.

9. The binding adjustment should be checked from time to time. New adjustment is always essential when changing ski, boot or binding and when mounting a ski stop.

10. Maintenance of the binding and its protection against dirt and corrosion are essential.

Lower leg diameter at tibia head	Torsion fall release		Frontal fall release		Adjustment value
	Release torque	Lateral force on boot	Release bending moment	Vertical upward force at heel	
cm	daNm	daN	daNm	daN	
Children and youths					
6	0,8	4,5	3	20	$^1/_2 \ldots$ **1**
6,5	1,2	5,5	4	25	**1** $\ldots 1^1/_2$
7	1,6	7,0	6	30	$1^1/_2 \ldots$ **2**
7,5	2,2	8,5	8	35	**2** $\ldots 2^1/_2$
8	2,8	10,5	10	40	$2^1/_2 \ldots$ **3**
8,5	3,5	13	13	50	3 . . . **4**
9	4,5	16	17	65	4 . . . **5**
9,5	5,5	19	22	80	5 . . . **6**
Adults up to 50 years					
7,5	3,0	12	11	45	**3**
8	3,5	14	13	50	3 . . . **4**
8,5	4,5	16	16	60	**4** . . . 5
9	5,5	18	20	70	5 . . . **6**
9,5	6,5	20	24	80	**6** . . . 7
10	7,5	22	28	90	7 . . . **8**
10,5	8,5	25	33	105	8 . . . **9**
11	9,5	28	38	120	9 . . . **10**

Figure 13. IAS—Adjustment table for ski bindings, 1976.

REFERENCES

Asang, E. 1961. Der typische Skiunfall im Wandel der Abfahrtstechnik, (The typical skiing accident in the change of the downhill technique.) Mü. Med. Wschr. 103:2433-2435.

Asang, E. 1964. Skiunfälle: Anderungen in der Häufigkeit der verschiedenen Verletzungen seit 1950. (Skiing Accidents: Changes in the frequency of different injuries since 1950.) In: VI Kongress der SITEMSCH, Chamonix, 6:81-84. C. R. Rapports.

Asang, E. 1966. Lesioni typiche da sci e attacchi di sicurezza. (Typical skiing accidents and release bindings.) VII Kongress der SITEMSH, Cortina d'Ampezzo; Medicina dello Sport 20:441-451.

Asang, E. 1967. Typische Skiunfälle und Sicherheitsbindung. (Typical ski accidents due to safety bindings.) Arch. Klin. Chir. 319:37.

Asang, E. 1970. 20 Jahre Skitraumatologie. Grundlagen zum Verletzungsschutz im alpinen Skisport. (Twenty years of traumatology of skiing. Basis for injury prevention in Alpine skiing.) Med. u. Sport. 1:23-26.

Asang, E. 1972. Verletzungsschutz beim Skisport. (Prevention of injury in skiing.) Sportarzt und Sportmedizin 8:209-222.

Asang, E. 1972. Die Bedeutung der biomechanischen und biodynamischen Eigenschaften des menschlichen Beins in der Sporttraumatologie des Alpinen Skilaufs. (The importance of biomechanical and dynamic properties of the human leg in the traumatology of Alpine skiing.) Arch. Klin. Chir. 332:870.

Asang, E. 1972. Biomechanische Untersuchungen am menschlichen Bein. (Biomechanical investigation of the human leg.) Hefte zur Unf. Heilkd. 114: 310-313.

Asang, E. 1973. Experimentelle und praktische Biomechanik des menschlichen Beins. (Experimental and practical biomechanics of the human leg.) Med. und Sport 8:245-255.

Asang, E. 1973. Skifahren und Sicherheit: Experimentelle und angewandte Biomechanik des menschlichen Beins. (Skiing and safety: Experimental and applied biomechanics of human legs.) Forum Davos 6:101-107.

Asang, E. 1974. Individuelle Belastungs-und Verletzungsgrenzen des menschlichen Biens. (Individual loading limits and injury tolerances of human leg.) Biopolymere u. Biomechanik von Bindegewebssystemen, pp. 51-57. Springer-Verlag, Berlin, Heidelberg, New York.

Asang, E. 1974. Les efforts dynamiques en ski et les limites de Lesion de la jambe en chute. (The dynamic forces in skiing and the injury limits of the leg when falling.) XI Congress der SITEMSH, Val d' Isere 4:25-28. Kongress Bericht.

Asang, E. 1976. Experimental Biomechanics of the Human Leg—A Basis for Interpretation of Typical Skiing Injury Mechanisms. First International Conference on Ski Trauma and Skiing Safety, Riksgränsen, Schweden. Orthoped. Clin. N. Amer. 7 (1):63-73.

Asang, E. 1976. Applied Biomechanics in Alpine Skiing—A Basis for Individual Protection from Skiing Injuries. First International Conference on Ski Trauma and Skiing Safety, Riksgränsen, Sweden. Orthoped. Clin. N. Amer. 7(1):95-103.

Asang, E. 1975. Biomechanik des Bein in der Skitraumatologie. (Biomechanics of the leg in the traumatology of Alpine skiing.) Mschr. Unfallheilk 78:58-71.

Asang, E. 1975. Experimentelle und angewandte Biomechanik des Beins. (Experimental and applied biomechanis of the leg.) Mechanica Polymerow (USSR) 3:504-510.

Asang, E. 1976. Biomechanik des Beins beim Alpinen Skilauf. (Biomechanics of the leg during Alpine skiing.) International Symposium Biomechanik des Skilaufs, XII Olymp. Winterspiele, Innsbruck, Inn-Verlag, Innsbruck, pp. 27–36.

Asang, E., and H. Schmid. 1966. Typische Skisportverletzungen und Sicherheitsbindung. (Typical skiing injuries and release bindings.) Mu. Med. Wschr. 108:2064–2071.

Asang, E., P. Posch, and R. Engelbrecht. 1969. Experimentelle Untersuchungen über die Bruchfestigkeit des menschlichen Schienbeins. (Experimental research on the loading capacity of the human tibia.) Mschr. Unfallheilkunde 72:336–344.

Asang, E., and G. Wittmann. 1973. Skifahren und Sicherheit: Experimentelle und angewandte Biomechanik des menschlichen Beins. (Skiing and safety: Experimental and applied biomechanics of human leg.) Forum Davos, Kongress Bericht. pp. 39–48 and pp. 101–107.

Asang, E., and G. Wittmann. 1974. Experimental and applied biomechanics of the human leg. Biomechanics IV, International Series on Sport Sciences, Vol. 1, University Park Press, Baltimore, Maryland.

Asang, E., G. Wittmann, H. Höpp, and P. Watzinger. 1973. Experimentelle und praktische Biomechanik des menschlichen Beins. (Experimental and practical biomechanics of human leg.) Medizinische Welt 24:576–581.

Asang, E., C. Grimm, H. Krexa, and G. Wittman. 1974. Skitelemetrie (Ski telemetry). Wissenschaftlich Schriftenreihe des IAS, TÜV-Verlag, München.

Asang, E., C. Grimm, and H. Krexa. 1975. Telemetrische Elektromyographie und Elektrodynamographie beim alpinen Skilauf. (Telemetry of Electromyographic and electrodynamic data during Alpine skiing.) EEG-EMG, pp. 1–10, Stuttgart.

Asang, E., and J. Lange. 1976. Belastungsfähigkeit der Tibia von Kindern. (Loading capacity of the tibias of children.) Forum Davos 2:191–193.

Diem, A. 1962. Ein Beitrag zur statistischen Auswertung von Skisportverletzungen. (The importance of statistical evaluation of ski injuries.) Inaugural Dissertation, Technische Universität, München.

Engelbrecht, R. 1970. Experimentelle Untersuchungen zur Torsionsfestigkeit des menschlichen Schienbeins. (Experimental investigation of torsional strength of human tibias.) Inaugural Dissertation, Technische Universität, München.

Grimm, K. 1973. Ergebnisse telemetrischer Messungen von elektromyographischen und mechanischen Signalen beim Skilauf und ihre Auswertung. (Results of telemetric measurements of electromyographic and mechanical signals during skiing and their evaluation.) Inaugural Dissertation, Technische Universität, München.

Guttenberger, R. 1974. Veränderungen der Elastizität und Bruchfestigkeit des menschlichen Schienbeins im fortgeschrittenen Lebensalter. (Changes in the elasticity and resistance to fracture of human tibias in progressive age groups.) Inaugural Dissertation, Technische Universität, München. Kongress.

Hauser, W. 1977. Torsionsfrakturen der menschlichen Tibia im dynamischen Zeitbereich. (Torsion fractures of human tibias in dynamic time ranges.) Inaugural Dissertaion and Technische Universität, München. Kongress.

Höpp, H. 1976. Experimentelle Untersuchungen zur Kombinierten Biege- und Drehbelastungsfähigkeit des menschlichen Schienbeins. (Experimental investigation of combined bending and rotational strength of human tibias.) Inaugural Dissertation and Technische Universität, München.

Holzinger, J. 1971. Fortschritte in der praktischen Prophylaxe typischer Skiverletzungen. (Improvements in the practical prevention of typical ski injuries.) Inaugural Dissertation and Technische Universität, München. Kongress.

Hauser, W., P. Marz, and E. Asang. 1976. Bindungseinstellung des Bayerischen Landesinstituts fur Arbeitsschutz. (Bindings adjustments by the Bavarian State Institute for Protection in Working.) Im Druck. (In press.)

International Association for Safety in Skiing (IAS). 1969. IAS-Richtlinie Nr. 100: Sicherheitsbindungen, Anforderungen and Prufung. (IAS Specification Number 100: Ski release bindings requirements and testing.) Meisenbach-Verlag, Bamberg (Ausg. Okt. 1969).

IAS. 1974. IAS-Richtlinie Nr. 100: Skisicherheitsbindungen für Erwachsene, Anforderungen and Prüfung. (IAS Specification Number 100: Ski Release bindings for adults, requirements and testing.) Verlag d. TUV-Bayern e. V. Munchen (Ausg. Febr. 1974).

IAS. 1974. IAS-Richtlinie Nr. 101: Skisicherheitsbindungen für Kinder und Jugendliche, Anforderungen and Prüfung. (IAS Specification Number 101: Ski release bindings for children and youth, requirements and testing.) Verlag d. TÜV-Bayern e. V. München, February 1974.

Kolb, P. 1973. Verlaufs - und Funktionsstatistik typischer Skiverletzungen aus dem Krankengut des Klinikums Rechts der Isar der Technischen Universität München 1967-1969. (Progress and functional statistics of typical skiing injuries from the Surg. Clinic Rechts der Isar of the Munich Technical University 1967-1969.) Inaugural Disseration, Technische Universität, München.

Kuhlicke, V. 1974. Elastizität and Bruchfestigkeit der menschlichen Tibia bei dynamischen Biegebelastungen. (Elasticity and resistance to fracture of human tibias with dynamic torque.) Inaugural Dissertation and Technische Universität, München.

Krexa, H. 1973. Grundlagen telemetrischer Messung von mechanischen and elektromyographischen Signalen beim Skilauf. (Basic telemetric measurements of mechanical and electromyographical signals during skiing.) Inaugural Dissertation, Technische Universität, München.

Lange, J. 1976. Elastizitat und Bruchfestigkeit der Tibia von Kindern und Jugendlichen. (Elasticity and resistance to fracture of tibias of children and youth.) Inaugural Dissertation, Technische Universität, München.

Mathoul, M. 1974. Angewandte Biomechanik im Verletzungsschutz des alpinen Skisports. (Applied biomechanics in injury prevention in Alpine skiing.) Inaugural Dissertation, Technische Universität, München.

Meynen, M. 1975. Fortschritte beim Verletzungsschutz im alpinen Skilauf. (Progress in injury prevention in Alpine skiing.) Inaugural Dissertation, Technische Universität, München.

Olzowy, J. 1974. Verlaufs - und Funktionsstatistik typischer Skiverletzungen aus dem Krankengut 1969/70/71 der Chirurg. Klinik Rechts der Isar der Techn. Univ. München. (Progress and functional statistics of typical skiing injuries from the surgical clinic, Rechts der Isar of the Technical University of Munich, 1969-1971.) Inaugural Dissertation, Technische Universität, München.

Pachl, G. 1963. Skisportverletzungen bei Kindern und Jugendlichen. (Ski injuries to children and juveniles.) Inaugural Dissertation, Universität, München.

Posch, P. 1970. Experimentelle Untersuchungen zur Biegebruchfestigkeit des menschlichen Schienbeins. (Experimental investigations of the resistance to fracture of human tibias.) Inaugural Dissertation, Technische Universität, München.

Pulkowski, K. 1972. I: Verletzungen in Münchener Skischulen. II: Experimentelle Untersuchung der Bruchkräfte bei verletzten Skifahrern an der Funktionseinheit Ski-Bindung-Schuh. (I: Injuries in Munich ski schools. II: Experimental investigation of fracture force of injured skiers at the functional unit ski binding shoe.) Inaugural Dissertation, Technische Universität, München.

Scherm, G. 1975. Biomechanik des Beins: Untersuchung von Rotationsbewegungen in Dynamogramm und Elektromyogramm. (Biomechanics of the leg: Investigation of the rotational movement with torque recordings and electromyograms.) Inaugural Dissertation, Technische Universität, München.

Schipek, E. 1975. Biodynamik des menschlichen Beins: Vergleichende elektromyographische und mechanische Untersuchungen zur Dreh—und Zugkraft. (Biodynamics of human leg: Comparative electromyographic and mechanical investigations of the torsional and tension forces.) Inaugural Dissertation, Technische Universität, München.

Schwesinger, G. 1971. Untersuchungen zur Zug - und Drehmuskelkraft des menschlichen Unterschenkels. (Investigations of the tension and rotational muscle forces of human tibias.) Inaugural Dissertation, Technische Universität, München.

Ter Welp, P. 1971. Experimentelle Untersuchungen zur Schlagfestigkeit und Härte des menschlichen Schinebeins. (Experimental investigations of the impact resistance and hardness of human tibias.) Inaugural Dissertation, Technische Universität, München.

Uhl, B. 1974. Sicherheitsbindungen für Kinder. Bindungseinstellung, Fahrtest, Anforderungen. Ein Beitrag zum Verletzungsschutz beim Skilauf. (Release bindings for children. Binding adjustments, skiing tests, requirements. A contribution to injury prevention of skiing.) Inaugural Dissertation, Technische Universität, München.

Walker, U. 1970. Typische Skisportverletzungen und Sicherheitsbindungen. (Typical skiing injuries and release bindings.) Inaugural Dissertation, Technische Universität, Munchen.

Watzinger, P. 1977. Experimentelle Untersuchungen zur Biegefestigkeit des menschlichen Schienbeins in frontaler and dorsaler Belastungsrichtung. (Experimental investigation of flexive strength of human tibias to the frontal and dorsal loading directions.) Inaugural Dissertation, Technische Universität, München.

Weidenthaler, P. 1973. Analyse von Skiunfällen einer Münchener Skischule. (Analysis of ski accidents in a Munich ski school.) Inaugural Dissertation, Technische Universität, München.

Wittmann, G. 1973. Biomechanische Untersuchungen zum Verletzungsschutz in alpinen Skisport. (Biomechanical investigations of injury prevention in Alpine skiing.) Inaugural Dissertation, Technische Universität, München.

Typical Injuries Caused by Skiing Equipment and Methods to Reduce Them

S. Pechlaner and G. Philadelphy

Due to the rapid development of Alpine skiing into a sport participated in by thousands, the total number of skiing injuries has reached such dimensions to warrant studies that will lead to the reduction of the injury rate. The increase in the total number of injuries is not the only factor of interest. In the last few years there has also been a significant difference in the type of injuries incurred, and these seem to be clearly differentiated between adults and children. In children, the occurrence of injuries to the lower extremities has shown very little change. In adults, however, their occurrence has sharply decreased and has been replaced by more serious injuries to the upper extremities and skull. Some causative factors are the condition and overcrowding of the ski slopes and changes in skiing technique due to recent developments in skiing equipment. For this reason, the types of injuries most commonly observed from 1958–1960 will be scrutinized, because during this time safety bindings were used by very few skiers (see Figures 1 and 2).

Statistics show that safety bindings have caused a significant reduction in the number of spiral fractures observed in the lower leg. However, after the ski has been released, it becomes the potential cause of an accident to another skier.

Ankle straps made from either a firm material or from an elastic material should be used so that the skier will retain his ski. These straps can also cause an injury if the skier falls, because the skis often whip around unexpectedly, the edges thus cutting and bruising the fallen skier. In some cases, these injuries have proven to be fatal. In an

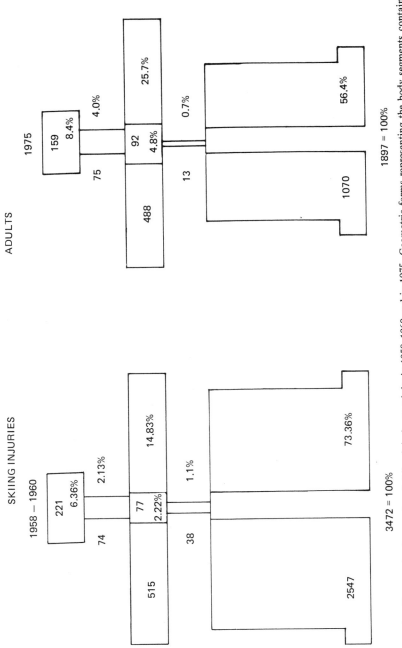

Figure 1.   Comparative frequencies of skiing injuries to adults in 1958–1960 and in 1975. Geometric forms representing the body segments contain the number and percentage of injuries to that body part.

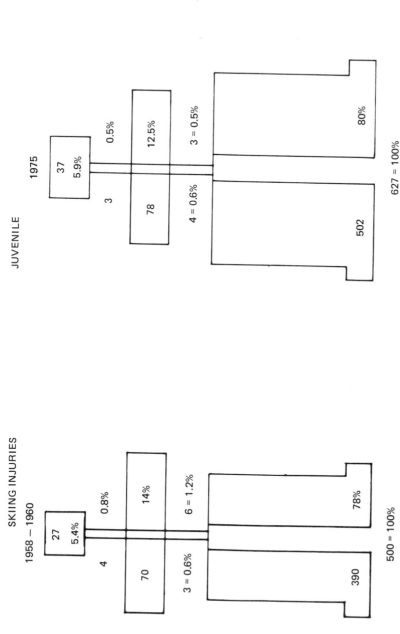

Figure 2. Comparative frequencies of skiing injuries to juveniles in 1958–60 and in 1975. Geometric forms representing body segments contain the number and percentage of injuries to that part.

YEAR	NUMBER		
1933	350		
1957	730		
1967	1860		
1970	2492	= 12.27% OF ALL INJURIES	
1975	2524	= 9.14% OF ALL INJURIES	

AUTHOR	TIME	♂	♀
PETITPIERRE	1930–1937	68.2	31.8
MARBERGER	1953	71.4	28.6
SCHÖNBAUER	1957–1958	59.5	40.5
TERBIZAN	1956–1963	64.0	36.0
PHILADELPHY	1970	66.0	34.0

Figure 3.   Reports of skiing injuries—number of spiral fractures of lower leg.

effort to reduce this danger, the "Ski Stopper" was developed. When the skis are released from the boot, a braking mechanism that should prevent the skis from sliding further is triggered. Ski stoppers have only been in use for a short time and statistical information regarding their effectiveness in injury prevention is not available, yet they do reduce the chances of someone being injured by loose skis.

Modern skiing technique demands that the foot be firmly attached to the ski. This requires a perfectly fitting high boot that is firmly bound to the ski so that the heel cannot be lifted. In the past, this was

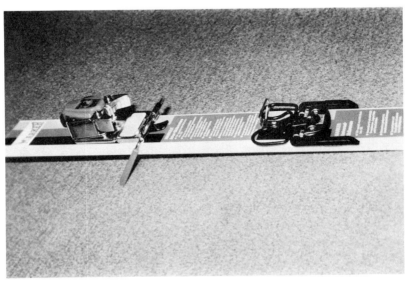

Figure 4.   "Ski stoppers" or brakes in the released position.

possible. The short ski boots used years ago came just above the malleoli and were made of soft leather. When the skier had to stop suddenly the line of force ran through the ankle joint causing dislocation or fractures. The use of hard plastic boots, as Frank explains, causes a total arthrodesis of the foot so that even minute movements in the joints of the foot are impossible to perform. However, the use of new materials and style has led to the observation of a new family of fractures in different areas of the foot and lower leg. Sudden stops, such as those caused by skiing into an obstacle or by the boot hitting the slope after the ski has been released, result in the now typical "boot top" fracture. It is related to the boot only insofar as an hypomochlion works on a "locus minoris resistentiae" of the metaphysis. Because of this, the "boot top" fracture typically appears as a transverse, oblique, or short spiral fracture, but it has also been observed as a compound fracture in the distal third of the lower leg.

Articular fractures of the pilon tibia result when compressive, bending, and sheer forces occur. Bandi showed that individual forces acting on the lower leg during a sudden stop can be represented as a vector. By using these vectors, it became possible to explain how each type of fracture occurred. Increasing the height of the ski boot from 20 to 25 cm does not significantly change the force vectors acting during a sudden stop, although the bending force is reduced by 6-7%. The greater height also moves the location of the fracture a few centimeters proximally to bring it into the cortical region. Some alteration in the forces acting during a sudden stop would be more helpful in injury prevention than increasing boot height.

The primary force acting on the tibia when it is perpendicular to the ground is reduced as the tibia is inclined forward. When the tibia makes an angle of 30° to the ground, the pressure is reduced by approximately 13%. Pressure can be reduced further by increasing the height of the boot by 5 cm; then pressure on the tibia when it is inclined at an angle of 45° is reduced by 30%. During an abrupt stop, the lower leg should be able to rotate forward to decrease the angle between the anterior tibia and the ground in order to reduce the bending forces acting on the tibia. The sheer and compressive forces that occur at this time are not affected by this rotation.

The majority of ski boots at this time are 20 to 30 cm high, with a forward inclination of 15-18° and an elastic component of approximately 10°. Some boots have a hard, stable, lateral joint built in. The newest products have, in addition, a shock absorber over the instep. Boot tops have become increasingly softer, so that the occurrence of fractures of the distal tibia will become less frequent.

Because of its shape, the ski pole is a relatively dangerous piece of

Figure 5.   The modern ski boot of hard plastic.

sports equipment. The most common injuries occur during ab-
duction of the thumb. When the skier holds the pole tightly, his
thumb is slightly abducted. If he should fall forward, the thumb is
abruptly hyperextended and abducted, resulting in a strain or rupture

of the first MP joint and often accompanied by lesion of the joint capsule. This is the most common injury of the thumb incurred during downhill skiing; it has been referred to as "skier's thumb" in the literature. Compression forces act on the abducted thumb, causing dislocation of the proximal, middle, and distal joints or fractures of the first metacarpal. The fractures characteristic of this force are transverse fractures near the base, osteoepiphysiolysis of the first metacarpal, as well as Bennets Fracture.

When the pole gets stuck during a run, strong rotational and tractional forces occur. The shoulder is the most vulnerable joint under these conditions, but sometimes the hand or the elbow is injured. As the pole becomes stuck, the arm abducts and outwardly rotates, causing a dislocated shoulder. In most cases, luxatio omi occurs anteriorly and inferiorly as a part of the labrum glenoidale from the edge of the bony capsule of the shoulder joint is torn away, as in Bankarts lesion. Here, the danger of reluxation is increased.

A small although serious proportion of ski injuries occurs on the casualty list when the body is struck by the pole grip or is impaled on the pole or a fragment of the pole. Injured parts include the facial bones, the eyes, the ribs, and the sternum as well as the abdomen. A fatal puncture wound to the neck has been observed, caused by a pole grip after collision. The post mortem autopsy of this person revealed bleeding in the musculature of the neck and a thrombosis of the internal carotid artery. Perforation wounds of the chest wall and heart have also been observed. Serious injuries do not generally occur when the grip of the pole strikes the chest as long as the deformation of the chest is less than 4 cm. This involves a pressure of approximately 3 kg/cm², or, within an area of 20 cm², a force of 60 kg/cm².

In West Germany, the number and seriousness of ski pole injuries has led to the creation of specifications for the manufacture of ski poles. These specifications include:

1. A cushioned, telescopic grip with a large cross-sectional area, so that a pressure of 60 kg/cm² causes the stick to retract
2. Wrist straps that are released by an upward force
3. A caroty like a crater instead of a point on the end of the stick (see Figure 6)

In conclusion, approximately 12.5% of all skiing injuries are caused by the equipment. Of these, 46% are caused by the poles, 38% by the boots, and approximately 14% by the skis themselves. It is hoped that an alliance of science and industry can improve the equipment more and more in order to reduce the number of skiing injuries occurring each year.

Figure 6.   Specifications for West German ski poles. Right: Cushioned telescopic grip and release strap; Center: Pole retraction accessory; Left: Tip of ski pole.

REFERENCES

Ahrer, E. 1965. Injuries of the shoulder. Klin. Med. 20:101.

Baetzner, W. 1928. Injuries at the sport. Med. Klin. II:1905.

Baumgartner, W. 1960. Safety of the Skiing posts. Münch. Med. Wschr. 102: 2220.

Bezouglis, C. P. 1967. Rupture of the Achilles tendon. Acta chir. hellen. 308.

Gelehrter, G. 1966. Injuries in the wintersport. Enke Verlag, Stuttgart.

Marberger, H. 1952. Skiing Injuries. Med. Wschr. 110.

Maurer, P. 1967. Safety bindings and typical skiing injuries. Dtsch. Ges. Unfallheilkunde, Berlin.

Patscheider. 1961. Death-rate in the wintersport. Wien. Med. Wschr. 111:669.

Philadelphy, G. 1970. Skiing injuries. Ärztl. Praxis 15:1525.

Rowe, C. R. 1962. Acute and recurrent dislocation of the shoulder. J. Bone Surg. 44A:998.

A New Method for Determining Setting Values of Release Bindings

F. G. Höflin, W. van der Linden, and U. Noelpp

Release bindings can only be of use if they are properly adjusted. This is a generally accepted fact; however, this adjustment is effective only if it suits the needs of the individual skier. If it does not, the skier will be tempted to increase the setting and will do so after an occasional fall that will be blamed on "inadvertent release." These post-adjustment increases are probably one of the main reasons for the increase in skiing-related fractures that have occurred in spite of the introduction and general use of release bindings. If, on the other hand, the skier is convinced that the adjustments are correct, he or she will be less inclined to increase the setting. The greatest advantage of the method for determining the release setting of ski bindings described below is that the skier is actively involved in determining the setting values. This should motivate the skier to accept and use the setting. This chapter evaluates the PRIS method for determining the release setting and compares it with the three principal methods now in use.

MATERIALS AND METHODS

The Perryman Retention Index System (PRIS) method measures the maximum quasistatic torsional effort the skier can apply in the skiing position. Standing on a calibrator with ski boots buckled, the skier applies a slow twisting torque sideways until the threshold of discomfort is reached (Figure 1). The skier's maximum inward and outward torsional capability are both assessed in this manner. The lower of the two

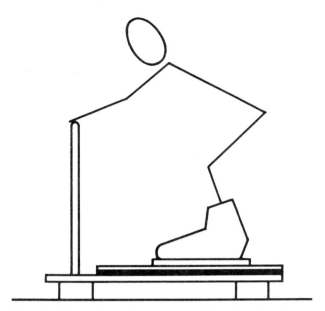

Figure 1.   Measuring maximum torque with the PRIS method.

values is used, and this torque is transformed into the setting value
with a special caliper. The caliper allows for differences in lever arm
due to boot size and binding design. Separate measurements are taken
of the right and left legs.

One hundred and fifty-five (155) employees of the Swiss
National Insurance Company participated in the investigation. There
were 30 women and 125 men. Age ranged from 12 to 59 years, with a
mean age of 39 years. Weight ranged from 47 to 99 kg, with a mean of
67.7 kg. When asked to note their own skiing ability, 49 of the 155
subjects (31.6%) described their skill level as good, 58 (37.4%) as fair,
and 4 (2.6%) as poor. Twenty-two (22) subjects were nonskiers (14.2%)
and 22 (14.2%) were excellent skiers and had participated in races.

In all 155 subjects, setting values were determined according to the
following four methods:

1. Perryman Retention Index System (PRIS).
2. International Association for Safety in Skiing (IAS), a German
   method widely used in Europe. It is based on experimental evidence
   that correlates the strength of the tibia with its breadth, which is
   measured with a sliding caliper just below the knee joint. The setting value can then be read from a table that takes age and skill
   level into account.

3. BfU, a Swiss method based on the skier's weight. Again the release value can be read from a table that takes sex, age, and skill level into account. The same value is used for both legs. (BfU stands for "Bund für Unfallverhütung," which could be translated as "Union for the Prevention of Accidents.")
4. Lipe, which also determines the setting value for both legs in terms of sex, age, weight, and skill level.

After all the data had been collected, they were analyzed using the appropriate computerized statistical treatments. To estimate any error inherent in the IAS method, the setting values of 18 skiers were determined by skilled sport shop attendants who were unaware that they were participating in an investigation. Error in the PRIS method was estimated in the same way.

RESULTS

Table 1 presents the means and standard errors of the setting values established using each of the four methods. The highest values were determined using data from the BfU method. When analyzed using the Student's t-test for paired samples, BfU values are higher than those obtained using any of the three other methods ($p < 0.001$). The lowest values were obtained using the data from the IAS method. When analyzed with the Student's t-test, the IAS values were significantly lower than those of the other methods ($p < 0.001$). The Lipe and PRIS values occupied an intermediate position. When the data were divided according to sex, all four methods assigned higher values to men than to women.

Table 2 presents correlation coefficients among the various methods. It also presents the correlation coefficient of method and breadth of the tibia. The methods are all significantly correlated with each other. The correlation coefficient of IAS and breadth of the tibia was the highest value observed in that category, while the lowest was found between the Lipe method and tibial breadth.

Table 1. Mean adjustment values with standard errors of different methods (in daNm)

Method	Mean	Standard error
PRIS ex[a]	5.461	0.093
PRIS in[b]	5.696	0.097
IAS	4.998	0.069
BfU	6.127	0.055
LIPE	5.828	0.065

[a] PRIS ex = value at exorotation.
[b] PRIS in = value at endorotation.

Table 2. Correlation coefficients[a] between different methods and tibia breadth

	PRIS ex[b]	PRIS in[c]	IAS	BfU	LIPE	Tibia
PRIS ex[b]						
PRIS in[c]	0.83					
IAS	0.55	0.58				
BfU	0.61	0.60	0.58			
LIPE	0.58	0.64	0.67	0.70		
Tibial breadth	0.37	0.43	0.65	0.53	0.34	

    [a] All coefficients are significant at the 0.001 level.
    [b] PRIS ex = value at exorotation.
    [c] PRIS in = value at endorotation.

Table 3. Mean values of four setting methods in different age groups[a] (in daNm)

Method	Age				
	≤ 20 (N = 13)	21–30 (N = 30)	31–40 (N = 33)	41–50 (N = 45)	> 51 (N = 34)
PRIS	4.52	4.78	5.29	5.59	5.28
IAS	3.90	4.59	4.80	5.34	5.51
BfU	5.62	6.01	6.44	6.28	5.91
Lipe	4.32	5.24	6.13	6.17	6.18

    [a] N = Number of subjects in each age group.

Table 3 presents the mean setting values of the four methods when the subjects were divided according to age. Both the IAS and the Lipe values show a constant rise with increasing age. By contrast, the BfU and the PRIS values decrease for the older age groups. The BfU values begin to decrease in the 41–50-year-old bracket, and the PRIS values decrease after age 50. Using methods described by Kendall to study covariation with age, and IAS and Lipe methods, the values were found to be significant.

    In order to study the effect of skill level on setting values, the 155 subjects were divided into three groups. One group consisted of good skiers and racers; the second, of fairly good skiers; and the third, of poor and nonskiers. Table 4 presents the IAS and PRIS results of the groupings. With both methods, a significant difference was observed among the three categories. In both methods, trained skiers required higher values than untrained individuals. The contingency coefficient was 0.35 for the IAS and 0.31 for the PRIS. When the Lipe values were studied in the same way, the differences among the three groups were more pronounced, with a contingency coefficient of 0.56. When calculating this coefficient, the same value was assigned twice to each

Table 4. PRIS and IAS adjustment values in three categories of skiing ability

Skiing ability	PRIS Age					IAS Age					
	≤3	3.1-4	4.1-5	5.1-6	>6	≤3	3.1-4	4.1-5	5.1-6	>6	N[a]
Good	13	22	41	34	32	20	33	32	32	25	142
Fair	23	35	27	15	16	26	36	38	15	1	116
Poor	15	15	15	5	2	13	21	13	5	0	56
	$\chi^2 = 33.37$; d.f. = 8; $p < 0.001$.					$\chi^2 = 42.17$; d.f. = 8; $p < 0.001$.					

[a] N = Number of determinations (left and right leg of each skier).

individual. The coefficients are comparable since they are determined using contingency tables of the same size. Surprisingly, the differences among BfU values in each of the three categories of skiing skill was far less marked. However, the chi-square value was significant at the 0.05 level, although the contingency coefficient was only 0.23.

Finally, the error inherent in the PRIS method was determined and compared with that of the IAS method. The error in each method was low, although that of the PRIS was slightly higher than that of the IAS.

DISCUSSION

This study evaluates a new method for determining the adjustment of release bindings. Values obtained using the three principal methods (IAS, BfU, and Lipe) properly used were compared with the values obtained using the PRIS method. The BfU values were significantly higher than those obtained using any of the other methods, and the IAS values were significantly lower. The PRIS and the Lipe values occupied an intermediate position.

The fact that the IAS values were significantly lower than those of the other methods was not surprising because IAS values have already been considered too low by some platebinding manufacturers. These manufacturers recommend a setting dictated by the IAS tables but with 1 cm added to the tibial breadth of the skier.

All setting methods try to measure torques that—with some safety margin—approximate the fracture limits of the tibia. However, results of this study show that they are poorly correlated. It is impossible to decide which one of the methods provides the best estimate of the strength of the tibia; knowledge of this strength stems from studies of laboratory specimens in which the influence of the musculature and the protection given by the ski boot to the lower end of the tibia were not taken into consideration. Still, it seems possible to determine criteria by which merits of the various methods can be judged.

Since Asang and his co-workers (Asang, 1970; Lange, Asang, and Nagel, 1976) have shown that the strength of the tibia is a function of its diameter, the correlation between each of the four methods and the breadth of the tibia was determined. Tibial breadth was significantly correlated with all four methods. When compared after a z-transformation, the correlation between tibial breadth and the IAS method was higher than that of any of the other methods. This was to be expected since the IAS method is based on measurements of tibial breadth.

It seemed that women should have lower values than men, and this was supported by the study. No differences among the various methods were found.

From what is known about the effects of age on bone strength, it may have been deduced that an adjustment method should assign lower values to the older age groups. This was not true for each method tested in this study. The Lipe and especially the IAS values increased with age. In contrast, the PRIS and BfU values decreased in the older groups. This finding suggests that the corrections for age in the IAS and Lipe tables are not adequate.

Because it is generally assumed that trained sportsmen have stronger bones than untrained individuals, three of the four methods make corrections for skiing ability. PRIS is the exception. When the effect of skiing ability was studied, it was found that trained skiers obtained higher values than untrained skiers using PRIS. The differences among the various categories of skiing ability were about the same for the PRIS as for the IAS method. In the PRIS method, the correction is based on differences in muscular strength, and not on the individual's own opinion of his skiing ability, which may not be a reliable criterion. The largest differences among the various categories of skiing ability were found with the Lipe method, and the smallest with the BfU method. Clearly, it is impossible to say which of these corrections is most suitable.

Several studies have shown that a large percentage of skiers have overadjusted bindings (Hoflin and van der Linden, 1976; Moraeus, 1976; Ulmrich, 1976). When binding adjustments of fracture cases and of skiers on the slope were studied (Hoflin and van der Linden), it was found that overadjustment was seldom caused by an error made in the ski shop. Instead, it seemed that the skier would not accept the setting values and later increased the adjustment. It seems likely that the skier will accept the adjustment values when he or she actively participates in the determination. This is considered to be the main advantage of the PRIS method. This study shows that the PRIS values hold an intermediate position between the BfU and the IAS values and that the PRIS method is correlated with tibial breadth. This method assigns higher values to trained skiers and lower values to the older age groups. The first two characteristics are common to the other methods. The last one is shared with the BfU method.

REFERENCES

Asang, E. 1970. 20 Jahre Skitraumatologie (20 years of ski traumatology). J. Heinkelein and F. Lechner (eds.), Kongress bericht 9 Internat. Kongr. f. Ski-Traumatologie und Wintersportmedizin. Garmisch-Partenkirchen.

Hoflin, F. & van der Linden, W. 1976. The importance of proper adjustment of safety bindings. Orthop. Clin. North America. 7:143.

Lange, J., Asang, E., and Nagel, A. 1976. Belastungsfähigkeit der Tibia von

Kindern (Strength of tibia of children). In: P. Matter, S. Perren, and B. D. Gerber (eds.), Skiing and Safety 2:191.

Moraeus, L. 1976. Report on a binding-test in a lift queue. Orthop. Clin. North America 7:149.

Ulmrich, E. 1976. Sichere Bindungseinstellung (Correct adjustment of ski bindings) In: P. Matter, S. Perren, and B. D. Gerber (eds.) Skiing and Safety 2:220.

IAS Recommendation for Safety Binding Adjustment

G. Wittmann

Since 1967, the International Association for Safety in Skiing (IAS) has consistently followed one objective—the prevention of typical skiing injuries. Looking back to the beginning of the Association, the first step in the development of a basic safety philosophy was the analysis of skiing injuries and of the circumstances and conditions that generated them. Some very simple facts were discussed: when a skier falls, he loses his balance because of active and passive forces between ski and ground. But typical injuries occur only when the binding fails to release and the unphysiologically long lever that is the ski can generate external loads on the lower leg so that a specific biomechanical threshold is exceeded. However, if a skier tries to set his binding at a very low load level, inadvertent, uncontrolled release occurs, which is also potentially dangerous. In that case the necessary skiing forces can no longer be transmitted, and another specific threshold is exceeded. These observations lead us to the following basic but opposing requirements for a real safety binding:

1. Interruption of the forced coupling between leg and ski before reaching a dangerous load level (release), but
2. Transmission of all forces necessary for active steering and of all passive short-time disturbing forces from the ground not dangerous for the leg (retention).

The next step must be research on these two related boundaries in order to define them statistically. The following values must be obtained:

1. The individual injury threshold of the lower leg, and
2. The lower limit of holding forces necessary for skiing without inadvertent dangerous release.

The last conclusive step must then be to develop from these two boundaries a safe adjustment recommendation and the essential technical criteria for suitable and reliable function of safety bindings.

Asang, Vogel, this writer, and other members of the IAS have reported frequently in the past years on the biomechanical and technical research. Therefore, here is a summary of the essentials:

—The transverse diameter at the tibia head represents the best and most suitable dimension in vivo for forecasting the individual load capacity of the lower leg.
—Under various load conditions such as twisting, bending, and combined loads, the tibia shows elastic deformation up to a certain elastic limit. Beyond this point, a significant plastic deformation can be observed. The fracture load limit is evidently located about 50% higher than the elastic limit.
—The elastic load limit related to the tibial diameter gives a very good measure for the biomechanical injury threshold.
—The steering forces reach their maximum with high snow removing resistance, in difficult terrain, and with high skiing speeds. They have a duration of about one-tenth of a second.
—With cumulative frequency distribution curves, it is possible to take into consideration the essential influencing factors such as weight, speed, skiing performance, etc. Therefore, the retention level, the lower limit of holding forces necessary for skiing, can be defined.

For establishing a safe adjustment recommendation, it is very important to select the static release value in the area between the two boundaries so that the risk of injury (distance from the injury threshold) and risk of inadvertent release (distance from the lower limit of holding forces) are minimized.

The results of all experimental work on injury threshold can be summarized in a diagram showing the relationship between the tibial diameter measured on a skier and the moments M_z and M_y for twisting and forward release (Figure 1). The most important equations can be determined by regression calculations. Figure 2 shows some of these formulas and should give a general impression of the scientific background, but for application in practice we need a simple and understandable setting table.

Figure 3 shows the IAS Adjustment Recommendation Table. It is separated into an area for children and juniors up to about 18 years and into an area for adults up to about 50 years. This separation

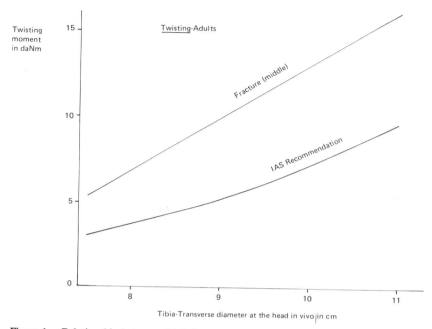

Figure 1.   Relationship between tibial diameter and twisting moment.

occurs because the relationship between tibial diameter and injury threshold is somewhat different for these groups. The column on the left
gives the tibial diameter in centimeters as the basis for the release
setting. The following double columns show the corresponding release
values recommended respectively for twisting and for forward release.
The twisting moment and the forward bending moment, respectively,
are given in daNm on the left of each double column.

Since equipment for checking the settings is normally calibrated in
force units, the corresponding force values are needed. On the right of
the double columns, the values of the lateral release force at the boot
toe and the vertical release force at the heel are given.

The outer column at the right gives the IAS Adjustment code
figure. Its value corresponds by definition to the twisting moment. The
intention is that all binding producers should use this code figure and
should mark it on the setting scale of the toe and heel elements of their
various binding systems. Compared with the present method of setting
bindings, there would be two decided advantages for the skier:

1.   When choosing a binding, the skier could consider the application
     range. He or she could determine by the code figures whether a

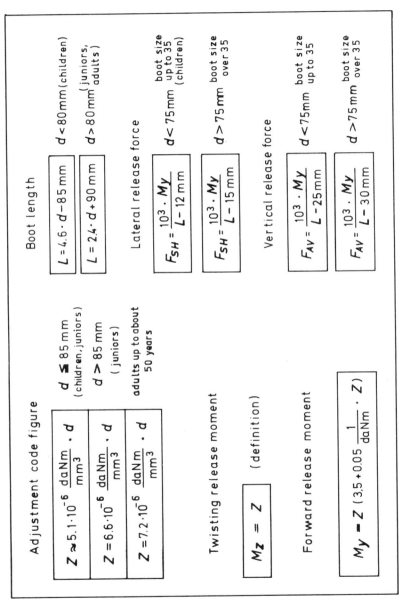

Figure 2.   Formulas for calculating release moments and forces for IAS safety binding adjustments.

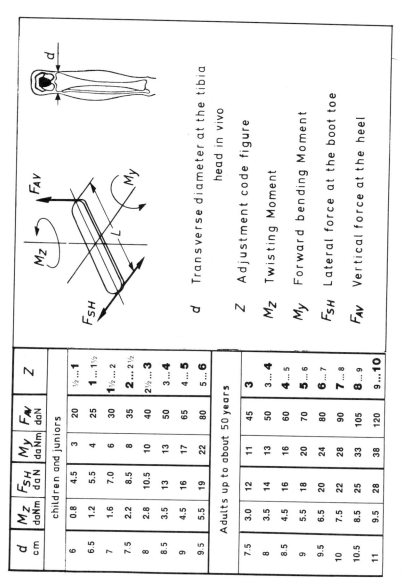

Figure 3.   IAS Adjustment Recommendation Table for ski safety bindings.

binding is suited for a child or a junior, for a normal adult, or for a racing skier.

2. A certain code figure would mean exactly the same adjustment and release level for all the various bindings offered on the market.

This method seems to be coming into use now. At the ISPO sport exhibition this year in Munich, there was one known German binding producer who used these methods on his bindings. It is hoped that others will follow.

The application of this table in practice is very simple, but before setting a binding, two essential requirements must be met:

1. A binding must be used in compliance with the technical rules and with IAS Rule No. 100 or 101, and the boot must have an appropriate boot sole with certain defined geometrical dimensions and material properties.
2. The sole must be adapted exactly to the binding elements so that correct function is insured before setting the release values.

The first step is to measure the transverse diameter of the tibia head with a slide rule while the skier is sitting with his knee bent. The correct measuring plane is located directly above the head of the fibula. The tissue should not be pressed by the slide rule. With this measured diameter, the table can be used to find the correct binding setting. Let a value of 9 cm measured on an adult skier be assumed. The table provides a corresponding twisting moment of 5.5 daNm with a lateral release force at the toe of 18 daN. The corresponding release values are a forward bending moment of 20 daNm with a vertical release force at the heel of 70 daN. These recommended release values found in the table should be set on the binding with an accuracy of ± 5%. Normally, two or three set-check cycles are needed to approach the correct values on the boot binding system. In the future, with the use of the code figure marked on the scale, the adjustment could be reduced to one cycle: setting the code figure at the value indicated by the table.

The table does not include the following recommendations for special applications:

—Skiers more than 50 years old should use a lower release level—one-half to 1 cm should be subtracted from the actual diameter.
—On the other hand, well-trained and experienced skiers can set a higher level by adding one-half to 1 cm to the true diameter.

If higher values than indicated by the table are needed for skiing, this generally points to a lack of suitability of the binding or the boot sole or to an incorrect fitting of the boot binding system.

Experience with thousands of skiers using bindings adjusted to comply with IAS recommendations shows that the 10 years of IAS work has been a successful path to more safety in skiing. The IAS will continue in this way during the next 10 years.

The Role of the Ski Resort in Accident Prevention

M. A. Molino

Ski resorts should try to reduce the number of accidents that occur during skiing in order to increase the number of skiers and to leave them with good memories of their skiing vacation. Accidents must be kept to a minimum. Those that do occur must be given special attention by resort personnel.

INFORMATION

Before leaving for the slopes, the skier should be informed of the weather conditions and the slope conditions. This can be best accomplished by ski forecasts over the radio or television. Hotels and condominiums within a certain area from the slopes should be notified so that they can make this information available to these guests. Finally, a snow report can be posted close to the place where lift tickets are purchased.

A slope map or plan should be made available so that the skier has a clear image of the type of drop, the length, and the condition of each slope in the resort. One system recently implemented in several resorts involves the use of blackboards or electronic panels to inform skiers of changes in the weather throughout the day.

It is important that the skier has a good idea of what type of clothing to wear on that particular day. Many accidents occur because the skier has not worn the correct clothing to keep him well insulated against the cold and wind.

SUMMER PREPARATION

Slope preparation during the summer can add to the skier's comfort or discomfort during the winter season. These preparations help prevent accidents, as well as ensure that slope designs exhibit a wide variety of steepness and relate to the capacity of their lifts. Here there is a difference between European countries and the USA; in some parts of Europe, it is not unusual to find five lifts for one popular slope, while in the USA there is often only one lift for five slopes.

Slopes should be diversified, natural, and pleasant. Vegatation, especially trees, help to make this possible. A slope should have good orientation, look as natural as possible in order to be interesting to the skier on each trip down, and be safe.

The safety of slopes is based on two things: the presence or absence of narrow passages, bottlenecks, or obstructions; and the surface on which the slope is built. Resorts have studied surfaces in recent years and found the ideal surface to be free of stones, to be well cut, and to have good drainage. When covered with 5 cm of snow, the ideal slope can be prepared with machines for skiing.

It is important to study the relative percentage of skiers using each slope in order to determine the skier/hectare ratio for each one. Then each slope can be adequately prepared during the summer to meet the skill and frequency requirements of the skiers.

The personnel who staff the slope services and machine services during the winter should prepare them during the summer. These people are most likely to know the demands of each slope in terms of safety.

WINTER PREPARATIONS

Specially trained personnel should oversee safety programs at the ski resorts. Such personnel exist in many countries. Spain, for instance, is in the process of professionalizing safety personnel. In the USA these personnel are referred to as the "Ski Patrol." In many parts of Europe, they are called Pisteurs; in Spain, they are called Pister. Members of the safety patrol should be knowledgeable about safety, have a good communications system, and be knowledgeable about first aid and victim removal procedures.

Insofar as machinery is concerned, the only machines previously available pressed powdered snow. Now there is such a wide variety of machinery available that the resort can meet its snow treatment needs.

It should be remembered that the skier saves money all year in order to enjoy a week of skiing, and the resort is obliged to send him home on Monday in good condition. By working carefully throughout the summer and by treating the winter snow carefully, the resort can make the weekend skier's stay happy and problem-free.

Prevention of Skiing Accidents by Action of the National Swedish Board for Consumer Policies

K. Danielsson

Many authorities work for the benefit of the consumer. The main objective of the National Swedish Board for Consumer Policies is to keep product development and service to the consumers in line with the real needs of the consumers. In the Sports and Transport Department, questions concerning safety and health are of high priority.

During the years 1973 through 1976, the Board had to work for product safety in many fields by means of voluntary agreements with the commercial organizations to bring out better products and fair marketing and information. If such an agreement was broken, there were no legal means of enforcing it. Through the Board's monthly journal, the daily papers, and TV, information giving details of the agreement served as the most effective pressure to control the trade. Since any statement from the Board has a great influence on the consumer, this kind of information also affects the producers, making them more inclined to develop better products.

Since July 1976, the Consumers Board has administered a new Marketing Act. This Act deals with unfair marketing practices, information, and product safety. It has proven to be a good tool for bringing about better product development and better information, which can prevent unnecessary accidents.

The first four sections of the Marketing Act are those of interest regarding safety in sports. The first two sections have already been in force for some years and concern improper marketing in general. The third and fourth sections are new and are more closely described in this chapter.

The third section states that a tradesman must present all information that is of special significance to the consumer. This includes negative information, such as warning labels and directions dealing with restrictions in usage. This is, of course, not very popular among the business people and could hardly be applied by a voluntary agreement. The use of such warning labels has been enforced many times, particularly with sports products, such as when certain rules or limitations of use have been necessary for safety.

The fourth section deals with product safety and with the situation where the product is unfit for its main purpose. It is applicable not only to a product that causes accidents because of its nature, but also to so-called safety equipment that does not fulfill its purpose of protection. This section is one that can be applied to ski release bindings and protective helmets.

A release binding that does not release at the right moment because of poor quality or inappropriate construction may be prohibited. The same holds true for a protective helmet that has insufficient shock-absorbing qualities. The reason for this kind of prohibition is that people relying on safety equipment may take greater risks than they would if they did not use it, and are therefore induced into a false feeling of security. The result is that they are worse off by using the equipment.

RELEASE BINDINGS GUIDELINES

At the first international conference on ski trauma in Riksgransen in 1974, measures taken by the Consumers Board to reduce accidents in skiing were described. Work on product safety in this field had just begun. The results from the injury statistics in skiing during the winter of 1973–1974 had shown that a properly working release binding was an essential detail in safe equipment. The first objective was therefore to purge the market of unsuitable bindings and to encourage positive product development and good repair service. With intense support from TV and the press, consumers were made aware of the problem. A data sheet was published with a list of those bindings that fulfilled the safety requirements according to test certificates.

In a press release, a list was also published of unsuitable cheap bindings for children, some of them sheer fakes. A voluntary agreement was made with ski shops and large warehouses to sell release bindings only in shops where skilled personnel could adjust the bindings with the help of test instruments. Within one year, more than 1,000 test instruments were installed in the shops. To help the ski shops, a manual on how to test the bindings was published. This manual was also given free of charge to all the local leaders of the Association for Development of Outdoor Life, a big Swedish organization that, among other activities, arranges skiing schools for children all over Sweden.

By the winter of 1975–1976, only bindings approved by the International Association for Safety in Skiing (IAS), BfU or American bindings of equivalent quality were imported into Sweden. Old bindings remaining in the shops were destroyed instead of being sold. Because there is still a fairly large difference in quality among the approved bindings, the Consumers Board also took part in a comparative test of children's bindings with the German organization Stiftung Warentest. The bindings that showed the best results were presented in our journal, *Råd & Rön 1975-9*, and on TV programs. The following winter, no retailer took the risk of importing bindings that the Consumers Board would not approve.

Together with a working group from the trade, the Board is now working out guidelines for marketing release bindings. The Market Act will give these guidelines a legal character, so that, if a binding does not fulfill the requirements in the Act, the case can be brought before the Market Court. The court will then decide if the binding shall be prohibited or not.

The guidelines consist of two parts. One concerns the quality of the binding: the vender must, upon request, show a certificate of quality and performance of the binding. The other part concerns information and service. All information on mounting, adjusting, and caring for the binding must be in Swedish when it is sold in Sweden. The ski shop must be able to fit and adjust the binding in a professional manner. These rules are also applicable on rented bindings.

ACTIONS AGAINST MINI-SKIS

In order to find out whether the safety work and propaganda for safer skiing had had any influence on the injury rate, a second set of skiing injury statistics was made for the winter of 1975–1976. Like the previous survey that was carried out by the Consumers Board, the investigation was in cooperation with Dr. Ejnar Eriksson of the Karolinska Sjukhuset, Department of Traumatology. This investigation is published in the report "Skador vid Skid Åking" Konsumentverket 1972:3-01 (English and German summaries are available). Forms were sent to all hospitals in Sweden.

When filling in the questionnaires, one surgeon at the children's hospital in Stockholm noticed that an astonishing number of the skiing accidents were caused by mini-skis. This is a kind of short plastic ski that can be tied onto the boot by means of straps (Figure 1). They are

Figure 1.   Mini-skis.

Table 1. Activities on mini-skis, Winter 1975–76.

Activity	Injuries
Downhill skiing	141
Cross–country skiing	4
Outings	28
Skijumping	23

intended for play on gentle slopes. This year, when the first white winter appeared after three green ones, a great number of young children bought these cheap skis. Having seen on TV their hero Ingmar Stenmark speeding easily downhill, they longed to the sport, although they had no idea of the risks involved. So they went up with the lift and down the slalom tracks and even tried ski jumping with these small skis (Table 1). Because they had very little or no experience in skiing, accidents were frequent. In ten days, 33 children (representing 73% of the skiing accidents) were injured while skiing with miniskis and were brought to the St. Gorans' Children's Hospital in Stockholm. A closer look at the statistics revealed that the injuries caused by mini-skis showed a different pattern than did injuries caused in downhill skiing (Figure 2).

Injuries on various parts of the body (%)

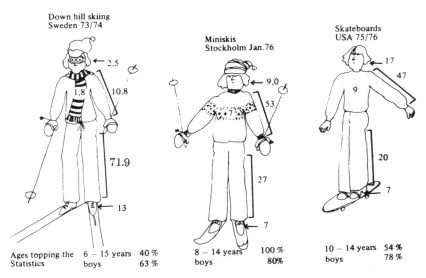

Figure 2. Injury patterns in children compared for downhill skiing, mini-skis, and skateboards.

Nine percent of the injuries were to the head, compared with 2.5% in downhill skiing. More than half of the injuries occurred to the upper part of the body, and only 27% to the legs. In normal downhill skiing, 62% of injuries are to the legs. This pattern shows that the mini-skiers must have fallen headlong down the hill. Pictures taken of mini-skiers show that when they reach a certain speed they totally lose the control over the skis and tumble down the hill. Since they use ordinary soft boots that are loosely tied onto the skis, they do not break their legs or hurt their ankles or knees in the same way as when using the stiff, tightly fastened boots that are used in downhill skiing. All accidents happened to children between the ages of 8 and 14 years. To prevent accidents of this kind, the Board decided to act quickly. Because more than 100,000 mini-skis had already been sold, there was no way to stop the accidents by forbidding the sale of mini-skis. From all reports it was clear that excessive speed was the main reason for the accidents and that the mini-skis used on gentle slopes could be considered fairly harmless.

It was concluded that the best way to reduce the accidents was to prevent children with mini-skis from using the lifts. On January 21, the Board wrote letters to all those responsible for sports and recreation arrangements in the municipalities asking them to contact the lift owners in their respective districts and to get the owners to prevent children with mini-skis from using the lifts. The press was also informed about the action and the reason for this request. This had a striking effect (Figure 3). It also affected the injury rate considerably. The statistics from the winter of 1975–1976 show the total number of injuries caused by mini-skis to be 252. Two hundred of these happened before the action on January 21, and only about 50 after that date, although most of the winter season still remained (Table 2). It is also

Table 2. Injuries caused by mini-skis, Winter 1975–1976

Place (Date)	Injuries		Mini-ski injuries (as percent of skiing accidents)
	Mini-skis	Other skis	
St. Görans Hospital			
Jan. 6 –Jan. 17	33	12	73
[Jan. 21 Warning! Mini-skis banned from lifts]			
Jan. 24–Feb. 7	18	18	50
All Sweden			
Before warning	202		
After warning	50		
Total all winter	252	2,444	10

Figure 3.   Press campaign against mini-skis.

noticeable that nearly all the accidents happened in mid-Sweden and very few in the north, where children are more skilled in skiing.

To comply with Section 3 of the Marketing Act, the producers of mini-skis are now required to put warning labels on the skis. The label draws attention to the risks when mini-skis are used at high speeds (Figure 4). Very few mini-skis were sold this year in comparison with previous years, and most lift owners are enforcing the safety rules and are stopping the children with mini-skis from using the lifts in spite of the loss of revenue.

ACTIONS TO PREVENT ACCIDENTS BY SKATEBOARDS

The above example with mini-skis illustrates how a central authority can act to prevent unnecessary accidents. However, prohibiting an activity or a product may not always be the best way of preventing injuries. Many people, particularly youngsters, find a certain pleasure in taking risks. Boys in their early teens are the ones generally topping the lists in all injury statistics. If one product is banned, they will soon find another with which to hurt themselves. The most realistic ambition

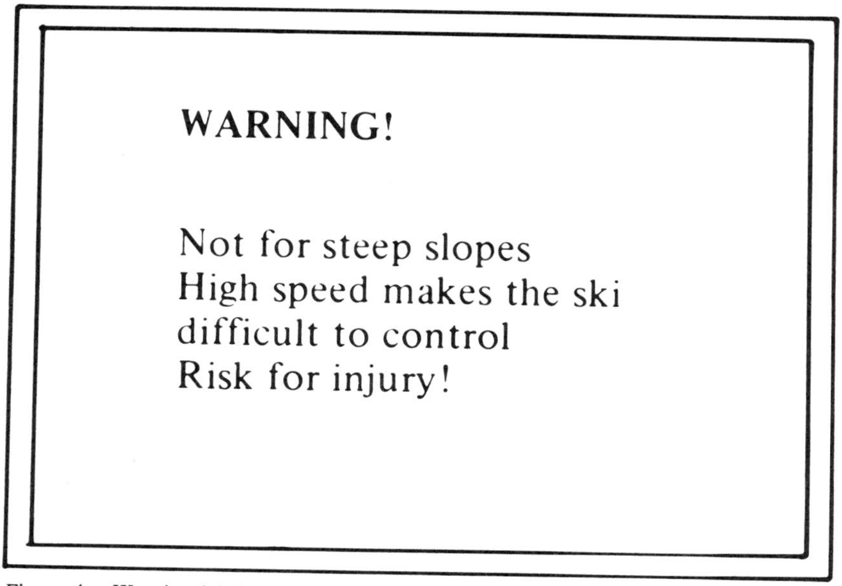

WARNING!

Not for steep slopes
High speed makes the ski
difficult to control
Risk for injury!

Figure 4.   Warning label on mini-skis.

must therefore be to conduct the activities so that the youngsters do not hurt themselves too seriously and do not annoy or hurt other people. Sports activities should thus be channeled to the right age and ability of the participant. Sports should also be practiced in the right places and under the right conditions. The Board's actions against skateboards can exemplify how this can be realized.

Last autumn alarming reports came in that a new sport, skateboarding, was to be introduced in Sweden. It was already very popular in the USA, where there were 20 million skateboarders according to the latest reports; it had also been shown to have a bad injury rate, with young boys topping the list as usual (Figure 5). The high percentage of head injuries and fractures were of additional concern. Skateboarding was introduced to young people in an irresponsible and cynical way. Articles in the daily papers appeared where daring tricks were encouraged and severe injuries made to look silly and called by nicknames.

Through the Ministry of Foreign Affairs, injury statistics were quickly obtained from the U.S. Consumer Product Safety Commission. Figure 2 shows the high percentage of injuries to the head and the upper part of the body. Further investigations of 70 accidents are summarized in Tables 3–7.

To prohibit skateboarding on public roads, in underground stations, etc., the Board wrote to the State Traffic Security Board with an

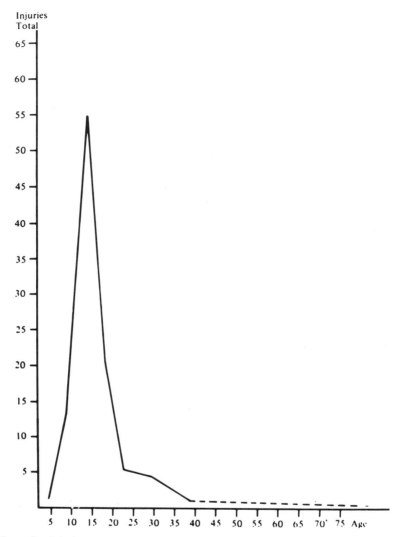

Figure 5.   Injuries caused by skateboards in the USA (1975-1976). Of 10-20 million skateboarders, about 55,000 are injured every year.

appeal to forbid skateboarding in streets and public places. Because a central traffic law takes a long time to ratify, the Traffic Board sent a note to all the local Traffic Security Commissions with a draft for local regulations on skateboarding. Within a few weeks, skateboards were forbidden on public roads and in public places in most communities.

Table 3. Where did the accident occur?

50% in roads and streets
25% in other public places

Table 4. What caused the accident?

More than half the skaters simply fell off the
skateboard. They were too young or too unskilled
to control the board.
25% of the accidents were caused by a small
obstacle—a pebble, a small pool of water—that
suddenly stopped the skateboard.
Only 10% of the skaters had been "showing off."

Table 5. How did the skaters fall?

Forward	50%
Sideways	10%
Backwards	10%
Complicated falls	30%

Table 6. The severity of the accidents

Fractures	70%	(Mostly hands and wrists)
Concussions, contusions	20%	(often faces and heads)
Lacerations, inner injuries	10%	(e.g., injuries of the spleen)

Table 7. Conclusion

Skateboards are not harmless toys. Skateboarding is quite a dangerous and
   difficult sport.
It should be practiced in special areas where it does not interfere with other
   traffic or pedestrians.
It should not be practiced by too young children. To avoid serious injuries,
   protective equipment should be worn.

In the meantime, the Consumers' Board negotiated with importers,
mostly young sportsmen with small firms. They have now formally
agreed to put warning labels onto the boards (Figure 6). All skateboards delivered after April 15th of this year will have such labels.
Sellers of skateboards shall provide information about the local traffic

---

WARNING!

Not for children under 12 years old
Obey the local traffic prohibitions
Be aware of the injury risks
Don't skate down steep slopes
Use protective equipment
Before skating — Read the instructions

Figure 6.   Warning label on skateboards.

rules and the necessary protection equipment, and they will give instructions about how to skate and how to handle the board (Figure 7). When skateboarding is introduced in full scale in Sweden, it is hoped that these actions taken beforehand will prevent the most serious consequences of this sport.

OTHER SNOW TOYS

As mentioned earlier, it is not possible to stop all dangerous products and activities. As soon as one of them is rendered fairly harmless by restrictions and warning labels, a new one is introduced onto the market.

All kinds of plastic sleighs and snowracers are available, even snowboards, which are a combination of the skateboard and the mini-ski. A kind of snowskate is also about to be imported into Sweden. Before deciding to import them, the tradesmen requested the Consumers Board's opinion. A quick look revealed that the snowskates would be new tools with which to break arms and legs if used on steep slopes. Using the experience gained from skateboarding and mini-skiing, these products will be treated in the same way. If they are found to be still more dangerous, they can even be prohibited by the Market Court.

Figure 7. Protective equipment for skateboarders: protective helmet, knee and elbow pads, and gloves.

FURTHER WORK

The results from last winter's ski injury investigation in Sweden show that a lot of work remains to be done in improving skiing safety. Slopes and lifts must be better controlled to maintain satisfactory standards. Hand injuries, particularly of the thumbs, show that ski poles are not designed to minimize injury. Problems concerning ski stoppers and ski straps also remain unanswered.

SKATING

Next season, the Consumers Board plans to hold a great deal of work to promote safety in skating. The following is a short glimpse of the background that has caused the Board to start this project.

Because the last winters in Sweden have had very little snow but were perfect for skating on the numerous lakes, there has been an increased number of skating injuries, many of them severe. Long, low skates, predominantly with wooden boards, are normally used, but new light metal types that enable faster skating are being introduced. People of all ages, from the very young to those long past middle age, enjoy skating on local lakes. Many take it up as a sport and travel long distances during a day. Dr. Eriksson of the Karolinska Hospital sent a questionnaire to a long-distance skating club of about 4,000 members, asking for details of injuries that had occurred to the members. He received about 3,000 answers and could register 1,300 injuries. The age among the skaters ranged from 30–60 years, with a peak at the age of 55 years.

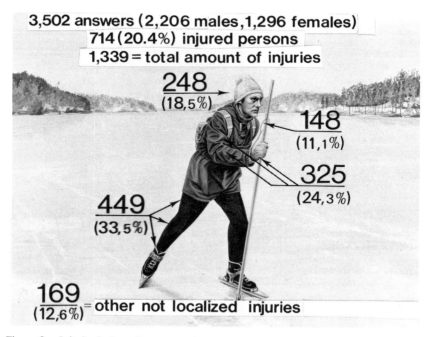

Figure 8.   Injuries in long-distance skating.

The injury rate was found to be about the same as in downhill skiing, i.e., about two per thousand. The injuries were distributed as shown in Figure 8. The number of injuries to the head is particularly remarkable. The investigation was sponsored by the Consumers Board. A prospective registration of injuries in skating is being carried out this winter. A questionnaire about skating injuries of all types has been sent to all hospitals in mid-Sweden. After the causes for the accidents have been analyzed, the data will be evaluated to see if any measures can be taken to reduce their numbers.

In conclusion, it should be stressed that safety work must start with statistics and analysis to find the real causes of accidents and adequate means to prevent them. One link in the safety work that has proved quite useful is legal restrictions applied on marketing and the use of the products or on service connected with the products. In many countries, there are now product safety acts that may be more efficiently used in the safety work.

REFERENCES

Danielsson, K. 1974. Rätt rustad billigt Försäkrad. (Correctly equipped-Cheaply insured.) Råd och Rön 10:8-15.
Danielsson, K. 1975. Barns brott i backen begränsas. (Reduction of skiing-fracture accidents in children.) Råd och Rön 9:3-7.
Danielsson, K. 1976. Swedish Measures for Reduction of Skiing Accidents with Special Reference to Children. Orthop. Clin. North Am. 7:3-9.
Danielsson, K. 1977a. Skador vid skidåkning. (Injuries in skiing.) The National Swedish Board for Consumer Policies. Report 3-01.
Danielsson, K. 1977b. Snölek. (Playing in snow.) The National Swedish Board for Consumer Policies. Report 3-03.
Danielsson, K. 1977c. Rullbrädor—risker och skadeförebyggande åtgärder. (Skateboards—Risks and preventions of injuries.) The National Swedish Board for Consumer Policies. Report 3-02.
Danielsson, K., and Basun, B. 1976. Miniskidor. (Mini-skis.) The National Swedish Board for Consumer Policies. Report.
Danielsson, K., Eriksson, E., and Strand, O. 1976. Skador Förorsakade av miniskidor. (Injuries caused by mini-skis.) Läkartidningen 13:1216-1217.
Danielsson, K., and Moraeus, L. 1975. Handledning för testning av skidbindningar för utförsåkning. (Instruction for testing ski bindings.) The National Swedish Board for Consumer Policies. Report 10-2.
Eriksson, E. 1976. Ski Injuries in Sweden: A one year Survey. Orthop. Clin. North Am. 7:3-9.
Lindberg, R. 1975a. Skador vid skidåkning. (Injuries in skiing.) SIFO, The Swedish Institute for Opinion Polls. (Mimeographed report.)
Lindberg, R. 1975b. Vintersport. (Winter Sports.) SIFO, The Swedish Institute for Opinion Polls. (Mimeographed report.)

Safety in Skiing—
A Complex Problem

E. Ulmrich

Any safety measure can be dangerous because it generates careless behavior. This idea is almost always overlooked in the development and execution of individual safety measures for the sport of skiing. Attention is focused on an isolated source of danger, an isolated countermeasure is invented, and then everyone is astonished when completely unforeseen events occur. Some examples will illustrate this process.

The principles employed in the construction of modern ski slopes are such that passenger capacity of the lift or of the cable car line divided by ten gives the width of the slope. For a lift having an hourly capacity of 400 persons, a slope with a general width of 40 m is necessary; a cable car capable of carrying 1,000 persons per hour calls for a slope having a width of 100 m.

Interviewed skiers indicated that they preferred easier slopes. Using safety as an excuse, the group conducting the interview perpetrated the idea that slopes should be designed not only with sufficient width, but also as easy and as flat as possible. Curves with a narrow radius were to be avoided and undulations of the terrain smoothed over. The result is a slope expressway that is as monotonous psychologically as the vehicle express and therefore just as dangerous. The width of the skiing space gives the deceptive impression of freedom of movement, but the danger of collision increases with the possibility of increased speed, and it increases above all else with the width of the slope. The latter paradox can be explained by the fact that skiers easily lose sight of what is going on over the entire slope. Skiers traveling diagonally across the slope are seen too late or not at all.

If guidelines for slope construction considered calculated minimum free space as well as both individual and psychosocial factors, the preferred design would be different. The excessive speeds, aggressive behavior, and boastful actions observed on many slopes made it seem that designers should build slopes that hinder the skier. When the above displays are coupled with decreased braking distances, consequences become even worse.

Instead of one mammoth slope, several modest ones should be built. All slopes should not be so easy as to induce everyone to race down them. The slope should fit its natural milieu so that no excessively long distances or long schuss stretches are included. The high speed course of a World Cup slope should not be taken as a model for leisure sport. Slope design consistent with these principles would have to be coordinated with the instructional goals of the ski schools. Slopes should not be made so accessible that everyone can move without concern for the natural surroundings; the skiers should be trained instead to handle the terrain adequately. Training in the selection of the correct types of slopes for their ability levels should be emphasized. The teaching of skiing technique becomes dangerous whenever it is not accompanied by instruction in skiing conduct.

Conditioning slopes with slope rollers originated in order to make the runs fit for skiing as rapidly as possible after a new snowfall. Routes so conditioned and smoothed made for much faster skiing because the surface of the slope was made considerably harder. Shaded areas that formerly exhibited a variety of snow covers, depending on the season, were now sheer slope all during the winter. Instead of a soft fall in these areas, the skier was now susceptible to injury. By eliminating the deep snow slope, new sources of danger were created by technologically conditioned snow. The popularity of the crash helmet, even among leisure skiers, is justified because of the slope tractor.

Another interesting consideration is the effect of altitudes from 2000-4000 m on people who live at lower altitudes. They often over-exert themselves from early morning until evening and then subject themselves to the social dictates of the après ski. In effect, they are overtraining, a practice that even a modestly schooled trainer would discourage.

Accident statistics reveal a great deal about the nature of the accidents and their consequences, but nothing about the actual accident causes. It would therefore be advisable for medical scientists to initiate studies concerning the correlations among overstimulation, fatigue, lack of concentration, and ski accidents. That some correlations exist can easily be seen from the peak of the daily accident frequency curve that occurs toward the end of the afternoon. If, in fact, the actual "healthy" aspects of skiing are the recuperative effects of the entire winter holiday rather than the physical activity in itself, suitable suggestions must be made by physicians about the types of activities skiers should emphasize. If the results of biometeorology are also taken into consideration, there would be other points to consider in planning the ski and winter holiday. Problems of safety in skiing would then achieve an entirely new dimension and one can imagine the extent of the effects on the ski industry. Attention should be focused on the consequences of the accidents, rather than on the causes. However, will anxiety about the elimination of these causes also eliminate some of the unique phenomena of the sport?

The development of skiing can be attributed to the development of ski equipment. The major contributors to safety have been in the sector of safety bindings. Despite this, only 30% of the skiers have correctly mounted and adjusted bindings. After all, safety is not just a technical problem, but also a human one. As long as skiers believe that others are taking care of their safety, they will not concern themselves with such things. Misled by dubious advertising, they believe that everything will function properly. Actually, skiers must learn that even correctly adjusted bindings do not prevent all injuries. They do protect the foot and lower leg up to and immediately below the knee. The increase in the number of knee injuries has been correctly interpreted statistically, yet it must be recognized that by protecting the lower leg from injury, the knee has become more vulnerable. The timely release of the safety binding necessarily results in a fall, and every fall is necessarily accompanied by the danger of injury. The safety binding can help to eliminate only those injuries occurring in the aforementioned areas, which are, on the average, the worst ones. Skiers must realize that they must adjust their skiing methods to avoid falls as much as possible.

Technological improvements in the field of safety bindings are useless unless the ski boot industry adheres to the necessary standards regarding the functional unit of the ski-binding-boot-holding. How long will manufacturers be allowed to market boots that block the function of the binding? This is analogous to the installment of malfunctioning brakes in an automobile. The difficulty lies in the fact that the skier, unlike the driver of a car, does not receive a completely assembled functional unit, but rather a modular set whose composition he decides himself. Is the interrelationship of this explained carefully so that the customer can decide properly?

The development of the plastic boot has had a significant effect in altering skiing technique. The alleged function assigned to the calf spoilers as safety devices remains of questionable value in terms of the slope skier, especially for those of low skill levels.

The combination of a low skiing position and an extreme backward leaning can be observed on all slopes. This boot is praised as a safety device because it helps to prevent backward falls. This is certainly true for racers and very good slope skiers, but not for the majority of slope skiers, who are not in good enough condition to rescue themselves from this marginal position to a more normal stance. A poor skier in the backward-leaning position resembles a car in which neither the steering nor the brakes work. One fatality in Germany proved to have been caused by this type of situation.

In connection with modern boot construction, the ski schools of some countries have created a skiing technique that cannot be approved by orthopedics. Beginning on swings in a position of extreme knee flexion with a simultaneously high isometric holding action causes strains on the knee joint. If people in sports medicine were to state clearly that this technique is recommended only for racers and champion skiers, and is a potential source of accidents for all others, perhaps it would disappear from ski instruction classes.

Too little attention is paid to safety aspects connected with advertising and sport journalism related to the conduct of skiers. Anyone using Fischer skis doesn't want to embarrass a Franz Klammer. The heroic adoration of the World Cup athletes unquestionably presents models for imitation for the average man on skis. It's hard to find anyone willing to listen to appeals for defensive skiing conduct when they are being drowned by cries of jubilation for "Rosi! Rosi!" Psychlo- ogists and sociologists concerned with such phenomena tend to be regarded as annoying interlopers in the skiing sphere. However, no prophet is needed to see that the complex field of promoting safety in skiing will be hindered without the cooperation of such scientists.

This incomplete list of examples represents the dialectic of isolated safety measures in the sport of skiing. It is time to pursue new and better methods. The sport of skiing should not be sliced like a cake whose individual pieces are devoured by sports physicians, slope designers, cable car builders, ski instructors, ski manufacturers, tourist directors, and sport specialists. The development of slope construction in the future must be coordinated with psychosocial studies of behavior patterns of groups of skiers, with development in ski construction, and with the objectives of the ski schools. Boot manufacturers can only make their boots in adherence to standards necessary for the auxiliary products, and should not make their boots without the advice of those who ski daily in them. For this reason, an interdisciplinary promotion of safety in skiing must be sought in place of the previously fragmented promotion. This is the only way to prevent one group from placing obstacles in the way of others. Research projects must not be restricted to a single field but must be placed in the hands of teams composed of experts from all disciplines.

A merely technical solution of the problems, however, does not achieve much. How the results obtained are to be conveyed to the skier is not just a theoretical problem. Over thirty million skiers all over the world must be reached. This presents a task that requires considerable expenditures of money, material, and personnel.

There are a number of periodical meetings in the field of sport skiing—the Forum Davos, the Kapruner Discussions, the Ski Slope Congress in Innsbruck, to name a few—all of which are conducted along the lines of single talks delivered in a tightly scheduled program. At the very most, there are short discussion periods, but no detailed discussions. Perhaps a new format should be considered for such meetings. Much could be learned through small group discussions composed of interdisciplinary teams tackling a precisely defined subject related to safety promotion. This might provide better accomplishment in terms of the common goals of various efforts through a more intensive coordination of ideas.

Methodology for the Control of Ski Accidents at Port del Comte

J. Tresserra, F. Prats, and F. Borrás

The ski station Port del Comte, in the foothills of the Pyrenees at Lerida, was provisionally inaugurated in the 1973-1974 season and began as a ski station in 1974-1975. At present it has eight ski-tows and one chair-lift, and the installation of 15 more lifts is planned. The skiable areas range from 1700 m to 2400 m. Although a major plan for urbanization is now underway, the present hotel capacity is limited and the station must depend on weekend and holiday skiers. Since Port del Comte has only recently opened, long-term statistics are not available, but the methods used to investigate and medically treat accidents can be described.

All lift systems have automatic counters that simultaneously count the number of skiers transported and the elapsed time. A topographical plan of the slopes was drawn using a scale of 1:1,000, and the gradients were designated. Using information related to the geographical characteristics of the lifts of different mounting systems, it is possible to obtain the absolute number of accidents per skier transported on a given lift.

At the medical center located at the foot of the slope, a victim-data card is prepared. It consists of personal data, means of transportation, type of injury, treatment administered, and the slope and the last lift used. The reverse side of the card contains technical and environmental data and the mechanism of the injury. The site of the accident is located as accurately as possible on the topographical map.

In this study, medical data and technical details are omitted in order to concentrate on a statistical analysis of the injuries that occurred in the last two seasons.

SKI ACCIDENTS

1975

	slope	grade	travelers	descents (meters)	fractures			other injuries			total		
					n°	×1000 p	×1000 km	n°	×1000 p	×1000 km	n°	×1000 p	×1000 km
PRAT BERLA	39 m.	10%	37 782	1473 498 m	6	0.15	4.07	8	0.21	5.43	14	0.33	9.50
LA PEDRA	70 m.	14%	48 465	3 392 550 m.	2	0.04	0.50	5	0.10	1.47	7	0.14	2.06
DEBUTANTES	26 m.	15%	60 600	1 575 600 m.	2	0.03	1.27	16	0.26	10.15	18	0.29	11.42
PRAT DUNADO	98 m.	18%	109 319	10 713 262 m.	4	0.03	0.37	43	0.39	4.01	47	0.42	4.38
grade 10% - 18%			256 166	17 154 910 m	14	0.05	0.81	72	0.28	4.19	86	0.33	5.01
LA RATA	220 m.	22%	108 481	23 865 820 m	14	0.12	0.58	33	0.30	1.38	47	0.43	1.96
PRAT DE BUTONS	235 m.	24%	32 400	7 614 000 m	1	0.03	0.13	10	0.30	1.31	11	0.33	1.44
LA BOFIA	276 m.	26%	65 034	17 949 384 m.	3	0.04	0.16	15	0.23	0.83	18	0.27	1.00
SUCRE	235 m.	27%	104 065	24 552 275 m	9	0.08	0.36	26	0.24	1.06	35	0.33	1.42
grade 22% - 27%			309 980	73 884 479 m	27	0.08	0.36	84	0.27	1.13	111	0.35	1.50
LA COMA	218 m.	35%	66 000	14 388 000 m.	2	0.03	0.13	18	0.27	1.25	20	0.30	1.39
grade 35%			66 000	14 388 000 m.	2	0.03	0.13	18	0.27	1.25	20	0.30	1.39
TOTAL			632 146	105 427 389 m	43	0.06	0.40	174	0.27	1.65	217	0.34	2.05

Figure 1. Statistical summary of skiing accidents during the 1974–75 season. (In addition to those listed here, there were 51 non-skiing accidents reported.)

| | **1976** | | | | SKI ACCIDENTS | | |
	hours	days	travelers	descents (meters)	nº	x 1000 p	x 1000 km
PRAT BERLA	132	25	10810	421.590 m.	4	0.37	9.50
LA PEDRA	70	11	19440	1.360.800 m.	0	0	0
DEBUTANTES	218	46	27430	713.180 m.	28	1.02	39.27
PRAT DUNADO	312	42	57021	5588.058 m.	42	0.73	7.51
grade 10 % -18%			114701	8083.600 m.	74	0.64	9.15
LA RATA	415	67	32595	7170.900 m.	12	0.36	1.67
PRAT DE BUTONS	-	-	?	?	-	-	-
LA BOFIA	219	42	27395	7561.020 m.	10	0.36	1.32
SUCRE	405	65	39734	9.337.490 m.	20	0.50	2.14
grade 22%-27%			99724	24.069600 m.	42	0.42	1.74
LA COMA	305	53	52327	11.407.286 m.	22	0.42	1.92
grade 35%			52327	11.407.286 m.	22	0.42	1.92
TOTAL			266752	43560280 m.	138	0.51	3.15

Figure 2. Statistical summary of skiing accidents during the 1975–76 season. (In addition, 35 traumatic injuries suffered by non-skiers were treated.)

Figure 3. Topographical map with the location of ski accidents that occurred during the 1974–75 season.

The slopes were divided into three groups according to difficulty and the averages for partial gradients and for the whole station were computed. In Figure 1, which corresponds to the 1974-1975 season, slopes are classified as *easy* with an average gradient of 10-18% and a lift that doesn't exceed 98 m, of *medium* difficulty with a gradient between 22-27% and a maximum gradient of 276 m, and *more difficult* with a gradient of 35% and maximum gradient of 218 m.

The number of skiers transported was tabulated automatically and the gradient was measured for the corresponding lift. Accidents were analyzed in terms of treatment administered and other injuries, as long as x-rays demonstrated no interruption of the bone integrity. The total number of accidents, regardless of their gravity, was determined per 1,000 persons as well as per 1,000 km skied.

A similar schema was devised for skiing accidents that occurred in the 1975-1976 season (Figure 2). In both seasons, accidents suffered by nonskiers approached 25% of the total.

The 1974-1975 season can be considered of short duration, and normal with regard to the quantity and quality of snow in the different months. In the 1975-1976 season, skiable time was at a minimum;

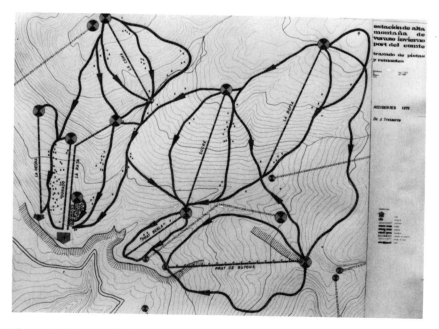

Figure 4.   Topographical map of the "Port del Comte" ski resort, with location of ski accidents that occurred during the 1975-76 season.

the slopes were in poor condition most of the time, making skiing difficult. Therefore, the overall analysis of station activity shows that the number of skiers and the number of kilometers skied decreased until they numbered one-third more than in the previous season. The number of accidents was also reduced in absolute terms. However, in relative numbers, accidents increased both per skier and per kilometer skied. In the study of slopes and gradients, the largest coefficient of accidents occurred on the easier and shorter slopes. There were fewer accidents on the difficult slopes with greater skiing areas. These were not long-term results because measurements included only two seasons. In the figures, it is seen that the greatest number of accidents occurred among inexperienced skiers on easier slopes. The worse the condition of the snow, the greater the number of accidents in all categories.

Knowledge of the topographical location of these accidents (Figures 3 and 4) will be used to study the sites of potential danger in order to correct possible deficiencies of the slopes, or to mark them more clearly.

These data along with similar data from other stations indicate the security level for each station. This information must be used to improve measures against accidents during skiing, sledding, or unrelated activities.

An Approach to Safety and Control of Skiing Accidents

J. M. Figueras, J. A. Merino, C. Algara, and M. Llobet

This chapter summarizes three papers presented at the Second Conference of the International Society for Skiing Safety at Sierra Nevada (Spain) in late April, 1977. Their respective titles were: "Exogenous causes of the ski accident;" "Considerations regarding the regulation of the adjustment of the safety binding;" and "Control of skiing accidents."

Since 1957, the skiing accidents occurring at the winter station "La Molina" (Spain) have been recorded. During the next three years, records of lesions incurred will also be made. The number of accidents at the station increased, and in 1969 a special perforated file was designed for this use. As its practicality became evident, a new model of perforated card was designed in 1965 and proved to be better adapted for systematic classification. In 1975, a codified card (Copies available from Dr. Figueras, Hospital Cruz Roja, Dos de Mayo 301, Barcelona 25 Spain) designed for computer use began to be used. It was supposed to simplify statistical analyses, but has led to some problems that are related not to the computer, but to the physicians who use it. The physicians at the winter station claim that the card is fine as long as there are few emergencies, but it is too long when a large number of accidents have occurred.

This problem was presented when the perforated card was introduced at the meeting in Chamonix in 1964, and again in Cortina d'Ampezzo in 1966. At that time, suggestions from interested parties were sought so that a model could be designed that would be practical, time-saving, and complete. This should be one of the main goals of future ISSS programming.

In Sierra Nevada, it was suggested that ski injuries may be caused by factors intrinsically related to the skier or to others independent of him. The former may be called endogenous causes, while the latter would be exogenous. Basically, endogenous causes depend on two factors: the person (the skier) and the equipment. The first factor includes: the skier's natural complexion; his or her physical health, related to a number of psychophysical circumstances (e.g., not enough sleep the previous night, alcohol ingested, age, etc.); and technical training. This last factor is important in any physical activity and may even compensate for some deficit in the skier's complexion or physical condition. Quality, maintenance, and inspection of the equipment are endogenous factors that may help avoid accidents. An example is the proper adjustment of safety bindings.

Statistical analyses, which were presented to the Department of Investigation and Prevention of Ski Accidents, show that 56% of the men, 74% of the women, and 70% of the children who suffered ski injuries ignored the proper use and adjustment of their safety bindings. After these statistics were revealed, a meeting of ski equipment merchants/distributors was held. Because of their position, it is their duty to alert future skiers to the importance of knowing and caring for the equipment they buy. The meetings yielded a list of guidelines that were distributed to all purchasers of safety bindings (Table 1). A card was also designed to register information from the client and the seller regarding the adjustment of the safety binding. The safety binding is most effective as a protection device if these three rules are followed:

1. Provide for maximum safety in any movement. Protection during movements such as lateral bending and extension should be added to the usual adjustments for rotation and flexion.
2. Proper adjustment should not be compromised. If handling is troublesome, the skier is usually not as careful as he or she should be regarding the proper adjustment of the safety binding. Safety is therefore reduced.
3. Allow for easy checking. The proper adjustment should be checked by the skier himself because he must be able to handle all the safety mechanisms. Age, sex, skier's physical constitution, etc., may be useful parameters, but they have no absolute values. Therefore, it is advisable that checking be done manually, just as Olympic skiers do after a race.

As previously mentioned, ski accidents may also be due to exogenous causes. In a chronological sequence, the first cause may be found in the mechanical lifts. Some extremely severe injuries may have

Table 1.

Hospital Cruz Roja Barcelona	Spanish Ski Federation

Department of Research and Prevention of Ski Accidents

GENERAL REGULATIONS FOR THE PROPER USE OF THE SAFETY BINDING

1. The specialized stores should advise which individual type of safety binding is most suitable for each particular skier.
2. Filling out the personal card of the user is important for the proper adjustment of the safety binding.
3. The specialized store should properly adjust the safety binding.
4. It is advisable that each skier have the corresponding booklet of instructions and maintenance of the safety binding.
5. The skier himself should verify the state and condition of the safety binding each time he uses it.
6. It is advisable that each time the ski is fitted it be checked to be sure the boots, safety binding, and antifriction devices are free of snow.
7. Antifriction devices have a great influence on the safety binding, and should therefore be carefully cared for.
8. The safety binding should be checked and lubricated at least once a year.
9. It is advisable that, if the safety binding fails, it be adjusted by experienced personnel.
10. Monitors and aides in the winter stations may be people experienced in the correct adjustment of the safety binding.

their origins in poorly arranged accesses, technical problems related to design failures, or careless maintenance. However, the most conspicuous causes of ski accidents are undoubtedly found on the ski slopes. The skier must face a number of obstacles, some of them stationary (such as unprotected milestones, rocks, fences, or trees), others moving (such are other skiers, or moving equipment—a loosened ski, a sleigh). The latter are responsible for unexpected collisions.

Weather must also be taken into account; fog or the possibility of an avalanche may be important factors in slope control. The winter station should control all factors except those depending on the skier himself. When conditions warrant, the station should limit access to or even close the ski lifts. If our country had outlined clear and specific regulations on this matter, some accidents may have been prevented. For example, of three fatalities that occurred in one area during the 1976–1977 season, one was caused by the lack of protection of a milestone, one by the bad condition of a slope that remained open, and one by the failure to recognize the warning signs of an avalanche. The lack of ski regulations in Spain becomes even more evident when the accident is due to another skier's conduct. It is concluded from the available information that many accidents could have been prevented if safety rules had been followed, and that the majority of ski injuries would then have been of endogenous causes.

Sliding Control of Ski Garments

B. vonAllmen

"Skiing accident dynamics" by vonAllmen and Glenne (pp. 199–208) is the technical foundation of this chapter. The presented testing method has been used since 1971 in several parts of the U.S. and is proposed in its concept to the International Society of Skiing Safety (ISSS).

Soon after the wet look was introduced in ski-wear fashion in 1971, the sliding and collision hazard connected with low-friction ski garments became obvious. In Europe in particular, numerous efforts to point out this danger (Schweizerische Beratungs/stelle fur Unfallverhutung, 1972; Greiter and Prokop, 1972–1973) captured public attention via television. The ski industry learned that the wet look ski clothes are dangerous.

Extensive research on the frictional behavior of ski garments on snow in Vermont (1971) and in Utah (1974 and 1975) convinced the author that the skiing public was relatively unaware of the sliding risk taken when skiing in low-friction ski garments. A more recent test of fashionable ski outfits for their frictional properties on snow by the Swiss Advisory Committee for Accident Prevention (BfU) was alarming. Reasonable friction criteria were met by only one of sixteen samples (Test, 1975).

The intent of this paper is to achieve sliding control of ski garments by an understanding of simple and reliable friction tests in various skiing environments, first by the ISSS and second by the skiing public.

BASIC CONCEPT

Ski garments come in such variety, ranging from a harness to exposed skin, that it seems hopeless at first to attempt to set standards so that the clothing itself will act as an active braking surface. Snow, a form of water strictly modified by the environment, is the passive breaking system. It also exists in such a number of states that it is hard to find a standard definition of snow.

National and international standards for frictional control between two sliding surfaces are only as good as the descriptions of the two surfaces. Friction generates heat that can bring about a change in the snow surface and further complicates the problem. Engineering solutions, in order to contribute effectively to the well-being of the skier, must incorporate an educational process intended to reach even those skiers who are likely to ignore the standards.

Therefore, meaningful and enforceable standards for the sliding control of ski garments seem to have failed to reach maturity in most nations because the criteria for formulating a control concept are delicate and opposed to norms. Technically, the problem will only find a solution if a unique description of at least one of the braking surfaces can be made. Environmentally, it is meaningless to isolate ice as the standard reference for the passive braking system, although it appears to be the only stable form of solid state water. Clearly, skiing is not an ice sport, but a winter recreation activity in the world of snow. On the other hand, the world of fabric, historically, has some basic roots that lend an opportunity to isolate a reference fabric and use this active braking surface as a standard to describe minimal frictional requirements for ski garments on variable slopes. Primarily, the fabric would have to approximate that of a basic and inexpensive ski garment so that it may be referenced easily over time and locality.

Research on ski-wear fabric, as in other fields, has initially introduced problems by ignoring the environment. It is now time to apply research and communication about the reaction of the environment to one fabric. Therefore, the industry as well as the standards committees will have to decide collectively on a reference fabric. This will carry the research into the environment where friction under various conditions and the direct risks of a sliding fall to the skier will be studied.

SUGGESTED TEST SPECIFICATIONS

1. The friction between the garment of a fallen skier, without skis, and various conditions of skiing surfaces should be investigated so that the dangerous conditions can be predicted comprehensively.
2. A conventional, non-stretching linen fabric (such as denim) should

be utilized as a reference for describing the friction between garments and skiing surfaces.

3. As soon as the reference fabric is both officially chosen and made available, a minimum friction coefficient of 75% of that fabric should be required for each fabric, regardless of snow condition and related environmental influences, to qualify it as a friction safety article.

4. The test methods for determining the friction of garments on skiing surfaces should be characterized by simplicity, mobility, and low cost.

5. The tests should be performed on natural skiing surfaces, using either random or selected samples of actual skiers without their skis attached, to take advantage of direct publicity for the cause within the curious public. The difficulty in reconstructing the exact test conditions perhaps involves a compromise, but it is insignificant when compared to the difficulties involved in simulating snow conditions in a laboratory.

6. The tests should be performed in various ski areas, each representing a different prevailing snow condition that may jeopardize a fallen skier because of the inadequate frictional properties of his clothing.

7. Reference tests should be performed at every site, at intervals no longer than one-half hour, by using a mat of reference fabric (Figure 1).

8. The mat of reference fabric should measure approximately 0.8 by 2 m (2.5 x 6.5 ft), should be nonelastic, should provide a grip for the test person and the friction measuring device, and should carry a clearly visible insignia of the supporting agencies.

9. The tests should be performed in principle according to Figure 2 in the three shown variations A, B, and C. The execution of the tests should be clearly explained in a separate description, and it should include at least that information shown on a typical data sheet (Figure 3).

10. The test site should be a natural ski slope that can easily be roped off to prevent traffic, should be of uniform slope, should have only large scale moguls undulating no more than 10 cm per 5 m in diameter, and should provide relatively uniform conditions as to:

    a. Temperature: 1) of the skiing surface, 2) of the ambient air
    b. Weather: 1) sun, 2) shade, 3) new snow accumulation
    c. Snow type: 1) hardness, 2) wetness, 3) grain of skiing surface

11. A typical friction test shall require:

    a. One reference fabric mat with grip and pulling reinforcement

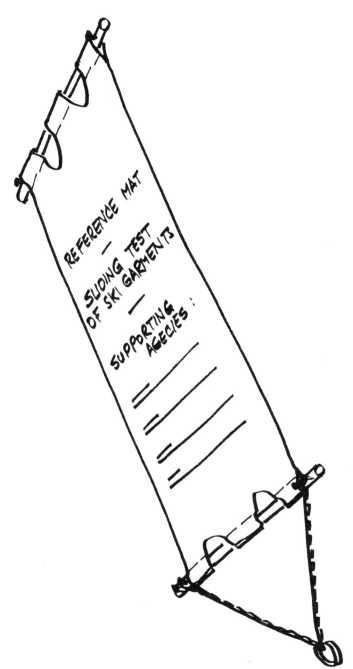

REFERENCE MAT
—
SLIDING TEST
OF SKI GARMENTS
—
SUPPORTING
AGECIES :

Figure 1. Mat of reference fabric.

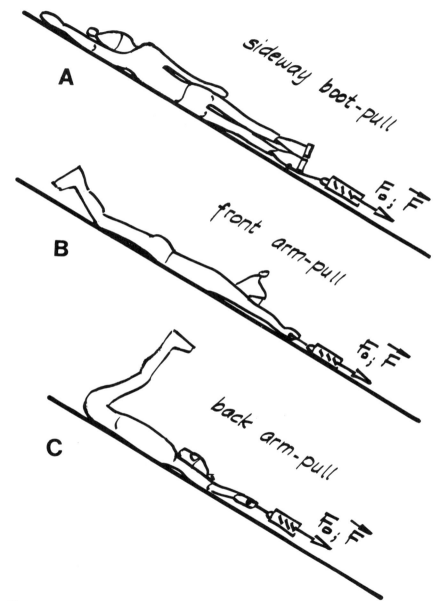

Figure 2.   The three variations of the test.

FRICTION TEST DATA -- SKI WEAR ON SNOW

Date: _____   Location: _____

Temperatures: a) Snow surface: _____ °C; b) Air: _____ °C.

Weather: ( )sunny; ( )cloudy; ( )snowing.

SNOW SURFACE CHARACTER
a) Hardness: pierce with hand; finger; pencil; knife
b) Wetness: dry; moist
c) Grain: new; grain <2 mm; >2 mm; cups; ice

SLOPE: ____ %
1 2 3 4
d m
+ · o <

SKI WEAR CHARACTER
Fabric "look" (see chart)
weight wet; fine; linen; coarse; rough; inserts

TEST PERSON age/ sex	weight (lb)	TOP						BOTTOM						FRICTIONAL FORCE (lb)		
														sideway boot-pull F_0/F	front arm-pull F_0/F	back arm-pull F_0/F
/		1 2 3 4 5 6( )						1 2 3 4 5 6( )						/	/	/
/		1 2 3 4 5 6( )						1 2 3 4 5 6( )						/	/	/
/		1 2 3 4 5 6( )						1 2 3 4 5 6( )						/	/	/
/		1 2 3 4 5 6( )						1 2 3 4 5 6( )						/	/	/
/		1 2 3 4 5 6( )						1 2 3 4 5 6( )						/	/	/
/		1 2 3 4 5 6( )						1 2 3 4 5 6( )						/	/	/
/		1 2 3 4 5 6( )						1 2 3 4 5 6( )						/	/	/

Figure 3. A typical test data sheet.

b. One spring gauge for a maximum pull between 25 and 50 kg (50 to 100 lb) according to slope of skiing surface
c. One inclinometer
d. One thermometer
e. Rope and one information board
f. Two persons, one measuring the friction force, the other taking notes

12. The mechanical execution of the standard friction force test should supply measurements of sufficient accuracy if taken at a uniform sliding velocity at an angle of no more than 5 degrees different from the tangent of the slope of the test surface.
13. The clothing of the test persons should be classified under six categories, and additional remarks should further distinguish between unusual fabrics and unusual test results, particularly when fabrics are unusually elastic in more than one direction.
14. The six different fabric classes are entered into the test sheet independently for the upper and the lower part of the garment, and the fabric should be typified primarily according to its look and secondarily according to a special description (reference is made to the Swiss "BfU" research carried out in 1971-1972):

a. Wet look: 1) glossy cire nylon (BfU-1, steel blue), 2) cire nylon (BfU-2, turquoise)
b. Fine look: 1) coated fine structured nylon (BfU-3, beige), 2) coated crepe nylon, rhubarb (-)
c. Linen look: 1) coated spun nylon (BfU-5, mustard), 2) raw spun nylon (BfU-6, light green)
d. Coarse look: 1) raw crepe nylon (BfU-4, dark brown), 2) coarse velvet (BfU-7, light brown)
e. Rough look: 1) boucle fabric (BfU-8, red), 2) corduroy fabric, fox gray (-)
f. Frictional inserts (Number): 1) Pistarex net (BfU-9, white), 2) safety spikes, very green (-)

CONCLUSION

Education of the skiing public on the sliding properties of ski wear needs international attention. The advanced skier in particular, because he enters into steeper terrain frequently, must understand how friction does and does not work to break him after a fall. Rather than isolating research in the laboratory where it is costly and impossible to simulate the proper snow conditions, a simple and inexpensive test like the one proposed in this paper should be permanently impressed upon the memories of as many skiers as possible.

REFERENCES

Greiter, F., and Prokop, 1972–1973. Untersuchungen mit Rutschfester Schibekleidung (Investigations of Sliding Resistant Ski Wear). Oesterreichisches Journal fur Sportmedizin. Special editions 1/72 and 4/73. Vienna, Austria.

Schweizerische Beratungsstelle fur Unfallverhutung "Die Gefahrdung der Skifahrer durch glatte Nylonstoffe" (The Hazard of Wearing Slick Nylon Fabric by Skiers). Bern, Switzerland.

Test, 1975. Vorsicht Rutschgefahr Stiftung Warentest. Berlin, Germany.

Liability in Ski Accidents Caused by Defective Bindings and Faulty Adjustments

D. Hummel

It is a fact that there are altogether too many ski accidents. It is the duty of technicians to maintain and to improve further the present high technical progress. It is the obligation of the lawyers to determine defects in this field.

THE SKI

The main interest of the skier is still concentrated on the ski. Its importance for skilled and safe skiing is often overestimated when compared with the influence of ski maintenance, which has been underestimated in the past. It is hardly possible to establish liability of a manufacturer in the case of a ski accident. The question of liability arises only if due to improper construction of the ski, such as when the screws of the binding do not hold in the ski material. In such a case the manufacturer may be liable for an injury to the skier as well as for injuries caused by the runaway ski sliding downhill and hurting another skier.

THE BINDING

Regarding liability for defects of bindings, there are substantial law cases.

Liability of the manufacturer

In the early days of safety bindings, devices sold as safety bindings were hardly worthy of the name. As a result of research in recent years, a standard has been reached that should reduce accidents to a fraction of previous figures. The International Association for Safety in Skiing (IAS) Regulations 100/1969 and 100/1974 as well as DIN Norm 7881 and IAS Regulation 101 for children's bindings guarantee a high standard of safety if observed. Other products that do not meet these technical requirements may still be produced and sold, but can no longer be called "safety bindings"; however, it will take years, as practice proves, before such older products cease to be used. The manufacturer is liable for thorough testing of the model itself for perfect technical function, and his liability also extends to each single product manufactured.

Mounting, Fitting, Adjusting

This is the area in which the majority of defects arise and which bears the largest risk of liability. Nearly all cases decided recently dealing with this matter involve practical use rather than defects of manufacture or workmanship.

The binding must be mounted properly; this is facilitated by templates. The binding must be adjusted to the boots that the skier will wear. It is important to check for due pressure, the proper level of the soleholder, and the absence of high friction loads among boot, binding, and ski. A proper antifriction pad and perfect boots (see below) are fundamental requirements; should the skier change his boots, a readjustment of the binding will be necessary. Furthermore, the binding must be adjusted to individual release values, and this adjustment must be checked by a modern binding control instrument.

New automatic bindings are indeed of such high quality that some manufacturer's advertisements suggest that the control instrument could be calibrated by their binding. Nevertheless, it is necessary to use this instrument in order to ascertain concealed friction forces. Investigations and criminal charges in recent years against sporting goods dealers and ski instructors, and also civil cases, were concerned exclusively with imperfect fitting and adjusting of bindings. The dealers are, of course, not responsible for subsequent changes of the binding adjustments. The skier himself has to be aware of the changing values during use mainly because of dirt and deformation of the boots. Maintenance of the binding, transportation in ski covers, and regular checks are sensible precautions against unpleasant experiences.

THE BOOTS

The ski boots have an immense influence on the style and safety of the skier. Many defects and ski accidents have been attributed to the binding though they have been caused, in fact, by the boots. The ski boot must have a standard sole according to DIN Norm 7880, or perfect functioning of the binding may not be guaranteed. The sole must have a specific hardness of the material because there should be no essential changes in the form and in the length of the boots caused by temperature, humidity, and use.

The front, the back, and the area of the antifriction pads must be smooth in order to avoid additional friction points, and the edges of the sole at the front of the boot must be rounded for proper function of the binding.

This does not mean that boots that do not meet the above requirements may no longer be sold. However, the manufacturers and dealers in such cases may only be released from liability if they have informed the customer of an eventual defect. The skier then has the option of choosing a plate binding with release characteristics that are independent of the boots.

It is expected from a ski boot that one may ski with it. Marketing reports have revealed, however, that a skier spends more time standing in his boots than walking in them and only a fraction of the time actually skiing in them. Therefore, standing and walking should have no negative effect on the health of the skier. Proper orthopaedic fitting is a question of not only comfort and health, but also of safety. Participants in ski competitions keep their boots buckled for only a few minutes at a time and, as may be seen in each competition, unbuckle them shortly after the end of each run.

The intentional "forward rake at the ankle of the boot" may lead to overburdened tendons and joints as well as cramping of the muscular system. Such tendencies can lead to sudden or premature tiredness. Of course, it would be difficult to prove that an accident had been caused by such defects in a ski boot; yet the need for the ski boot in which one may stand at the ski lift is not only an orthopaedic but also a legal requirement.

It is evident from the medical and technical research that a higher boot with a soft collar is to be preferred because it provides the skier with greater control, and because, in an accident, loads will be absorbed by a safety zone; a severe injury below the boot collar is evidence of improper boot construction.

RETAINING DEVICE

The newest development in safety considerations is the ski brake. Originally, skiers wore safety straps in order to avoid losing their skis after a fall. Later, safety straps came to be regarded as necessary to avoid danger to and injuries of other skiers from runaway skis. However, a great number of injuries in past years has also been caused by safety straps. After falling at high speed, skiers have been hit by their own skis, often resulting in cuts, fractures, and head injuries. In the literature, Mang has mentioned two cases of fatal brain hemorrhage caused by skis attached by safety straps. Therefore, in recent years ski brakes have begun to replace safety straps despite general skepticism and the initial resistance of lawyers and manufacturers. Since the last ski season, the ski brake has become an accepted safety device. While people were initially afraid of skis flying through the air, experience has shown a far better result. Ski brakes do not fail as often as safety straps break, and the ski tends to stop more quickly than the skier who has fallen and therefore endangers neither its owner nor other skiers. So far no report is available about accidents caused by ski brakes. However, because of the variety of designs and the usual boom in the development of different new types, one must be careful to use only ski brakes that meet IAS Rule 120 and have been approved by the Technical Supervisory Association (TUV).

The greatest danger from ski brakes is presently the mounting. In the past, binding parts of different manufacturers have often been mounted together; now ski brakes are being mounted with bindings for which they were not designed. While this does not affect the operation of the brake, it may cause additional friction loads. Since there is no standard mounting position for ski brakes, there may be an overlapping with rough parts of the sole of the ski boot that are permitted under the DIN Norm. The thickness of the brake may also require an adjustment of the soleholder. Various technical details have to be observed in order to avoid additional friction between the boot and the ski, thus preventing the release of the binding. Defects in this area almost certainly cause injuries and result in liability because all parties should be familiar with these new ski accessories. Only a simultaneous functioning of ski boots, binding, and brake will enable the skier to ski safely through the winter.

Biomechanical Factors

Skiing Accident Dynamics

B. vonAllmen and B. Glenne

Skiing provides confidence to people who are increasingly constrained by the limitations to freedom that society imposes. While many regulations are created for safety reasons, skiers in particular wish to abolish limitations to behavior. Therefore, the International Society for Ski Safety (ISSS) must define specifically those hazards involved in skiing.

This chapter addresses the specific physical principles that limit a skier's speed. Focus is on the accelerated sliding fall of a skier, which exemplifies one of the greatest skiing hazards.

The physical principles of the downhill motions of a skier standing upright and a fallen, skidding skier are very much alike. However, there is a dramatic difference between the conclusions of skiing and skidding. The principal author of this chapter had the experience of hitting a line of spectators during an international downhill race in Sestriere, Italy, in 1966. The spectators absorbed the momentum just feet away from a large tree. Another young skier did not have such a cushion as he hit the trees directly; he was paralyzed. Courts are deciding who is responsible for his narrow margin of survival (*Ludwig v. Sportscaster et al.*, 1976).

Who is to blame in this case? The skier? The tree? The ski garment manufacturer? The ski area for not cushioning the trees? Or perhaps the ISSS for not better informing the skiing public of an obvious hazard?

BASIC MECHANICS

The sliding or skidding motion of a skier is basically a function of four variables: the slope of the ski hill; the friction between snow and skier; the air resistance of the skier; and the inertia of the skier.

Sprague (1963) and Perla and Glenne (1977) have analyzed the mechanics of the schussing and turning skier. Figure 1 shows the attainable skier velocities as functions of ski slope, snow friction, and air drag as taken from Perla and Glenne. This figure proves that most terminal skier velocities are higher than the 5 m per second velocity that is commonly assumed to be the human impact tolerance velocity against hard obstacles.

Outwater (1968) and Perla and Glenne (1977) studied the friction coefficients between snow and skis while vonAllmen (1971 and 1974a, b) studied the friction between snow and skidding skiers. The air drag of skiers has been measured in wind tunnels (Eidgenossisches Flugzeugwerk, 1967) and the biomechanics of skiers have been examined by Fukuoka (1971) and Hull (1975). An extensive bibliography of skiing epidemiology has been collected by Schaeffer (1975).

SKIDDING SKIER ACCELERATION OR DECELERATION

vonAllmen (1974b) investigated the motion of skidding skiers as it

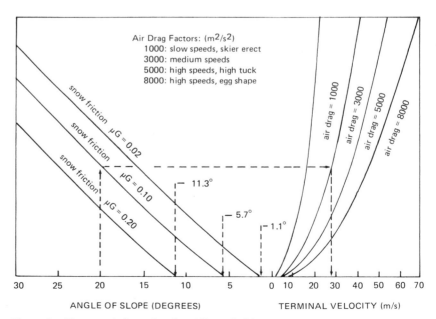

Figure 1.   Nomograph for estimating skiing velocities.

varied with different types of ski garments. This problem may be summarized as follows:

When the friction coefficient between the snow and the ski garment is less than the tangent of the slope, a fallen skier's speed will increase to a terminal velocity similar to that of an upright skier. While falling, he or she may reach even higher velocities than when standing on skis because the drag (air resistance) is less because of the lower profile.

The greater the difference between the coefficient of friction and the slope tangent (friction angle), the more acceleration potential (+a) exists. A deceleration potential (-a) exists only when the friction coefficient between garment and snow is greater than the tangent; breaking and eventual stopping of a fallen skier will occur. Figure 2 gives a representation of skier acceleration or deceleration as the function of ski hill slope and friction coefficient.

SKIDDING SKIER STOPPING DISTANCES

Velocities of fallen skiers were plotted parametrically by vonAllmen and Lux (1976) in order to represent the relationships among velocity (v), slope tangent (tan α), and the relative distance of the sliding fall (s). The following conditional values were used to solve the speed function:

Skier's weight	80 kg mass
Drag force at 100 km/hr	240 Newton
Temperature	-10°C
Air pressure	720 mm Hg
Density of air	1.29 kg/m

The analysis necessitated neglecting three factors:

1. The irrational braking due to moguls. This may be significant during falls over deep mogul surfaces. For that reason, the computed sliding distance must be divided by a roughness factor (RF). An approximation of this factor is based on tests:

$$RF = 1 + \frac{e - 10}{5}$$

where e = maximum mogul depth in centimeter (cm), based on a standardized 5 m span between mogul tops. The measured mogul depth must be reduced or enlarged in proportion to the span between the moguls.

2. The dynamic variation of pressure applied by a live versus a "dead" body.

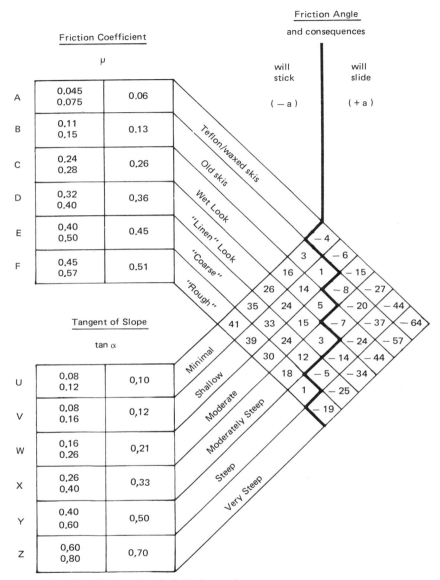

Figure 2.   Classification of typical friction angles.

3.   The water-ski effect—a combination of pushing and compacting snow ahead of the sliding object.

Figures 3a, 3b, 4, and 5 give computer calculations for skier stopping distances. Distances may be measured between any velocity curve and a

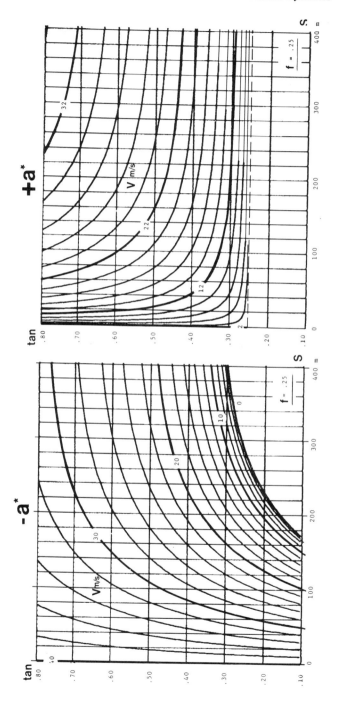

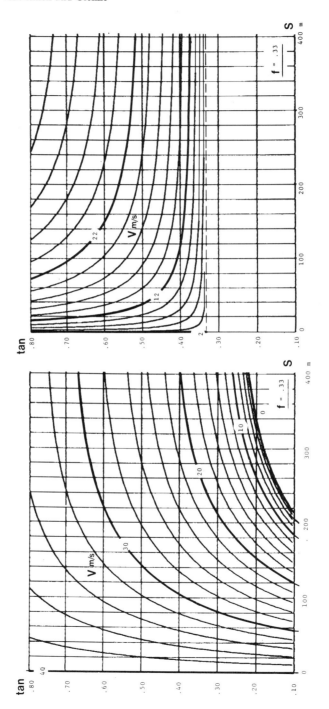

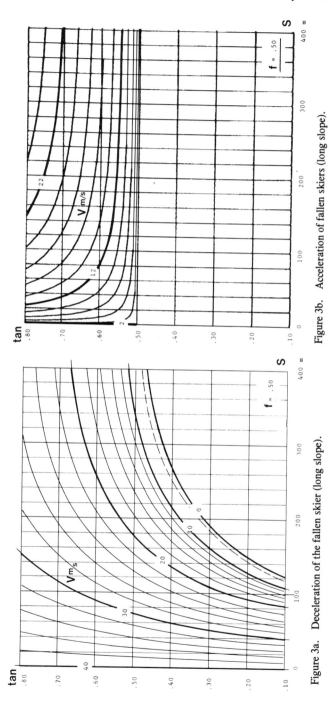

Figure 3b.   Acceleration of fallen skiers (long slope).

Figure 3a.   Deceleration of the fallen skier (long slope).

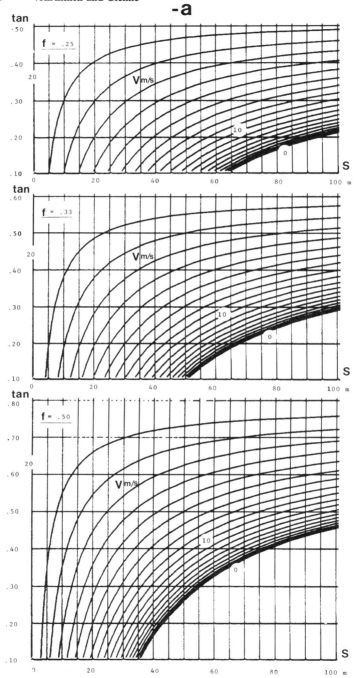

Figure 4.   Deceleration of the fallen skier (short slope).

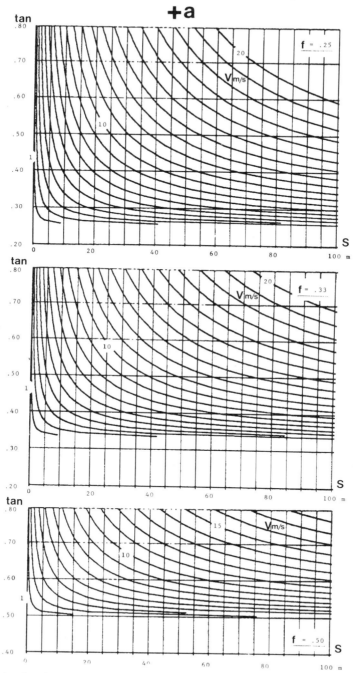

Figure 5. Acceleration of fallen skier (short slope).

representative slope tangent. Curves are shown for the respective friction coefficients (f) between snow and ski garment:

f = .25 (typical for wet look garments)
f = .33 (typical for nylon garments)
f = .50 (typical for coarse wear)

CONCLUSIONS

Care must be taken in choosing ski clothing. One cannot expect to slow down after falling if the ski clothing has a friction coefficient less than the tangent (gradient) of the ski slope.

Even when wearing proper ski garments, one should keep in mind the stopping distance required if falling and keep this separation from trees and other immovable objects. Race courses should be required to be separated from trees and other obstructions by the skier stopping distance. Ski garment manufacturers should notify the consumer about the friction coefficients of their garments.

REFERENCES

Eidgenossisches Flugzeugwerk. 1967. Luftwiderstandsmessung an Skifahren. (Measurement of air resistance in skiing.) Bericht FO-882. Emmen, Switzerland.

Fukuoka, T. 1971. Zur Biomechanik und Kybernetik des Alpinen Schilaufs. (The biomechanics of Alpine skiing.) Limpert Verlag, Frankfurt, Germany.

Hull, M. L. 1975. Skiing Injuries: Field loading and analysis. Department of Mechanical Engineering, University of California, Berkeley, California.

Outwater, J. 1968. On the Friction of Skis. University of Vermont, Burlington, Vermont.

Perla, R., and Glenne, B. 1977. Skiing. In: D. Gray (ed.), Snow. University of Saskatchewan, Canada.

Schaeffer, F. 1975. Bibliography for the ASTM Epidemiology submitted to Amer. Soc. for Testing and Materials Committee F8.14, Philadelphia.

Sprague, R. C., 1963. Skier Equation. Sprague Electric Company, North Adams, Massachusetts.

vonAllmen, B. 1971. Safety on Ski Slopes. University of Vermont, Burlington, Vermont (unpublished).

vonAllmen, B. 1974a. Unzweckmassige Bekleidung-Eine Unfallgefahr beim Skifahren. (Unsuitable clothing-an accident hazard in skiing.) Nr. 57, Neue Zurcher Zeitung, Zurich, Switzerland.

vonAllmen, B. 1974b. Die Textilbremse auf Schnee. (Textile brakes on snow.) Der Skilehrer, Nr. 2, Zurich, Switzerland.

vonAllmen, B., and Lux. 1976. Skier Skidding Distance Curves. Salt Lake City, Utah (unpublished).

Comparison of the Shinbone Loading Capacities of Children and Adults

J. Lange and E. Asang

As a consequence of the rapid growth of skiing to a mass sport, both adults and children are equally exposed to the risk of injury. In the past, the bone breaking point of children was calculated on the basis of the static muscular forces because there is a fixed relation between the muscular force and the breaking point. The experimental torsional strain applied to children's shinbones made it possible to find out the exact load limit and thus the lateral release force required of a child's safety binding.

A total of 115 adults' and 54 children's tibias were exposed to experimental strain. The shinbones were first measured and x-rayed in order to find any previous injury. They were then fixed at both ends in holding jaws in a device designed for the purpose.

The bone was twisted with a hydraulic press. The torsional moment and the angle of rotation were determined by means of extension strips and in inductive motion pick-up (Figure 1). The torsional moment and angle of rotation diagram was recorded by an X-Y plotter. Figures 2A and 2B show a few typical torsional moment-angle of rotation diagrams. In Figure 2, the right-hand diagram has been evaluated. After a short flat course that is due to the short idle movement during fixing, the curve has a linear rise until it reaches the elastic limit torsional moment. At this point, the bone twists around the elastic angle of rotation. After exceeding the threshold of elasticity, the curve bends off the straight line and the rise becomes less. The bone breaks, after the torsional moment of fracture, when twisted around the break-

Figure 1.   Device for measuring torsional strain.

ing angle of rotation. The following values can thus be determined from the torsional moment-angle of rotation diagram: breaking torsional moment, breaking angle of rotation, elastic limit torsional moment, elastic limit angle of rotation, and breaking energy. Using these results, further values interesting for the examination can be determined, such as: plastic angle of rotation, torsional rigidity until breaking, twisting rigidity in the elastic range, energy in the elastic and plastic ranges.

Shinbones of 5- to 15-year-old children and 20- to 60-year-old adults were evaluated. A correlation analysis was made for all values found in order to see what statistically significant interdependence exists among the individual variables. The interrelation of the different values is represented in Figures 3A and 3B: a black circle indicates a strong correlation. When the correlations for children's shinbones are compared with those for adults, it is clearly shown that, for adults, age has no influence on the dimensions and load characteristics, such as fracture torsional moment and elastic limit torsional moment. There is a marked intercorrelation among all values in the 5- to 15-year-old persons, with a correlation coefficient always higher than 0.75.

In 20- to 60-year-old adults, however, this fixed relation is only found in the tibia head diameter and, less frequently, in the total length. In adults, it must be assumed that the stability properties of the bone adapt themselves in case of loading from outside, which is dif-

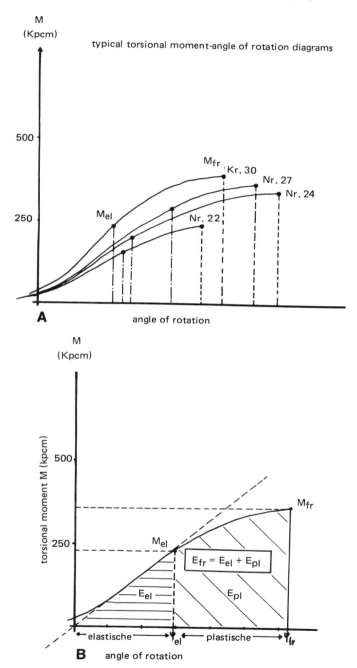

Figures 2A and 2B.   Torsional moment-angle of rotation diagrams.

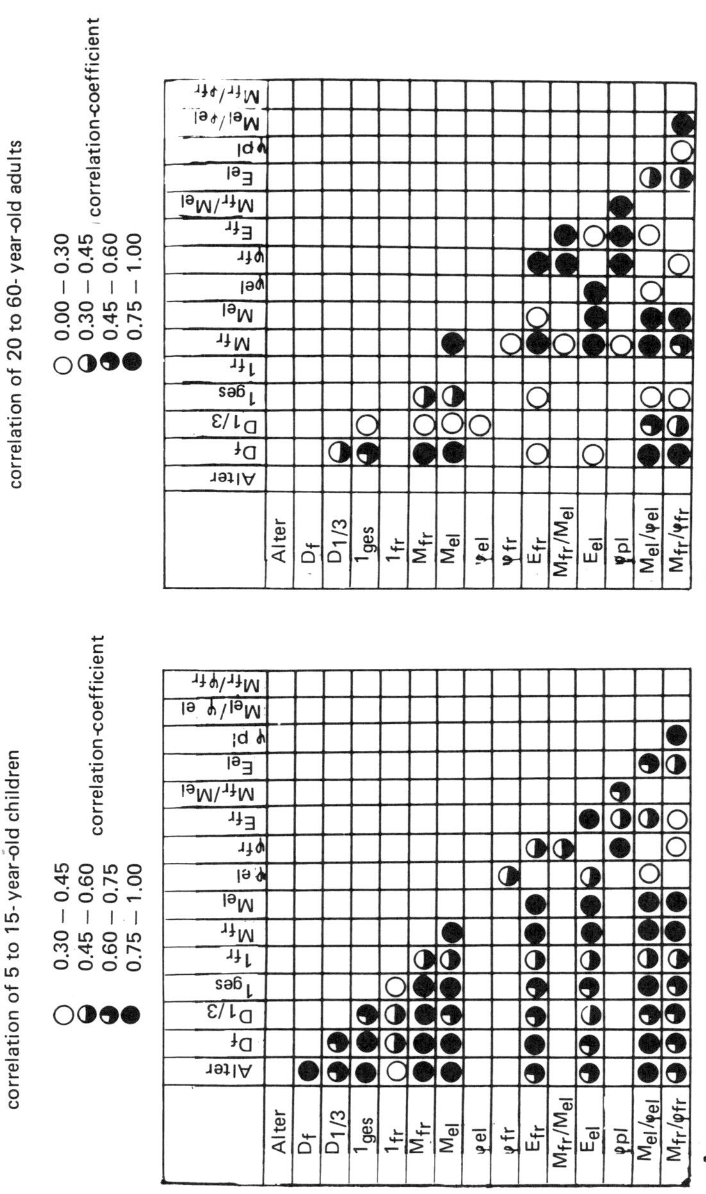

Figures 3A and 3B. Torsional strain intercorrelations.

ferent for each person. Children, however, seem to have relatively constant dimensions and material properties of the shinbone for their respective ages.

A fixed dependence among age, bone dimensions, and load characteristics is understandable in children. The dependence among the age and the frontal tibia head diameter and tibia length is shown in Figures 4A and 4B. For the tibia head diameter, the correlation coefficient is 0.88; in children, then, a determined tibia head diameter can, with certain restrictions, be allocated to each age.

Because there is a strong correlation among the frontal tibia head diameter and the fracture torsional moment and the elastic limit torsional moment, as was shown in earlier experiments, there must consequently be a fixed dependence between age and the load characteristics. Figure 5A shows the breaking torsional moment as dependent on age; Figure 5B reflects the elastic limit torsional moment as dependent on age. It would seem to be possible, then, to infer a breaking point from a child's age and then adjust the safety binding accordingly. However, this must be rejected for various reasons:

1. Proceeding on the assumption that there are children of the same age but of entirely different body weights, it is clear that a determined elastic limit torsional moment or fracture torsional moment cannot be allocated to every age of a child.
2. It would be absurd to start from different reference quantities for children and adults; only confusion would result.
3. The frontal tibia head diameter constitutes an exactly measurable quantity for the purpose. It is therefore rightly used as a measuring auxiliary from which loading characteristics can be inferred.

Consequently, regression lines for the threshold of elasticity or the breaking torsional moment of children depend on the frontal tibia head diameter with a static control and lower tolerance limit (Figures 6A and 6B). The average elastic limit torsional moment in the experiments was 234 kpcm, 498 kpcm less than that of adults. One cannot, then, properly speak of an average torsional moment in children because it constantly changes during growth as the diameter of the tibia head becomes larger.

The breaking torsional moment was 336 kpcm at an average diameter of 64 mm; it is thus 736 kpcm lower than in 20- to 60-year-old persons. On these two curves (Figures 7A and 7B) the elastic limit torsional moment can be seen above; the fracture torsional moment, depending on tibia head diameter of 5- to 15-year-olds, 16- to 20-year-olds, 20- to 60-year-olds, and those over 60 is represented below. It can be seen that the bones of children do not have the same breaking

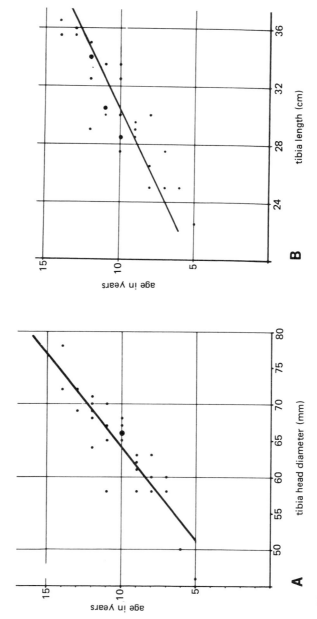

Figures 4A and 4B.   Age, tibia head diameter, and tibia length relationships in children.

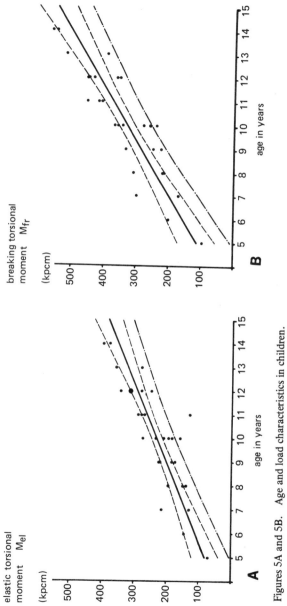

Figures 5A and 5B.   Age and load characteristics in children.

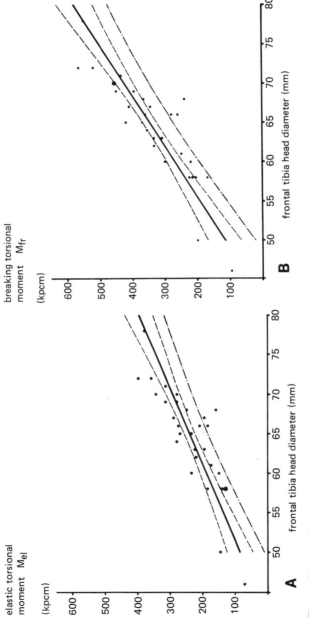

Figures 6A and 6B. Relationships of frontal tibia head with elasticity and breaking torsional moments.

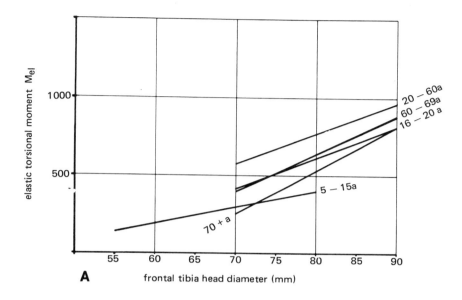

A   frontal tibia head diameter (mm)

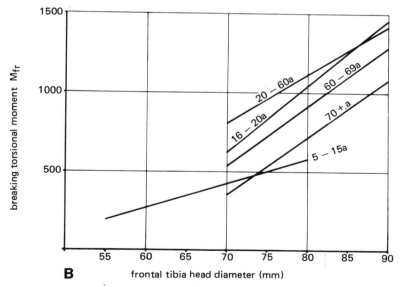

B   frontal tibia head diameter (mm)

Figures 7A and 7B. Comparison of elastic and breaking torsional moments with frontal tibia head diameter in children and adults.

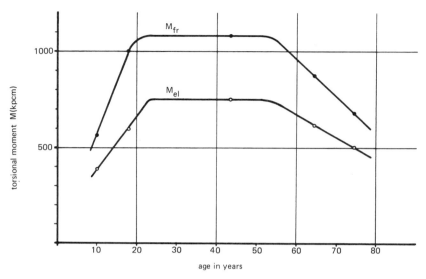

Figure 8.   Elastic limit torsional moment variations with age.

strength as those of adults. This is not attributable only to lower tibia head diameters. When considering the load limit of children's bones having the same dimensions as those of adults, it is clear that the breaking strength is nevertheless considerably lower than that of the 20- to 60-year-old group.

To provide a comparison of load characteristics under equal circumstances, Figure 8 represents the elastic limit torsional moment and the fracture torsional moment for the different age groups that have a constant tibia head diameter of 79 mm. The breaking point and the threshold of elasticity increase considerably until the twentieth year of life, reach a constant level, and then decrease again by the sixtieth year of life. This series of experiments made it possible to determine all dimensions and load values in children and adults and to calculate exactly the individual values of the adjusting table of safety ski bindings. In order to attain effective protection from ski lesions, the release value must have a sufficient safety margin from the breaking point of the shinbone. Because the tibia reveals a marked elasticity limit up to which no damage will occur, this threshold of elasticity must be used as the biological limit for the recommendation of the release torsional moment.

As mentioned above, the frontal tibia head diameter is used as a measuring auxiliary from which it is possible to infer the breaking strength of the tibia. For a practical application, the diameter measurable in a living person, i.e., that with the support of soft parts, must be taken into consideration.

Dynamic Torsional Loading of the Human Tibia

W. Hauser

Many investigations have taken place in recent years to determine the ultimate loading limits of the human tibia, the weakest link in the lower extremity and the most frequent site of severe injuries in Alpine skiing. The individual slow loading limits in bending and twisting using nondenatured shinbones and the relationships of bone dimensions, sex, and age to the biomechanical characteristics of the tibia are known by the extensive research in this field started in 1965 by Asang.

The active and passive forces and impacts in Alpine skiing were also studied to determine the retention force, the lower limit of the release adjustment. To avoid inadvertent release and atypical injuries that may be more serious (e.g., fractures of the skull) than typical skiing injuries involving the leg, the release adjustment must be set higher than the retention force needed under quasistatic and dynamic conditions.

To guarantee the protective function of release bindings that is most important in preventing typical skiing injuries, the release adjustment must be under the upper limit, too. The upper limit is determined by the injury threshold of the tibia. This limit is well known for quasistatic conditions and is related to the individual injury threshold entered in the International Association for Safety in Skiing (IAS) Adjustment Table for Ski Bindings. The upper limit of release adjustment with dynamic loading is known for dynamic bending but not for dynamic twisting. Therefore, the purpose of these investigations was to study the ultimate properties of whole human shinbones in dynamic twisting and to find out whether and in which order there is an increase of strength properties by decreasing loading time.

Dynamic properties of bone tissue were investigated by Bird and Becker (1965 and 1966) and by McElhaney and Byars (1965). The authors found a distinct increase in the failure strength when the loading time was decreased.

Whole bones were investigated by Sanmarco, Frankel, and others in 1971. They determined the effect of loading rate on ultimate properties by torsional tests of fresh dog bones. The findings indicated an increased maximum torque under rapid loads with a difference of 33.4% and a standard deviation of ± 28.4. The loading time for quasistatic fractures was 120-180 sec, for dynamic ones, 40-60 msec.

Asang and Kuhlicke (1974) were the first to investigate the strength properties of the human tibia under dynamic bending loads. Impacts 0.1 sec in duration generally revealed an increase of the fracture limits and of the threshold of elasticity of about 5% in comparison with that in slow loading. With impacts of 0.01 sec in duration, the fracture limits were almost 20% above those in slow bending.

LOADING TIME: ONE-TENTH OF A SECOND

Procedure

The shinbones were excised and the soft tissue was removed, leaving the periosteum intact. The bones were then packed in airtight plastic bags and deep-frozen. Before testing, the bones were thawed, x-rays were taken, and the bones were measured and kept wet. The apparatus used in dynamic twisting experiments of 0.1 sec was similar to the one Asang used in slow twisting tests (Figure 1).

The bones were placed in the torsion apparatus so that the distal and proximal epiphysis were held by jaws that were adjustable to the length of the tibia. Over a cardan joint and a sheave on which a wire rope was fixed, the force of a hydraulic testing machine was transferred to the bone. Data from the strain gauge force transducers were amplified and plotted so that vertical displacement indicated torque and the angle of twist and horizontal displacement indicated time.

Torque, angular deformation, and energy absorbed up to the elasticity threshold and up to the point of failure were analyzed and compared with experiments under quasistatic conditions. The mean diameter of the compacta at the site of fracture, the axial length, and the fracture pattern were also recorded. A picture was taken of each broken bone.

The bones tested were between 18 and 60 years old; their average age was 37.5 years. Between the extremes of this age range, the strength properties remained nearly constant. Twenty-nine shinbones were taken

Figure 1.   Apparatus used in dynamic twisting experiments of 0.1 sec.

from males and 21 from females; there was no basic difference between the properties of the human tibia with regard to sex. The bones were broken with a loading time of 0.12 sec for fracture, with a standard deviation of 0.07 sec.

Results

The basic aggregate of the 50 shinbones that were broken rapidly with a loading time of 0.1 sec did not differ in age or dimensions from those that were broken quasistatically with a loading time of several seconds required for fracture.

Correlations between the dimensions of the shinbones and the loading limits were calculated. Statistically, a highly significant correlation of more than 99.9% probability was found between the frontal diameter at the tibia head and the elastic and maximum torque. The same correlation was shown for the frontal diameter at the distal epiphysis of the tibia, but this dimension is difficult to measure in vivo. A high correlation, with 99% reliability, was also found between the circumference at the smallest region in the distal third point and the mean diameter of the compacta at the fracture site. No difference in these correlations between male and female bones was revealed. The left shinbones showed a slightly higher correlation than the right ones.

Analysis of a diagram of typical dynamic twisting demonstrates the elastic, plastic, and fracture behavior of the human tibia. There is no fundamental difference in slow twisting experiments (Figure 2), but the mean elastic and maximum torque show significant increase. The average of the maximum torque for dynamic twisting is 109.1 Nm related to the mean diameter at the tibia head; the relative value for slow twisting is 93.3 Nm. The difference of 15.8 Nm is equivalent to an increase of

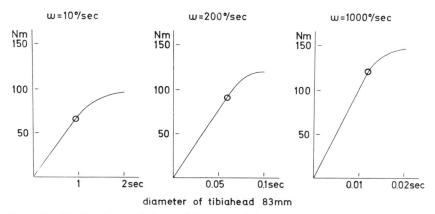

Figure 2.   Results of tests of slow and dynamic twisting.

16.9%. The t- and U-tests verify this difference with a reliability of over 95% ($p < 0.05$; $t_{60} = 2.032$).

Angular deformation, energy absorption, axial length, and site of fracture did not change significantly. In dynamic twisting with the applied torque at the elasticity threshold, the energy absorption and the angular deformation showed an increase 19% higher than the data at failure. In addition, in dynamic twisting, the regression lines for fracture indicated that the diameter at the tibia head was directly proportional to the maximum torque (Figure 3).

The regression line of the elasticity threshold in dynamic twisting was distinctly higher than the regression line in slow twisting experiments (Figure 4). The lower tolerance limit of 80% of the total elasticity threshold is very important for the adjustment of release bindings, because this curve constitutes the injury threshold of the leg. Over the total range of tibia head diameters, the lower tolerance limit is significantly higher in dynamic twisting than under quasistatic conditions.

LOADING TIME: ONE-HUNDREDTH OF A SECOND

Procedure

The procedure was similar to that conducted with a loading time of 0.1 sec. The torsion apparatus was modified as follows: the wire rope and

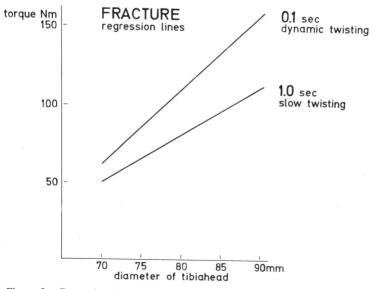

Figure 3.   Regression lines of fracture in slow and dynamic twisting.

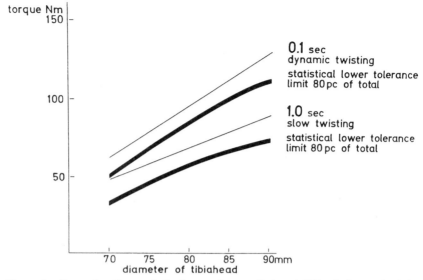

Figure 4.   Regression lines and the lower tolerance limits of 80% of the total of the elasticity threshold in slow and dynamic twisting.

the sheave were exchanged for a toothed rack and wheel, and the strain meter was transferred to a position under the jaws at the distal end of the tibia. Thus the moments of inertia of the testing machine did not influence the measurements. Twenty-six shinbones were taken from males and 19 from females. The mean fracture time was 30 msec, with a standard deviation of ± 10 msec.

Results

The applied maximum torque was 24% higher than in slow twisting experiments. Angular deformation decreased by 5 degrees. Axial length, site of fracture, and fracture pattern did not change significantly. The site of fracture was at the distal third point, and the gross fractures produced in dynamic twisting had a spiral configuration in all bones tested.

DISCUSSION

The results show a significantly higher maximum torque for undenatured human shinbones broken under rapid loads in comparison with the results of slow twisting experiments. The elasticity threshold, which is important for the adjustment of release bindings, increases still more. Knowledge of the ultimate properties of human shinbones under dynamic twisting loads helps to suggest the exact release adjustment in relation to the range of time in which fractures of the tibia may occur. Another important consideration is the finding that in dynamic twisting of about 0.01 sec, inertial effects of the whole human shank influence the injury threshold.

The release adjustment must therefore be between a lower limit (the retention force) and an upper limit (the injury threshold). The distance from each of these limits may be varied individually within a range that takes into consideration such important factors as skiing performance, protective muscle function (e.g., training conditions), weight, and age. The chances of inadvertent release and the risk of typical skiing injuries should then be minimized.

The duration of the forces in slow falls corresponds to the results of slow twisting and bending experiments, and these results determine the upper limits for long-acting forces. The lower limit for a long-duration force is represented by the steering forces. Using short-duration forces, the upper limits are determined by the results of dynamic torsional and bending loading of the human tibia; the lower limits are represented by the disturbing forces. Both, lower and upper limits show an increase with a decrease in the loading time.

For release adjustment, only slow loading results are useful in practice. When short-duration forces act on a binding system, the release value has to change automatically with regard to the loading time. Most of the present release bindings systems do not sufficiently increase the release value when the loading time is decreased. In the future, an electronically controlled force-time adjustment may provide a practical means of controlling release values in ski bindings.

REFERENCES

Asang, E. 1970. 20 Jahre Skitraumatologie. Grundlagen zum Verletzungsschutz im alpinen Skisport. (Twenty years of ski injuries. Basis for injury prevention in Alpine skiing.) Habilitation-Schrift., Technische Universität, München.

Asang, E. 1973. Experimentelle und praktische Biomechanik des menschlichen Beins. (Experimental and practical biomechanics of the human leg.) Med. und Sport 8:245–255.

Asang, E. 1976. Experimental Biomechanics of the Human Leg—A Basis for Interpretation of Typical Skiing Injury Mechanisms. First International Conference on Ski Trauma and Skiing Safety, Riksgränsen, Schweden. Orthoped. Clin. N. Amer. 7(1):63–73.

Asang, E. 1976. Applied Biomechanics in Alpine Skiing—A Basis for individual protection from Skiing Injuries. First International Conference on Ski Trauma and Skiing Safety, Riksgränsen, Schweden. Orthoped. Clin. N. Amer. 7(1): 95–103.

Asang, E., C. Grimm, and H. Krexa. 1975. Telemetrische Elektromyographie und Elektrodynamographie beim alpinen Skilauf. (Telemetry of Electromyographic and Electrodynamic data during an Alpine ski run.) EEG-EMG, pp. 1–10, Stuttgart.

Becker, H., F. Bird, M. Messer, and J. Healer. 1965. Report No. ARA 280-4. Allied Research Associates, Concord, Mass.

Bird, F., and H. Becker. 1966. Report No. ARA 322-2. Allied Research Associates, Concord, Mass.

Comparison of Conservative and Operative Treatments of Osteotomies of Rabbit Tibias

M. Jäger, W. Gördes, W. Kossyk, and M. Ungethüm

The number of active skiers is steadily increasing. In spite of technical improvements for the safety of the skier, the absolute number of skiing accidents is also climbing.

Fracture of the lower leg is still the most frequent injury. There are two principal methods of treatment: realignment, traction, and cast (conservative); and nail or plate osteosynthesis (operative).

PROBLEMS

When deciding between operative and conservative treatments, the physician has to consider a number of problems. Solutions to some of these problems have been approached through animal experiments.

There are two important problems after plate osteosynthesis.

Problem 1

Indications for operative and conservative methods have become standardized. In fractures of the tibia, for example, it is possible to act conservatively or surgically. A multitude of data determining the indication must be considered. Uncertainty remains about the flexural strength after absolutely stable internal fixation (such as plate fixation) and external unstable fixation (such as cast fixation with medullary splinting). Comparative results of flexural strength testing with regard to time and mechanical properties in identical fractures and osteotomies are lacking.

Problem 2

Refractures have occurred infrequently, but occasionally after osseous consolidation with stable osteosynthesis. A concern arises about the mechanical data of bone after removal of the implant, and the following questions must be answered:

1. What is the flexural strength in relation to:
   a. Type of osteosynthesis (without compression or dynamic compression plate)?
   b. Time until removal of the implant?
2. What is the comparable flexural strength after:
   a) Stable plate fixation?
   b) Cast and medullary K-wire?

MATERIAL AND METHOD

The experiments were standardized in terms of subject size and protocol. Fifty-five adult male rabbits averaging 3 to 4 kg were used. The right tibias were osteotomized between the lateral malleolus and the distal tibio-fibular synostosis after the animals were anesthesized with pentothal. Flexural strength testing was performed 4, 8, and 16 weeks after the osteotomies.

Series 1 was treated with loose medullary K-wires (2 mm) and fixated in above-the-knee casts after the osteotomies. The flexural strength was tested 4, 8, and 16 weeks after the fixation devices had been removed.

In Series 2, the osteotomies were stabilized with six-hole plates without compression. Flexural strength testing was performed 4, 8, and 16 weeks later.

Series 3 treatment was identical to Series 2 for the first 8 weeks. Then the plates were removed and the hind legs fixed in casts for 4 weeks. After that the casts were removed and the animals allowed to put weight on the extremities. Sixteen weeks after the osteotomies, flexural strength testing was performed.

In series 4, treatment involved the use of dynamic compression plates (6 holes) with dimensions similar to those of the plates without compression for the fixation of the osteotomies. Flexural strength testing was done at 4, 8, and 16 weeks.

In Series 5, the control group, the right hind legs were fixed in casts without prior osteotomy, and flexural strength testing was performed at 8 weeks after cast fixation. The flexural properties were tested on both tibias in each animal. The loss of flexural strength plus standard deviations of the individual test groups were calculated. Comparative flexural strength testing was done with the universal testing machine "Zwick," with three-point fixation.

RESULTS

Flexural properties showed two typical patterns in the force-elongation curve. The untreated control tibias showed a linear progression up to 40 kp.

A lesser angle of inclination in the diagram could be interpreted as evidence of a diminished moment of resistance in both the previously cast-stabilized and the previously plate-stabilized tibias. The loss of flexural strength of the treated tibias was obvious at all intervals.

The breaks never occurred abruptly in medullary rodded tibias

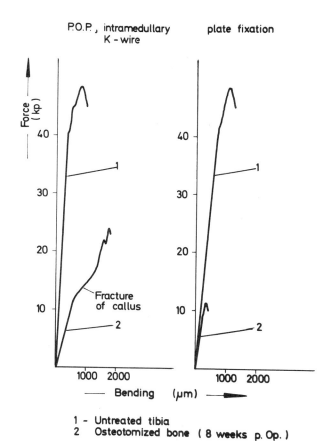

1 - Untreated tibia
2   Osteotomized bone (8 weeks p. Op.)

Figure 1. Fracture behaviors of tibias after different plate fixations.

that had healed with callus formation. They started within the calluses and ended in the previous osteotomies.

The breaks in previously plate-stabilized tibias were always abrupt after reaching maximal stress. The fracture lines went through the previous osteotomies at all intervals, giving the impression of refracture. The fracture behaviors of tibias after different plate fixations were identical (Figure 1).

The unstable fixations with long leg casts and K-wires (Series 1) gave continually rising flexural strength values. After 4 weeks, the loss of flexural strength was 60%, after 8 weeks 55%, after 16 weeks only 40%. Those tibias treated with plates without compression (Series 2) or dynamic plates (Series 4) showed a considerably slower return of flexural strength properties. Values for the dynamic plates were slightly higher than for the plates without compression. The steep rise of flexural strength 8 weeks after plate fixation with subsequent 4 weeks' cast fixation and 4 weeks' normal weight bearing (Series 3) was quite interesting. Eight weeks' cast fixation without previous tibial osteotomy (Series 5) did not lower flexural strength (Figure 2).

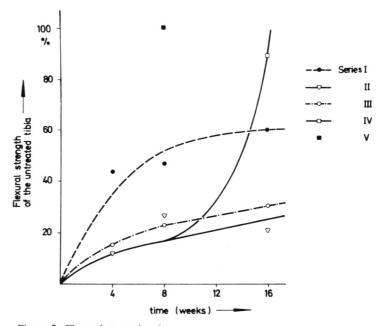

Figure 2. Flexural strength values.

CONCLUSIONS

The fracture line after removal of the implant material is partially dependent on the concentration of forces with three-point fixation, and partially on the loss of flexural strength subsequent to treatment.

Fractures healing with callus formation (secondary or indirect healing) exhibit initially better flexural strength properties when compared to so-called no-callus or primary vascular direct healing. After implant removal and graded weight bearing (long leg cast) a steep rise in flexural strength becomes apparent. The cortical structure seem to regain its mechanical strength faster after removal of the stress protection and graded weight bearing than does the fracture callus that has to undergo structural differentiation under mechanical stresses.

There seems to be no explanation for the minor differences between plates without compression and dynamic compression plates with regard to their flexural strength. It is possible that the lower rigidity of the dynamic plate because of its difficult construction has something to do with it.

Knee Mechanics and Analytical Modeling in Lower Limb Injuries

R. L. Piziali, D. A. Nagel, J. Rastegar, and T. K. Hight

While ski release bindings provide increased safety for skiers, there are still many aspects of skiing forces and lower limb response that are unknown and are limiting optimal design. The purpose is to develop an analytical model of the lower limb capable of predicting the dynamic response of the limb and stresses in the bones and ligaments. Such a model can be used with typical skiing force histories to establish desired ski binding characteristics. This requires the development of both a numerical model and the appropriate biomechanical data. Early analytical work (Piziali, 1973; Piziali and Nagel, 1976) modeled the leg in torsion and established the importance of dynamic effects and the need to determine the stiffness characteristics of the joints. Work on the static response of the tibia (Piziali, Hight, and Nagel, 1976) showed the importance of accurately modeling bone as an irregular, multiconnected solid for torsion and of including the twisted, curved geometry of long bones.

The current efforts within this research program are to establish the stiffness and strength characteristics of the human knee and to develop a numerical model capable of determining the nonlinear, large displacement response of the lower limb. Future efforts will include studies of the ankle and hip, muscle effects, and the limb response to skiing loads as measured by Hull and Mote (1976). By knowing the forces and moments present in downhill skiing and the response of the lower limb to these forces, as well as forces present in falls, the parameters necessary for the binding designer to improve binding performance may be discovered.

This research was supported by grants from the National Science Foundation (NSF ENG 03567) and the National Institutes of Health (NIH 18181).

RATIONALE AND METHODS

Both experimental and analytical programs have been directed at developing very complete and accurate data and models. These programs have been designed to interact with each other in analyzing leg response in an injury-producing environment.

Previous investigations of the structural characteristics of the human knee have been qualitative (Brantigan and Voshell, 1941; Hallen and Lindahl, 1965; and Kennedy and Fowler, 1971), restricted to one or two motions (Edwards, Lafferty, and Lange, 1969; Wang, Walker, and Wolf, 1973; Wang and Walker, 1974; and Noyes et al., 1976), or aimed at clinical diagnosis of injured ligaments (Markolf, Mensch, and Amstutz, 1976; and Pope et al., 1976). This experimental program is designed to produce quantitative data for twelve displacements (Figure 1) at loads near injury level. The program utilizes the stiffness influence coefficient method to study the load-displacement and stiffness-displacement characteristics of the knee. The experimental apparatus attaches six degree-of-freedom dynamometers to the femur and tibia. The femur is held stationary and the tibia is moved through a single displacement by specially designed fixtures attached to an electrohydraulic load frame. Thus, the six forces and moments on both the femur and tibia are measured as a function of displacement. These data are digitized, stored on line, and later reduced by fitting the data with a four-section least squares cubic spline. The analytical expressions are then differentiated to produce stiffness versus displacement curves.

The coordinate system for these experiments is shown in Figure 1. During an experiment the initial orientation between the tibia and the femur is established. A single displacement is then applied while all forces are measured. For example, if the tibia undergoes pure varus-valgus rotation, U_{11} is varied while all other displacements remain zero. The resulting force-displacement curves establish the primary and coupled structural characteristics of the knee. The derivatives of the above curves provide stiffness data; for example, $dF_1u_{11}/du_{11} = K_{1,11}$ (u_{11}) relates the axial forces and varus-valgus rotation to produce the coupled stiffness coefficient. For the limb in the anatomical position (Figure 1), certain displacements are reciprocal, e.g., $u_2 = -u_8$. However, once flexion or other initial displacement are applied, there is no reciprocal relationship. The above method and apparatus produce accurate data describing the nonlinear, large displacement, coupled nature of load transmission across the knee. A more complete description is available (Piziali, Rastegar, and Nagel, 1977).

Previous models of whole bones have been restricted to bone vibra-

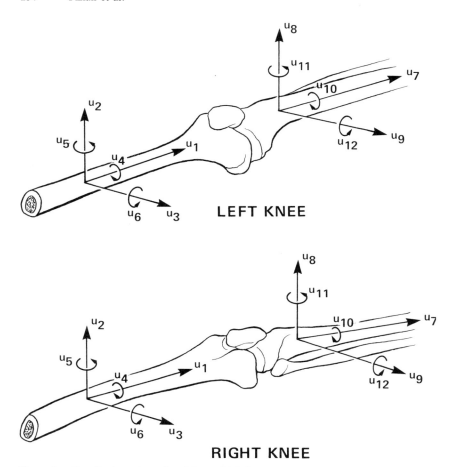

Figure 1.   Coordinate systems for right and left knees.

tions (Orne, 1974) or to static studies and have generally assumed circular or constant cross-sectional properties (Koch, 1917; Toridis, 1969; Piotroski and Wilcox, 1971). The structural response of the entire limb has not been developed in the literature. The analytical model developed in this research program utilizes two numerical models. The first, BONE, is a static model, and it determines the stiffness characteristics of a given cross-section and the stresses in a cross-section given the loading at that cross-section. A complete description of this program and the importance of various parameters are given in Piziali, Hight, and Nagel (1976).

The second program, DYLDBM, is capable of modeling the non-linear, large displacement, dynamic response of the lower limb to arbitrary loading. The current model consists of stiffness matrices from the matrix condensation of a 15-member beam finite element model of the femur and a similar condensation of the tibia and fibula. A stiffness-inertia approximation is used for the ankle, ski, and boot, and the knee is modeled as a nonlinear force-displacement relationship. The mass matrices are diagonal and are based on the total mass of each segment, including bones and flesh. The proximal end of the femur is considered fixed, and loads are applied to the ski. The lack of motion at the hip greatly affects limb response; however, the lack of hip stiffness data lead to this assumption.

The numerical integration and convergence criteria are based on Newmark's β method and Belytschko's total energy criteria (Belytschko and Schoeberle, 1975), respectively. Because the knee allows large displacements in three dimensions (nonplanar), rotation angles cannot be treated as vector quantities. Consequently, the rigid body motion of the bone is determined by summing the incremental changes in the direction cosine matrix of the local coordinate system fixed in each bone (similar to the procedure developed by Oran (1973)). At each time step, global mass and stiffness matrices are formed using these rotation matrices. A new load increment is then applied to the ski, and incremental displacements are calculated. The internal forces are then compared to the applied load plus the D'Alembert forces and a force error vector is found. The correct forces and displacements across the knee are determined in this step by utilizing the experimental data. This step is repeated until the work associated with the force error vector is less than some fraction of the total system energy. When the convergence criterion is met, the limb position and loading are established and the entire procedure is repeated for the next time increment.

RESULTS

Experiments were conducted on fresh human knees obtained at autopsy. The knees were stored at $-15°C$, thawed, and then maintained in a $23°C$, 100% humidity environment. Tests conducted include:

1. Axial tension and compression
2. Medial-lateral shear
3. Anterior-posterior shear
4. Varus-valgus rotation about different centers of rotation
5. Axial rotation about different centers of rotation
6. Hyperextension.

Tests 1 through 5 were also conducted for various joint orientations, e.g., flexion angles. Some typical results for human left knees are presented in this section.

Figure 2a shows plots of varus-valgus moments versus varus-valgus displacements as the axis of rotation is moved medially. It can be seen that the valgus moment is increased by the medial shift. This results from increased condular contact pressure for the same rotation angle. The varus stiffness remains almost constant with the medial shift in axis indicating that the decreased condylar pressure and increased lateral ligament tension have similar values. Figure 2b is a plot of the derivatives of the curves in Figure 2a and thus presents the varus-valgus stiffness versus rotation. The valgus stiffness increases with the medial shift of the axis, while the varus stiffness remains nearly constant.

The effect of axis shifts is also significant for some of the coupled loads. The axial load greatly increases for medial axis shifts and valgus rotations (Figure 2c). The roles of condular pressure and ligament tension are well established from this curve; for example, the axial force is always compressive for valgus rotation, but for varus rotation it becomes negative. Thus the relative force levels of condylar compression and ligament tension can be determined. When the axis of rotation is shifted approximately 1.0 inch medially, the axial force is nearly zero. Thus this axis is the appropriate axis of rotation for a pure varus moment.

The effect of the initial orientation of the tibia and femur on knee stiffness can be seen in Figures 3a and 3b. As the flexion angle increases (except for 45° flexion), the moment required for a given rotation increases.

Because the experimental method applies a specific displacement to the joint, the experiments can be repeated as ligaments are cut

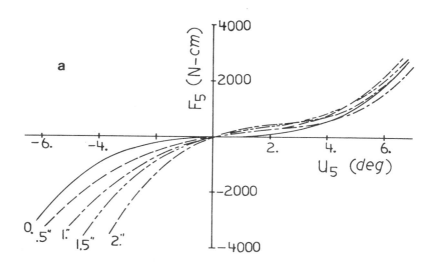

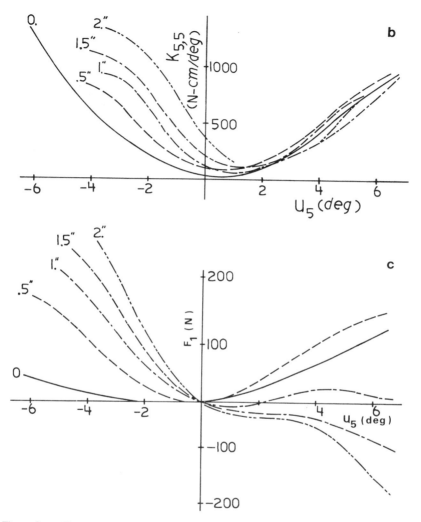

Figure 2.   a:Varus-valgus load versus varus-valgus rotation—effect of medial shift of axis of rotation. b: Varus-valgus stiffness versus varus-valgus rotation—effect of medial shift of axis of rotation. c: Coupled axial load versus varus-valgus rotation—effect of medial shift of axis of rotation.

without affecting the role of the remaining elements. A series of such tests was conducted for the intact knee, followed by the same tests with only the cruciate ligaments intact. Figure 4 is a plot of an ante-rior-posterior shear test. The results show that the posterior cruciate ligament supports essentially all of the load caused by a posterior tibial

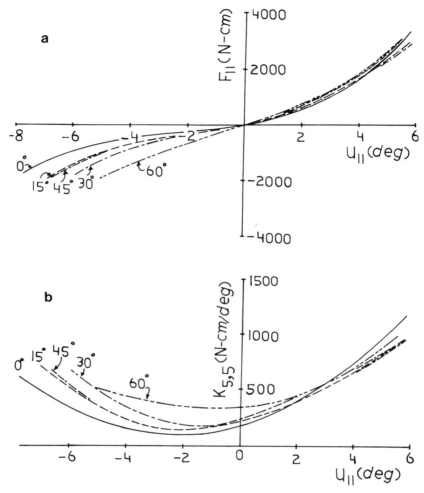

Figure 3.   a:Varus-valgus load versus varus-valgus rotation—effect of initial flexion. b: Varus-valgus stiffness versus varus-valgus rotation—effect of initial flexion.

displacement and that the anterior cruciate ligament supports 80–90% of the load caused by an anterior tibial displacement.

For a medial-lateral displacement, the joint capsule and ligaments other than the cruciates support approximately 25–35% of the load (Figure 5). The effects of condylar interference can be seen to reach 40 N in Curve 3 for a lateral femoral displacement of 0.65 cm.

In torsion, the cruciates wind up on each other for internal rotation and unwind for external rotation. This leads to the effect seen in

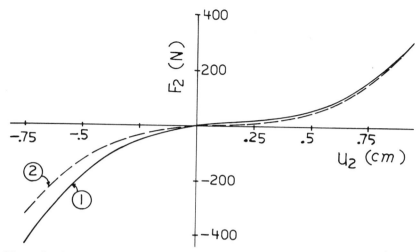

Figure 4. Contribution of cruciate ligaments to anterior-posterior load. ① = Intact knee. ② = Knee with only the cruciate ligaments intact.

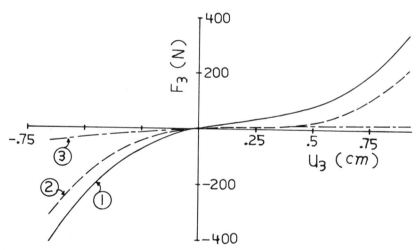

Figure 5. Contribution of cruciate ligaments to medial-lateral load. ① = Intact knee. ② = Knee with only cruciate ligaments intact. ③ = All connecting soft tissues removed.

Figure 6 where the cruciates contribute 30–50% of the load for internal tibial rotation but produce no significant load for external rotation.

The analytical model has been used only for the leg elements described in the previous section. Two impulsive, F (1 − cosωt) loads were applied simultaneously, each with a period of 0.1 sec. One was a

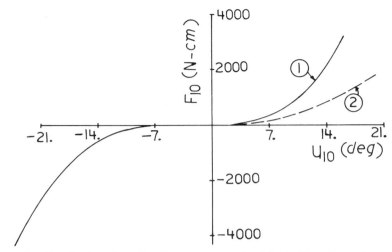

Figure 6.   Contribution of cruciate ligaments to torsional load. ① = Intact knee. ② = Knee with only the cruciate ligaments intact.

lateral load that reached a maximum value of 445 N, and the other was a torsional load that reached a maximum value of 34,000 Ncm. Figure 7 is a plot of the applied moment, the elastic moment at the distal side of the ankle and the moment at the distal side of the knee. The ankle moment follows the loading rather closely because it represents the applied load minus the inertia load. The knee moment lags by nearly 100 msec. The torsional moment is large and would either release a binding or fracture the tibia. The total rotation at the distal side of the knee and distal side of the ankle (the boot and ski) are shown in Figure 8.

The lateral displacements at the ski and proximal tibia are shown in Figure 9. They result primarily from the applied lateral load. As expected, the ski displacement is larger and slightly precedes the lateral displacement of the proximal tibia.

DISCUSSION

The experimental and analytical results to date clearly establish the need to measure accurately both the nonlinear and coupled structural characteristics of the knee. These data must be developed for all reasonable displacements and joint orientations in a manner consistent with analytical modeling. The experimental results have proven the methods described here to be efficient and accurate in collecting data both on the intact knee and on specific structural elements of the knee.

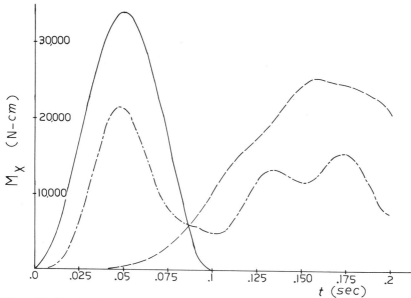

Figure 7.   Torsional moment versus time—applied moment at distal ankle (solid line); internal elastic moment at distal ankle (dotted line); and internal elastic moment at proximal tibia (dashed line).

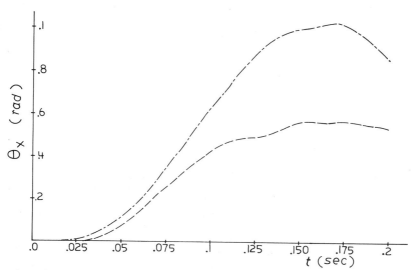

Figure 8.   Axial rotation versus time—rotation at distal ankle (dotted line); rotation at proximal tibia (dashed line).

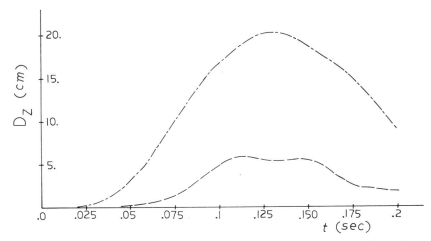

Figure 9.   Lateral displacements versus time—displacement at distal ankle (dotted line); displacement at proximal tibia (dashed line).

Once strength data are generated, predictions of knee injury will be possible. With the collection of data on the hip and ankle, the entire passive lower limb can be accurately described. The analytical model is currently able to model accurately the lower limb response and the stresses in the bones for arbitrary loading. Once sufficient data are generated, the model is capable of simulating both the passive and active lower limb.

    With the ability to model the human lower limb accurately, the mechanics of limb injury can be defined, and methods for preventing injury can be evaluated and established.

REFERENCES

Belytschko, T., and Schoeberle, D. 1975. On the unconditional stability of an implicit algorithm for non-linear structural dynamics. Trans. ASME, V. 97, J. Appl. Mech., V42, N4, pp. 865–869.

Brantigan, O. C., and Voshell, A. F. 1941. The mechanics of the ligaments and menisci of the knee joint. J. Bone and Joint Surg. 23:44–66.

Edwards, R. G., Lafferty, J. F., and Lange, K. O. 1969. Ligament strain in the human knee joint. Trans. ASME Winter Annual Meeting, November.

Hallen, L. G., and Lindahl, O. 1965. Rotation in the knee joint in experimental injury to the ligaments. Acta Orthop. Scandinav. 36:400–407.

Hull, M. L., and Mote, C. D., Jr. 1976. Pulse code modulation telemetry in ski injury research. II. Preliminary Results. Int. J. Bio-Telemetry. 2(5):276–296.

Kennedy, J. C., and Fowler, P. J. 1971. Medial and anterior instability of the knee. J. Bone and Joint Surg. 53A:1257–1270.

Koch, J. C. 1917. The laws of bone architecture. Amer. J. Anat. 21:177–298.

Markolf, K. L., Mensch, J. S., and Amstutz, H. C. 1976. Stiffness and laxity of the knee: The contribution of the supporting structures. J. Bone and Joint Surg. 58A: 5.

Noyes, F. R., Grood, E. S., Graves, G. A., and Burstein, A. H. 1976. Comparative mechanical properties of prosthetic, primate, and human anterior cruciate ligament. Orthopaedic Research Society, No. 15.

Oran, C. 1973. Tangent stiffness in space frames. J. Structural Division, ASCE. 99(ST6):987–1001.

Orne, D. 1974. The in-vivo, driving point impedance of the human Ulna-A viscoelastic beam model. J. Biomechanics. 7(3):249-257.

Piziali, R. L. 1973. The dynamic torsional response of the human leg relative to skiing injuries. Symposium on Mechanics and Sport, ASTM, AMD-Vol. 4.

Piziali, R. L., Hight, T. K., and Nagel, D. A. 1976. An extended structural analysis of long bones: Application to the human tibia. J. Biomechanics. 9: 695–701.

Piziali, R. L., and Nagel, D. A. 1976. Modeling of the human leg in ski injuries. Orthopedic Clinics of North America 7(1).

Piziali, R. L., Rastegar, J. C., and Nagel, D. A. 1977. Measurement of the nonlinear, coupled stiffness characteristics of the human knee. J. Biomechanics. 10:45–51.

Piotroski, G., and Wilcox, G. 1971. The stress program: A computer program for the analysis of stresses in long bones. J. Biomechanics. 4:497–506.

Pope, M. H., Crowninshield, R., Miller, R., and Johnson, R. 1976. Static and dynamic behavior of the human knee 'in vivo.' J. Biomechanics. 9:449–452.

Toridis, T. G. 1969. Stress analysis of the femur. J. Biomechanics. 2:163–174.

Wang, C. J., and Walker, P. S. 1974. Rotary laxity of the human knee joint. J. Bone and Joint Surg. 56A:161–170.

Wang, C. J., Walker, P. S., and Wolf, B. 1973. The effects of flexion and rotation on the length patterns of the ligaments of the knee. J. Biomechanics. 6:587–596.

Laboratory and Field Research on Ski Bindings

C. D. Mote, Jr., and M. L. Hull

Research in industry and universities on skiing injuries and ski binding design problems has been underway for some years. Visible progress in the marketplace has resulted more from the elimination of fundamentally poor designs than from any breakthrough in design concept. The binding design problem remains difficult because the failure criteria associated with leg injuries and the true excitation of the skiing process are still little known. Notable research has been established on the torsional and bending strength of the human tibia (Asang and Wittmann, 1973). Tibial fractures account for approximately 20% of all skiing injuries: tibial fractures in the absence of muscle and ligamentous forces are a minor fraction of those injuries. The dynamic response of the leg to external forces, and ligament failure in the knee are being studied by R. L. Piziali at Stanford University and R. Johnson et al. at the University of Vermont, but the distance between current leg modeling research and the ability to predict the threshold of injury remains large.

The forces on the leg encountered during skiing have been measured on several occasions (Wittmann, 1975; Outwater and Woodward, 1966; Hull and Mote, 1975; Svoboda). Accurate measures of the forces under the critical conditions of safety release and retention are rare. Severe loading has been recorded during skiing by Hull and Mote (1975) where relatively long duration forces in excess of the reported tibial fracture

This research was supported by a National Science Foundation grant.

strength in bending and torsion occurred at the boot. No injury to the test skier resulted. The measurements also included a premature binding release and legitimate forced binding release during aggressive skiing. Data of this type are necessary to identify the extreme loading environments for binding design. This work is continuing.

The binding problem is complicated by the dual design requirements of release and retention (Mote and Hull, 1976a) and the uncertainty surrounding the necessary or desirable number of release modes. The release function accounts for the binding safety features and the retention requirement is concerned with the skiing effectiveness. A release mode is a direction of relative motion between the boot and ski in which binding release is possible; e.g., laterally at the toe. As the number of release modes increases, optimal design for release and retention in all possible combinations of binding motion becomes increasingly difficult.

Progress in binding research is centered on four research areas:

1. Failure criteria for the leg and load transmission from the ski through the leg (Piziali and Nagel, 1976; Hight, Piziali and Nagel, 1975; Piziali, 1973)
2. Analysis of forces occurring in the skiing process under critical loading conditions where the release and retention criteria are challenged (Hull and Mote, 1975 and 1976)
3. Specification of optimal design properties for the binding mechanism (Mote and Hull, 1976a and 1976b)
4. Design of appropriate dynamic tests for bindings (Yam and Mote, 1976; Davidson and Mote, 1971; Ellis and Mote, 1972)

This subdivision outlines the elements of a successful research effort on the binding design problem; none can be neglected.

The objective of this chapter is to summarize the authors' current results from the testing of bindings, from the specification of desirable binding properties, and from the analysis of skiing forces. Results and materials from the previous work (Mote and Hull, 1976a) are preliminary to this paper and are not repeated here. The emphasis here is on current, fundamental results and ideas that have long-term importance in the design and understanding of any binding.

LABORATORY RESULTS

The purpose of this section is to discuss current tests and interpretations of mechanical binding properties. Emphasis is on mechanical properties that are significant for nearly all bindings. Consideration of binding properties, such as corrosion resistance, ease of maintenance, simplicity of design, etc., are not discussed.

Types of Lab Tests

There are two types of laboratory tests that are distinguished by loading rate. In the first group, the ski (or boot) is held and the boot (or ski) is twisted or pulled away as in Figure 1. This is a slow, or quasistatic test that is representative of nearly all binding tests. In the second group, the ski is knocked away from the boot-leg system with a sudden blow or impact as illustrated in Figure 2. Relatively few of these high-speed, dynamic tests are performed. As a general rule, a binding should be tested throughout the loading rate range of its intended application. The slow tests are important because the slow twisting and bending of the tibia is common in skiing; accordingly, they cannot be ignored in binding evaluation. By similar argument, the dynamic evaluation of bindings is important because the typical skiing environment is dynamic. Since dynamic tests are not generally performed, conclusions regarding dynamic performance have been drawn from static tests. These conclusions are often seriously in error. More on this point shortly.

Static binding tests[1] can be divided into three classes depending upon the purpose of the test:

1. Binding adjustment testing
2. Design evaluation testing for standardization purposes
3. Load-displacement tests for research on mechanical binding design function.

Adjustment testing, such as that typically performed in ski shops, is done to set the maximum static load at release, but it does not evaluate the design or give an indication of safety. This, by the way, points out a common misconception even among expert skiers who associate proper adjustment with good binding design. Design evaluation tests performed for standardization purposes following the BfU in Lausanne, the International Association for Safety in Skiing (IAS) in Munich and the soon-to-appear American Society of Testing Materials (ASTM) standard in the USA, determine whether a binding meets a minimum quality standard over a range of conditions. Attention is directed to uncovering designs that do not function satisfactorily. A binding either does or does not meet the standard whatever it may be. The third class includes research tests probing the detail of binding function under general loading. The twisting moment-rotation characteristic of the commercial toe binding in Figure 3 is such a test.

Dynamic tests have not been performed in sufficient number to warrant a parallel classification into the three groups. Tests to date

---

[1] The terms *twisting moment, torque,* and *torsion* are used interchangeably by researchers in this field. The terms *load* and *excitation* refer to any combination of forces and moments acting on the skier-ski system.

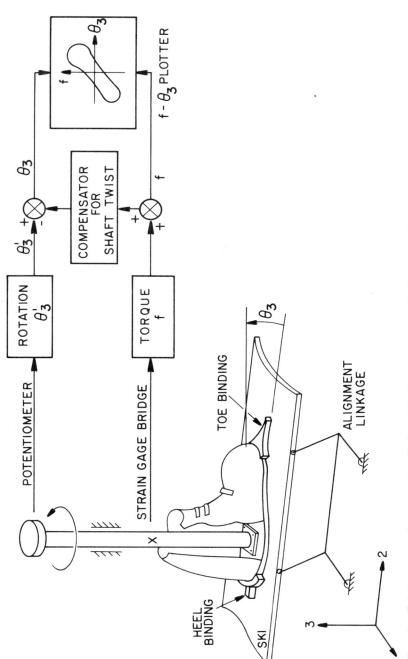

Figure 1.   Twisting moment f versus rotation θ_3 for a ski release binding toe unit. The system allows the binding to rotate about its axis by permitting the ski to translate in the 1-2 plane.

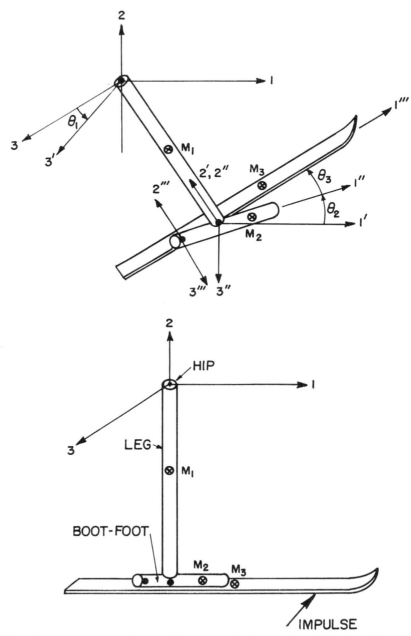

Figure 2.   Three degree-of-freedom laboratory and theoretical model for lateral impulse loading of the ski.

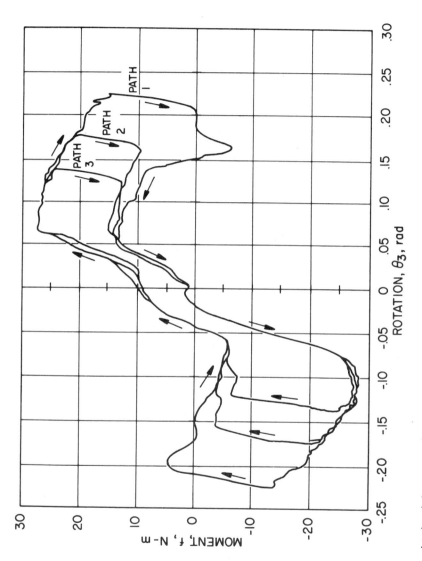

Figure 3.   Quasistatic twisting moment f, relative rotation Θ_3, for commercial toe binding along three arbitrary paths.

have been of the research type. However, dynamic tests covering the three testing areas will come in the natural development of the design and safety problem.

Long Stroke Bindings

Long stroke refers to the relatively large rotation or displacement of the boot in the binding prior to release. Test data for a particular toe binding are presented in Figure 3, where the stroke is the rotation Θ_3. The three characteristic paths displayed therein are distinguished by the $(\Theta_3)_{max}$ value in each test. The characteristics of the hysteresis loops in the figure have been discussed in Mote and Hull (1976a). Maximizing the external impulse[2] on the ski for release at a given binding setting f_{max} and minimizing the recentering time from the maximum displacement $(\Theta_3)_{max}$ to $\Theta_3 = 0$ following impact are desirable design characteristics for the binding.

Release in modern bindings is displacement-controlled. A leg moment f that produces a relative displacement $\Theta_3 = (\Theta_3)_R$ in Figure 4 causes the boot and ski to separate. The mechanical work done by the boot-binding interaction moment f is the area under the $f-\Theta_3$ path from Θ_3^1 to Θ_3^3 where the boot is moving toward release. Maximizing this area maximizes the work done to release the boot, and this arrests the relative motion of ski and boot most effectively. In Figure 4 the path $\Theta_3^1-\Theta_3^3$ maximizes the work done (area under the path) for a given f_{max} and $(\Theta_3)_{max}$. The purpose of this mechanical work in the design is to prevent premature release from subinjury level impacts or blows to the ski. For instance, the ski may experience a lateral impact. The ski instantly begins moving laterally while the boot initially remains stationary, as illustrated in the impact tests in Figures 5 and 6. The ski then interacts with the boot through the binding; the ski decelerates because of this interaction f and the boot accelerates. If the relative velocity between ski and boot vanishes before the release rotation $\Theta_3 = (\Theta_3)_R$, then the binding subsequently recenters. The maximum point $(\Theta_3)_{max}$ at which the relative motion ceases is determined by the area under the Θ_3^1 to Θ_3^3. The primary function of the long stroke in the binding design is to increase the minimum impulse required to release the binding without

---

[2] The impulse is defined to be the area under the applied external twisting moment (or force) versus times curve:

$$\int_0^T f(t)dt = \text{Impulse}$$

where T is the duration of the impact. The impulse is a measure of the severity of the external impact because it determines the sudden velocity given the ski following the impact.

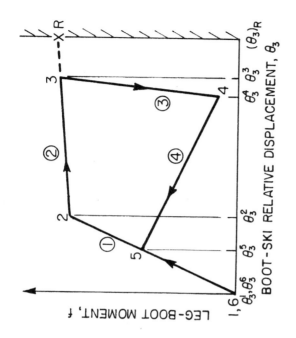

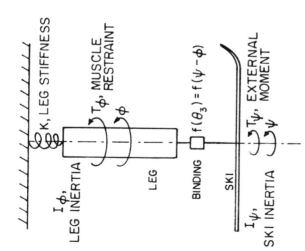

Figure 4. Conceptual model of the ski-binding-leg system and a piecewise-linear approximation to the twisting moment f-binding rotation Θ_3 relationship. The release displacement is $(\Theta_3)_R$.

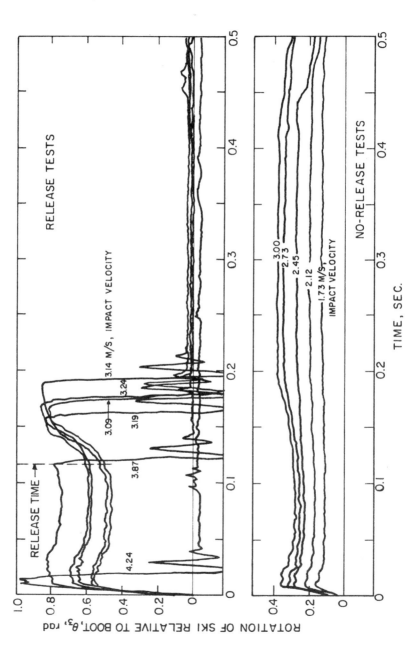

Figure 5. Measurement of the ski rotation relative to the boot. The initial impact velocity of the ski is indicated for each curve.

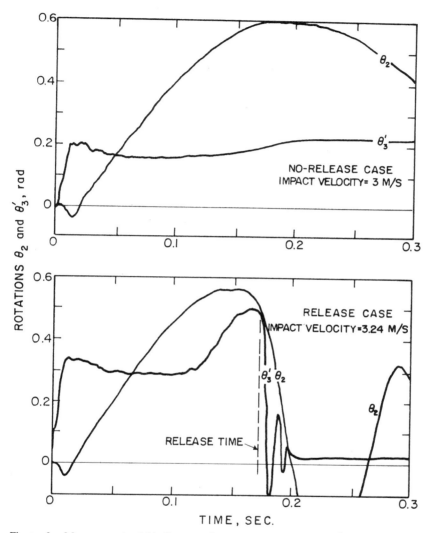

Figure 6. Measurement of binding rotation relative to the ski Θ_3', and the model boot-foot rotation Θ_2 relative to the leg. $\Theta_3 \cong 1.68\,\Theta_3'$.

increasing the static adjustment f_{max}. Increasing the setting f_{max} is an unsatisfactory alternative means of increasing the area under Θ_3^1 to Θ_3^3. The return path, Θ_3^3 to Θ_3^6, determines the rate of recentering, the binding oscillation upon recentering, and the hysteretic energy dissipated in the binding. The loop area inside Θ_3^1-Θ_3^3-Θ_3^5 is a measure of hysteretic energy lost or converted into heat. A small loop dissipates less energy, recenters quickly and is, in general, desirable. If the loop area is zero, then the binding would return the ski to center at $\Theta_3{}^6$ at the same rate at which it left center after the initial impact, and the ski would oscillate endlessly on the boot. This idealized, limiting condition will never be important in practice.

The discussion has utilized the quasistatic f-Θ_3 tests in Figures 1 and 3 to draw conclusions about the expected dynamic behavior. While this is acceptable in a descriptive context, it cannot lead to precise results in general. Most bindings exhibit an f-Θ_3 characteristic in a dynamic test that differs from the static measure. The difference is caused in part by the release path of the boot. In the static test, the boot is twisted out of the binding through a series of equilibrium positions that minimize f for each Θ_3. The boot and ski naturally adjust their orientation for each Θ_3 to hold the equilibrium with the least moment f. In the impulse test, the ski displaces on the boot through other non-equilibrium positions depending upon how the ski is impacted. The f-Θ_3 characteristic is very sensitive to the path or orientation of the boot relative to the ski; a different path leads to a different f-Θ_3 relationship.

The second point of difference is the absence of velocity dependence for f in the static test. Systems with large energy dissipation, such as ski bindings, show significant dependence of f upon loading rate. The only possibility to reduce the stroke of the binding is to design proper loading rate sensitivity into the binding. The f-Θ_3 curve must shift up as the loading rate increases. New designs with this feature will undoubtedly appear. As an example, an electronic binding designed at the University of California measures the torsion f and then electronically calculates the release decision. The circuit properties provide dissipation and allow distinguishing the slow from the fast loading rates.

Friction

Friction is the force that resists the relative motion of surfaces in contact. In the ski binding, friction occurring between the boot and the binding, the boot and the ski, and within the binding itself resists the motion of the boot in the binding. The integrated or summed frictional effect is illustrated in the hysteresis loop in Figure 3. The major problem with friction in the ski binding is that the release function becomes sensitive to interface pressures that are variable and difficult to control.

On the other hand, friction resists the motion and is a major source of mechanical work in the relative boot-ski motion. This work is important to prevent premature release as discussed. If the binding is designed to reduce friction through Teflon pads, etc., then the binding setting will necessarily be increased to compensate for the eliminated friction work.

The friction problem is a double-edged sword. Elimination of friction removes the variability of adjustment with interface pressure and contact surface conditions, but it worsens the binding dynamic quality through reduction of the work done along the release path Θ_3^1 to Θ_3^3. The design solution to the problem is removal of the uncontrollable friction and inclusion of controlled rate-sensitive work in the binding itself to compensate for the reduced friction work. This technique is not used in bindings the authors have seen, but future generations of designs are likely to have this feature.

Dynamic-Impulse Tests

The first dynamic tests for toe and heel release reported in the literature held the boot rigid and applied a known short duration impact to the test ski (Davidson and Mote, 1971). This test is quite good for standardization where specific and repeatable tests are an important element of the procedure; no better test has come to the authors' attention. However, the rigid boot cannot be a representative model of the leg response to impulse loading that is needed for research tests on design function.

A laboratory model illustrated in Figure 2 has been developed with rotation at the 'hip' Θ_1, at the 'ankle' Θ_2, and of the full size ski relative to the boot, Θ_3. The leg mass M_1 is that of the 50th percentile man (Sher and Kane, 1969). The boot-foot segment M_2 rotates through Θ_2 about the longitudinal axis of M_1. The full-size ski is attached to the boot and rotates through Θ_3 according to the test binding pivot. The toe binding is adjusted statically and then the skis are impact tested by applying a known lateral impact and recording the angles Θ_1, Θ_2, and Θ_3 as the leg-boot-binding system responds.

Typical data histories are illustrated in Figures 5 and 6 where the velocity of impact of the 28.1 kg pendulum is indicated. In Figure 5, the upper curves show binding release cases and the lower curves, at smaller impact velocities, are no-release tests. There are a number of significant and surprising conclusions from the data. First, there is no oscillation of the boot in the binding under any circumstances of release and no-release. The oscillations in Figures 5 and 6 occur after the ski has separated from the boot. The second point is that there are two characteristic intervals of binding release. The primary release occurs during, or just following, contact of the impact pendulum with the test ski at approximately 10–15 msec after impact. The initial velocity imparted to the ski by impact releases the ski from the boot before the leg and ankle can respond; see Figure 6. The secondary release occurs approximately 125–200 msec after impact and is caused by stiffening of the 'ankle' spring. The leg is resisting the motion of the ski. Primary release is independent of any biological properties; secondary release is a function of ankle and leg stiffness. In both cases the release is too fast for significant reflex action but shows initial ankle and leg stiffness to be significant. The third point is that the recentering times for the no-release cases are relatively long, greater than 500 msec, and the time increases as the setting is reduced. Rapid recentering, a desired characteristic in a binding, was never observed. The ski remains displaced and nearly stationary relative to the boot for long periods. The fourth point is that the magnitude of the relative rotation of ski to boot at release in these tests is approximately $\Theta_3 = 0.8$ rad, while this release rotation in the static test is only $\Theta_3 = 0.44$ rad. The boot rotates past the static release rotation without release occurring! The apparent paradox was resolved with 1500 frame/sec, 16 mm moving pictures that confirmed that the ski is actually pushed back onto the boot following impact. The lateral motion of the boot in the binding heel unit and the design of the heel unit caused this result. These data illustrate the potential error in predicting dynamic binding behavior from static tests. The release path, or motion of the boot in the binding during release, is critical to the performance of the binding. In multirelease mode bindings, the number of release paths is very large and the problem should be more acute. It is unlikely that static tests can duplicate the information given by dynamic release tests.

The maximum boot-foot rotation in these tests occurred between 100 msec and 200 msec, as illustrated in Figure 6. The initial motion of the boot toe is *into* the impact, as seen in the figure, because of the stiff binding contact with the heel of the boot. The magnitude of the boot-foot rotation in the model depends upon the pendulum impact velocity or the initial impulse.

The maximum rotation of the boot-foot increases steadily with impact velocity until binding release occurs. In fact, the critical impact separating release and no-release gives the maximum boot-leg-rotation. It is reasonable to consider this the most severe loading condition for the leg. For higher impact velocities the maximum Θ_2 rotation *decreases* with increasing impact velocity because the impulse to the boot-leg system decreases with decreasing release time. As an alternative view, the separation of the ski from the boot takes energy out of the leg-foot system in the form of kinetic energy of the departing ski. This result is expected theoretically (Mote and Hull, 1976b) and was observed experimentally (Yam and Mote, 1976).

ANALYTICAL RESULTS

The concern in this section is with analysis of the binding release function. The release function problems fall into two categories: no-release or too-late release, and premature, inadvertent, or too-early release. No-release is clearly a release function failure that can lead to injury. Premature release is also a release function failure that can lead to injury. Experience and research by Davidson and Mote (1971) and Ellis and Mote (1972) indicate that a no-release failure often occurs under conditions of quasistatic loading, while premature release is commonly associated with impact loading of the ski. Satisfying the release function requirement for both static and dynamic loading demands that the binding differentiate between slow and fast loading rates in the same way the leg differentiates between slow and fast loading.

The twisting moment-rotation properties of the binding, f versus Θ_3 under dynamic loading, determine the performance of the binding. It is of interest to discuss the desired f (Θ_3) shape for the binding release and retention requirements. An idealized analytical model has been constructed for the ski-binding-leg system and the model has been used to study binding design as a function of f (Θ_3). The remainder of this section will discuss some results of this analysis, which appears in more detail in Mote and Hull (1976b).

Model

The ski-binding-leg was modeled as a two-stiffness, two-inertia system, as shown in Figure 4. The two inertias I_Ψ and I_ϕ represent the ski and the entire leg, respectively, while f (Θ_3) and K are the binding and leg stiffness, respectively. The rotation of the leg inertia is described by the angle ϕ, the rotation of the ski is given by Ψ, and the binding displacement is $\Psi - \phi$. The moment-rotation curve in Figure 1 has been modeled as piecewise linear f (Θ_3) to simplify calculations. It is assumed in the analysis that f (Θ_3) does not vary with the loading rate. The assumption does not undermine the central observations to be presented.

The f (Θ_3) model is divided into the four segments shown in Figure 4. Segments 1 and 2 define the loading path or the separation of boot and ski, while segments 3 and 4 define the return path. Discussions of the loading path from points $\Theta_3{}^1$ to $\Theta_3{}^3$ and the return path are naturally separated by different design requirements.

Loading Path

The static release requirement depends upon the maximum static moment at release and is not dependent on the loading path. The leg model rotation is directly related to the maximum f (Θ_3), f_{max}, which corresponds to a leg rotation of less than critical value, ϕ_{crit}. The tibial fracture strength in torsion can be used as a measurement of f_{max}. From the standpoint of skiing control, the skier desires the connection between the boot and the ski to be as rigid as possible; this dictates a steep slope in region 1 with the value f (Θ_3) nearly equal to f_{max}. For dynamic loading, the critical leg displacement ϕ_{crit} following impulsive loading of the ski must be bounded through timely release of the binding mechanism. The conservation of momentum principle applied to binding release under dynamic loading has been discussed in Mote and Hull (1976b). This method of analysis is correct for small muscle restraint $T_\phi \cong 0$ and for a ski that comes to rest at $\Theta_3{}^3$ before the leg rotates significantly. This is supported in the data in Figure 5 and 6. Under these assumptions the f (Θ_3) curve does not effect the maximum model leg rotation. The binding design problem then becomes one of preventing release for impulse levels less than the design impulse that produces ϕ_{crit}. This is the function of the long stroke. In the skiing process, data are available which support the condition that $T_\phi \cong 0$. Asang, Grimm, Krexa and Wittmann (1973) recorded electromyograms of typically active muscle groups (adductors, quadriceps, femoris, triceps surae, and tibialis anterior) with surface electrodes. Grimm and Krexa (1972) note that electromyogram signals indicated little muscle activity during falls in their work. If muscle activity is significant (momentum is not conserved), then the impulse to cause the critical leg displacement ϕ_{crit} will be related to the binding design f (Θ_3), the leg stiffness, and muscle restraint. Selecting the design impulse will probably necessitate a compromise between skier safety and skiing utility.

Return Path

In discussing the desired return path, there is a conflict between a fast return rate and oscillation between the ski and boot. Oscillation has not been recognized as a practical problem because of inherent boot-binding damping. A high recentering rate is thought to be critical.

The ratio of the return time duration to the loading time duration was computed by solution of the model equations. The parameters varied in the binding model f (Θ_3) were the slope of the segment 4 and the value f $(\Theta_3{}^4)$.

The return time is shortest when the return path is identical to the loading path. This is an ideal case where the energy stored in the binding displacement $(\Theta_3)_{max}$ is completely recovered and the binding oscillates indefinitely. Inherent system dissipation does not permit this case to be realized and, in fact, oscillation was never realized in actual tests. The return rates for paths with identical energy dissipation are not equal. For a fixed energy dissipation, return time is a minimum when f $(\Theta_3{}^4)$ equals f $(\Theta_3{}^3)$.

Optimal f (Θ_3)

The optimal loading path for the piecewise linear f(Θ_3) model has nearly infinite stiffness in segment 1, which extends from $f = 0$ to $f = f_{max}$ and zero slope $df/d\Theta_3 = 0$ in region 2. Skiing control is maximized by the rigid boot-ski attachment. The design maximizes the impulse to release in this model. The optimal return path equates $f(\Theta_3^4)$ and $f(\Theta_3^3)$ so that return path time is minimum for a given energy dissipation. The specification of $(\Theta_3)_R$ determines the impulse to release. The optimal impulse is as yet unknown.

FIELD RESEARCH

Any laboratory or analytical investigation must ultimately model the actual skier and loading of the skiing process. The actual loads transmitted to the leg during skiing are at the heart of the injury problem.

The Measurement Problem

An important consideration in the force measurement problem is which forces must be measured. A distinction is made between boot-binding interactions and the forces between the leg and ski. This distinction is especially important for heel-toe type bindings because boot-binding interactions are not necessarily transmitted to the leg. They do however, effect the binding's mechanical function (Outwater and Ettlinger, 1969; and Bahniuk, 1972). The classic example of this is boot compression between the heel and toe binding units when the boot is jammed forward by the clamping action of the heel mechanism. Figure 7 shows the 12 independent loads, six at the toe and six at the heel, that are necessary to define completely boot-binding interactions and loading on the leg.

An instrumentation system was designed and used during the Springs of 1975 and 1976 to study the excitation of skiing. Force measuring devices called dynamometers were mounted inside the ski under the toe and heel areas of the boot. Figure 8 shows that this mounting method maintained a representative boot-ski profile. Dynamometer signals were radio transmitted in digital form to a stationary receiving station located about 2 km from the test site on the mountain. There the data were recorded on magnetic tape and subsequently analyzed by digital computer.

The field tests collected cruising data in three basic maneuvers: snowplow, stem christiana, and parallel christiana. Tests were skied through a five-turn slalom course and in a variety of snow conditions that ranged from freshly packed powder to hard, icy crust. Some rather spectacular falls in which the binding mechanism released were recorded. Parallel runs were skied aggressively and the instrumentation system did not interfere with the skier.

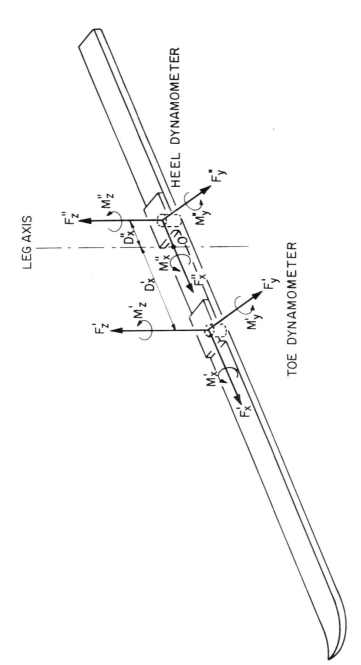

Figure 7. Complete boot-binding interaction forces and moments in the heel-toe type binding system. All twelve loading components were measured simultaneously.

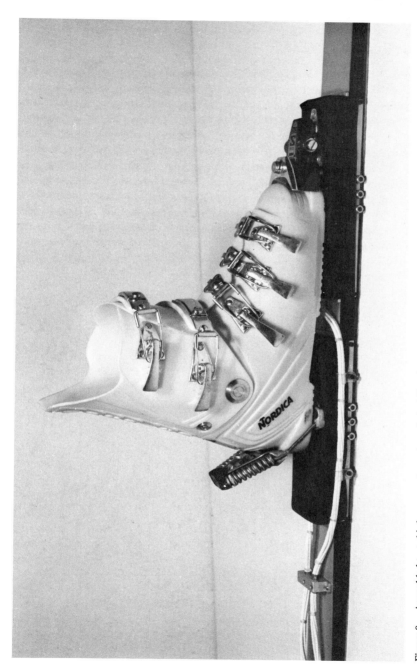

Figure 8.   Assembled test ski-dynamometer system. Imbedding dynamometers within the test ski gave a nearly normal boot-ski profile.

TEST RESULTS

Boot Compression

Figure 9 shows the longitudinal excitation (along the ski long axis) at the toe (F_x') and heel (F_x'') dynamometers[3]. The heel loading is nearly identical to that at the toe except that it is opposite in sign; the excitation depicted here is nearly pure boot compression and was observed in all tests regardless of speed, maneuver, or snow condition. Two separate compression sources have been identified in previous research. Outwater and Ettlinger (1969) discovered that spring compression in the heel binding mechanism as the skier leaned forward leads to increased release levels in static twisting test. Figure 9 shows that the boot compression does not oscillate about a zero mean value; the heel mechanism used here presses the boot forward when clamped. Boot compression due to ski flexure, first discussed by Svoboda, produced the principal compression observed in these data. The loading is increased during turns 1, 3, and 5

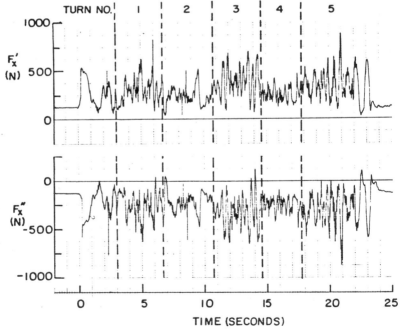

Figure 9. Boot compression during a five turn, stem christiana slalom run at speed ~25 km/hr. The test ski was weighted or driven hard in turns 1, 3, and 5.

---

[3] The prime/double prime notation refers to loads at the toe and heel dynamometers respectively.

because in these turns the instrumented ski was the weighted or outside ski in the turn. The average compression levels in the weighted turns would increase the quasistatic release moment for lateral release at the toe by 20–30% for the binding system tested. Data are not yet available from falls that actually call upon twisting moment release (lateral at the toe). Nonetheless, high twisting moment and boot compression have been measured in skiing, and the combination is expected to appear in forward twisting falls. The release function is impaired if lateral release at the toe is affected by boot compression; the ideal binding would eliminate this coupling.

Heel Release

A number of fast, aggressive parallel runs were skied in wet, heavy snow conditions that made execution difficult. During these tests, two unstaged falls resulting from inadvertent release of the heel binding mechanism were recorded. Both releases occurred during the weight transition at turn initiation, as Figure 10 depicts. In a right turn (turn 3), the instrumented ski heel binding released inadvertently; in a left turn (turn 4 of the following run), the heel of the uninstrumented mate released inadvertently and the instrumented ski heel was forceably released. Note that in the latter case the forced release occurred 1.8 sec after the inadvertent release because the skier was able to maintain his balance on one ski before falling. The accidents were quite spectacular and nearly identical in type, with the skier falling face forward at approximately 40 km/hr. The inadvertent and forced release loads are compared in Figure 10, which shows the vertical loads at both the toe and heel for each fall. The inadvertent and forced release levels compare identically at 750 N, which was the laboratory quasistatic adjustment. The inadvertent release was not a malfunction of the binding mechanism; that is, the binding performed as it was set to perform. Inadvertent release occurred because the muscle-induced loads required for difficult maneuver execution exceeded the loading for execution in smoother skiing situations.

The forward bending loading M_y on the leg during these falls indicates the severity of the accident. Figure 11 shows the maximum forward bending load is 350 N-m for both releases. The static tibial strength in forward bending for a 30-year-old man, predicted from the data of Asang (1972), Asang and Wittmann (1973), and Wittmann (1973), is also shown in the figure. The 350 N-m forward bending load at release exceeds the predicted fracture strength. The loading was measured at the boot sole and not the tibia, and muscle effects are, of course, not part of the tibial data. The bending moment approached the predicted fracture strength, though the binding released at the 'safe' laboratory quasistatic setting. While it is impossible to assess the injury proximity

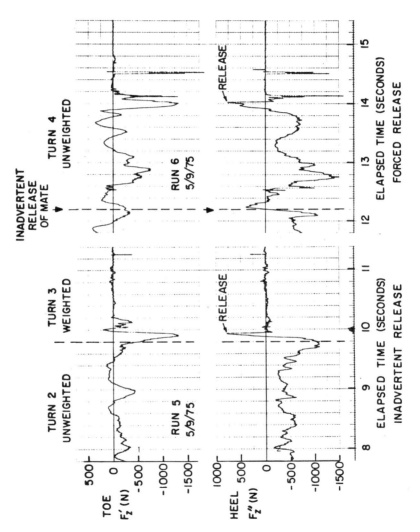

Figure 10.   Comparison of vertical dynamometer forces for the inadvertent and forced releases of the heel binding mechanism during skiing.

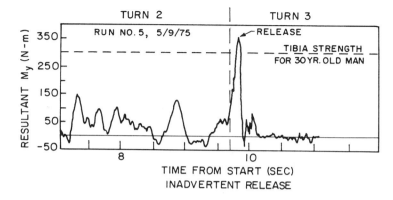

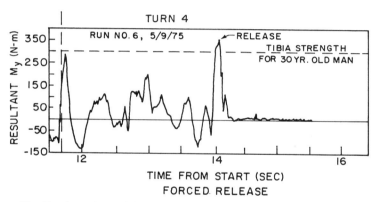

Figure 11.   Resultant forward bending moment M_y at the boot during the inadvertent and forced binding releases in Figure 10.

during these falls, the skier did not register pain and was not injured. The loading is higher than that recorded in previous research because the loading condition was critical and because the loading was completely and accurately measured. The loading duration of these significant loads is not particularly short.

High Amplitude Cruising Loads

High amplitude forces that were comparable to the tibial fracture predictions were measured frequently in cruising skiing maneuvers. These loads occurred for both the twisting moment M_z and forward bending moment M_y, often simultaneously as shown in Figure 12. The skier was not injured in any of these situations, and the bindings did not release. Release did not occur under the 415 N-m forward bending load in

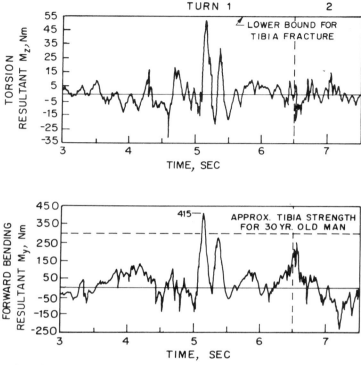

Figure 12. High amplitude cruising loads during skiing exceeded the predicted tibia fracture strengths in both torsion M_z and flexure M_y.

Figure 12 though this level exceeded the 350 N-m forward bending loads at release (Figure 11). This is possible in classical heel-toe type bindings because heel release is activated by the vertical heel load F_z'', which is not required to be large for large forward moment M_y. The conclusion is that a range of bending moments M_y and M_z are possible which exceed the tibia fracture strength without binding release occurring.

Additional Results

The data are related to maneuver type. The quasistatic lateral loading (i.e., F_y and M_x) is significantly different when snowplow is compared to unweighting type maneuvers. The snowplow technique produces a quasistatic twisting moment that acts on the leg of the unweighted ski and is approximately 20 N-m. Because the loading is quasistatic, the entire boot-leg system experiences this load. The tibial fracture strength in torsion is in the range 40–80 N-m so that this loading is significant.

Unweighting (christiana) type maneuvers did not exhibit this high static torsion load.

High amplitude (7–9 N-m), short duration (0.200 msec) pulses were observed in the twisting moment M_z' at the toe binding. High torsion on the leg M_z did not accompany the toe torsion pulses. The toe torsion pulses usually appeared at the initiation of turns in which the instrumented ski was being driven (i.e., the outside ski for turns 1, 3, and 5). These pulses emanated from the forces applied by the leg to the ski in initiating the turn. This toe binding pulse is an example of muscle-induced excitation. High amplitude binding pulses occurred most often in test runs where execution was difficult; their occurrence was not related to speed, snow condition, or equipment except as they related to maneuver difficulty. The muscle-induced loading is related to the inadvertent release of toe bindings that, as experience indicates, often accompanies difficult maneuvers.

The snow conditions during testing ranged from icy crust with fierce chattering of the ski to freshly packed powder with smooth low frequency loading. The loading rate determination is important to define the environment in which bindings operate. Data from the various snow conditions were subjected to a type of analysis—spectral analysis—that evaluated the distribution of excitation frequencies in each component, e.g., the leg twisting moment. As expected, the icy conditions resulted in much higher frequency excitation with significant energy as high as 100 Hz being measured. In the course of a normal skiing season, bindings must function over a broad range of loading rates. The ability of bindings to act as shock absorbers is especially important for high loading rate conditions that occur on ice or hard crust.

SUMMARY OF CONCLUSIONS

The Laboratory

The laboratory tests on a ski-binding-leg model utilizing a real ski and binding have identified two types of release under impact loading of the ski. Primary release occurs in 10–15 msec and is independent of the biological system. Secondary release occurs in 150–200 msec as the stiffening 'ankle' element resists the ski rotation. In both cases the time is too short for significant reflex action to effect the result. The times required for the boot to recenter in the binding in the no-release cases were greater than 0.5 sec in the designs tested; rapid recentering of the binding and oscillation between boot and ski were never observed. The relative displacement of the boot and ski for dynamic release under impact loading was almost twice that for static release. The difference occurred because the path or motion of the boot in the binding under impact loading of the ski is not the same as in the static test. The twisting moment versus rotation of the binding is sensitive to this path. Accordingly, the static test cannot be used to predict quantitative dynamic properties of bindings unless the static and impact loading release paths are identical and $f(\Theta_3)$ does not vary with loading rate.

Analysis

The quasistatic load-displacement relationship is approximately piecewise linear in most bindings with significant (hysteretic) energy converted to heat by friction. The dynamic analysis discussed here neglects muscle loading; this is justified by the binding response rate observed in the laboratory impact tests. The optimal bending moment versus rotation path, where one attempts to maximize protection against inadvertent release for a fixed static setting, leads to a rigid plastic design.

This assumes that design is independent of loading rate, a major assumption. Rate-dependent load-displacement paths are sensible designs and common in other technologies. More detailed attention to dynamic design of bindings can be expected in the near future. The return path from maximum binding displacement determines the return rate and the energy dissipated in the binding. Bindings examined return too slowly and dissipate too much energy. The probable design trends will tend to reduce the hysteresis loop size to increase the recentering rate.

Field Tests

Measurement of the complete forces on the boot during skiing identified boot compression, a boot-binding interaction that is known to effect the binding release in the particular binding system examined. Compression is significant regardless of speed, snow condition, maneuver, etc.

The recorded inadvertent release of the heel mechanism was caused by muscle loading when driving the ski into a difficult turn. The binding released at its adjustment. High turn initiation loading was measured at the toe unit as well as the heel unit. A potential inadvertent release problem, lateral at the toe, was also identified. The recorded forward bending at the boot sole during these falls was approximately equal to the static bending strength of the tibia in the absence of muscle loading. No injury occurred.

Forces measured at the boot sole often exceeded the reported static twisting and bending tibial fracture strength during normal cruising skiing maneuvers without injury to the test skier. This emphasizes two points, one old and one new. The old point is that muscle contributions to leg stiffness and leg loading capacity are significant. The new point is that the actual loading of skiing is considerably higher than previously measured.

ACKNOWLEDGMENTS

The authors are very grateful to Mr. Gilbert Delouche of Salomon and Mr. P. Blime of the LOOK companies for their contributions to this research. The authors are also pleased to acknowledge Mr. Peter Juen of Beconta, Inc., for his long and continuing interest. And, finally, they thank Ms. K. A. Sereda for her assistance with the preparation of the manuscript.

REFERENCES

Asang, E. 1972. 20 Jahre skitraumatologie. (Twenty years of ski injuries.) Med. and Sport 12:23–26.

Asang, E., Grimm, C., Krexa, H., and Wittmann, G. 1973. Grundlagen der ski-telemetrie: Mechanogramm and elektromyogram. (Foundations of ski telemetry: mechanograms and electromyogram.) Publication unknown.

Asang, E., and Wittmann, G. 1973. Experimentelle und praktische biomechanik des menschlichen beins. (Experimental and practical biomechanics of human bones.) Med. and Sport 13:245–255.

Bahniuk, E., 1972. The biomechanics of contemporary ski bindings. J. Safety Res. 4:160-171.

Davidson, R. W., and Mote, C. D., Jr. 1971. Impact testing of snow ski bindings. Department of Mechanical Engineering Report, University of California, Berkeley.

Ellis, R. W., and Mote, C. D., Jr. 1972. Short duration response of ski bindings: Toe and heel units. Department of Mechanical Engineering Report, University of California, Berkeley.

Grimm, C., and Krexa, H. 1972. Personal communication.

Hight, T. K., Piziali, R. L., and Nagel, D. A. 1975. An extended structural analysis of the human tibia. ASME Symposium on Biomechanics, Summer Applied Mechanics Conference, Troy, New York.

Hull, M. L., and Mote, C. D., Jr. 1975. Skiing injuries: Field loading and analysis. Department of Mechanical Engineering Report, University of California, Berkeley.

Hull, M. L., and Mote, C. D., Jr. 1976. Pulse code modulation telemetry in ski injury research. II. Preliminary Results. Int. J. Biotelemetry 2:276-296.

Mote, C. D., Jr., and Hull, M. L. 1976a. Fundamental considerations in ski binding analysis. Orthopedic Clinics of North Amer. 7:75-94.

Mote, C. D., Jr., and Hull, M. L. 1976b. A preliminary analysis of ski release binding dynamic properties. J. Dynamic Systems, Measurement and Control. Trans. ASME 98 (G):301-306.

Outwater, J. O., and Woodward, M. S. 1966. Ski safety and tibial forces. ASME Paper No. 66 WA/BHF 14.

Outwater, J. O., and Ettlinger, C. F. 1969. The engineering problem of ski bindings. Med. Sci. Sports 1:200-206.

Piziali, R. L. 1973. The dynamical torsional response of the human leg relative to skiing injuries. Applied Mechanics Division Symposium Volume. Mechanics and Sport AMD 4:305-315.

Piziali, R. L., and Nagel, D. A. 1976. Modeling of the human leg in ski injuries. Orthopedic Clinics of North Amer. 7:127-139.

Sher, M. P., and Kane, R. R. 1969. Alteration of the state of motion of a human being in free fall. Department of Applied Mechanics, Technical Report 198, Stanford University.

Svoboda (AMF-Tyrolia). Research in skiing by means of radio telemetry. Unpublished report.

Wittmann, G. 1973. Biomechanische untersuchungen zum verletzungschutz im alpinen skisport. (Biomechanical investigations of injury prevention in Alpine skiing.) Doctoral Dissertation, Technical University of Munich.

Yam, Lap Man and Mote, C. D., Jr. 1976. Analysis of a leg-ski-binding model under impact loading of the ski. Department of Mechanical Engineering Report, University of California, Berkeley.

Physiological
Factors

Glycogen Depletion Pattern in Leg Muscle During Recreational Downhill Skiing

E. Nygaard, E. Eriksson, and P. Nilsson

A person who has been injured during downhill skiing often refers to a feeling of extreme fatigue just before the fall, when asked for a possible explanation for the accident (Eriksson, 1976).

The aim of this study has been to search for objective signs for the perception of muscular fatigue experienced in connection with downhill skiing. Possible explanations might be lack of muscle carbohydrate and/or accumulation of lactate. One approach to the investigation of these possibilities has been to focus upon glycogen depletion in the form of total glycogen utilized by the working muscles as well as selective glycogen depletion of slow and fast twitch fibers, and to relate the findings to the skill and experience in downhill skiing of the subjects examined.

SUBJECTS

Twenty-eight healthy subjects participated in the study. Mean age was 32 years. Physical fitness in terms of maximal oxygen uptake ranged from below average to well-trained (32–62 ml O_2 per kg per min). Technical skill and experience in downhill skiing varied from the level of beginners through moderate skiers with some years of experience, to the level of competitors on a national scale.

This study was supported by grants from the Research Councils of the Danish and the Swedish Sports Federations.

METHODS

Muscle biopsies were taken with a needle technique (Bergström, 1962), with the muscle at rest in the morning and immediately after cessation of skiing in the afternoon, from the middle portion of the vastus lateralis of the thigh muscle.

Total glycogen determinations were made on muscle pieces according to the Lowry method as described by Karlsson (1971).

Muscle fibers were identified as slow twitch fibers (ST), and fast twitch a (FTa) and b (FTb) fibers by the use of histochemical stains for myofibrillar ATPase at various pH values, as described by Brooke and Kaiser (1970). The slow twitch fibers are mainly responsible for the oxygen-demanding work in activities like long distance running or cross-country skiing. The fast twitch fibers, on the other hand, are more responsible for the fast, explosive, anaerobic work as in sprinting or isometric contractions with heavy loads. Of the subgroups of fast twitch fibers, in untrained human muscle, the FTa fiber has the higher oxidative capacity.

Glycogen content of single fibers was evaluated histochemically on the basis of the periodic acid Schiff (PAS) reaction (Pearse, 1968). Staining intensity was divided into three categories: no staining, moderate staining, and dark staining.

RESULTS

Total Glycogen Break-down (Figure 1)

During a Week: When not told to take specific care of the daily carbohydrate intake, morning (pre-ski) levels of glycogen were found to decrease by 30 mM glucose units/kg wet weight over five days. A group of subjects that on day four was asked to have an extra-high carbohydrate intake showed a complete replenishment of glycogen stores on day five.

During a Day: After a day of free skiing, the glycogen content of the thigh muscle in excellent skiers showed a decline of around 40 mM/kg, while less experienced skiers showed a reduction of around 30 mM/kg. Similar results were obtained in the two groups on the first and the fifth day of a ski vacation, respectively.

Selective Glycogen Depletion (Table 1)

All three groups showed depletion of the ST fibers. This was most pronounced in moderate-good and excellent skiers, with 15–20% depleted and 80–85% partially depleted after a day of skiing, while, in

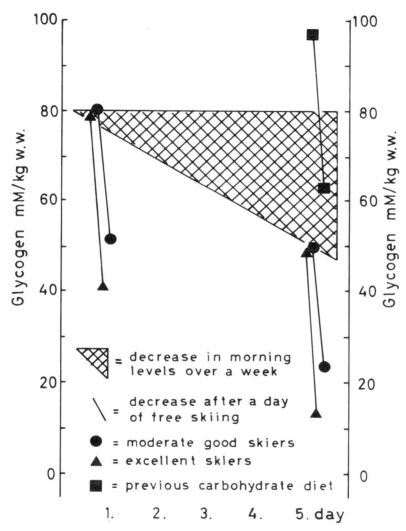

Figure 1.   Total glycogen breakdown. Shaded area shows that during a week of downhill skiing, morning (pre-ski) muscle glycogen levels decrease from 80 mM glucose units/kg wet weight muscle on the first day to 50 mM/kg on the fifth day. Symbols (circles, triangles, and squares) give the daily muscle glycogen decrease in groups of moderate to good skiers, of excellent skiers, and of skiers who on the previous day had an extra high carbohydrate intake. Note the high pre-ski muscle glycogen in the last group.

Table 1. Evaluation of glycogen content in muscle fibers of downhill skiers with various levels of technical skill, expressed as the percentage of total number of fibers counted

Technical level	Fiber type	No staining	Moderate staining	Dark staining
Beginner	ST	6	72	22
	FTa		10	90
	FTb	19	59	22
Moderate-good	ST	15	85	
	FTa		6	94
	FTb			100
Excellent	ST	18	82	
	FTa		80	20
	FTb		10	90

the group of beginners, some 20% of the ST fibers retained the glycogen, and only 6% were depleted.

The most remarkable finding was that among the group of beginners the FTb fibers showed a higher degree of depletion (19% depleted, and 59% partially depleted) than did the ST fibers. The FTb fibers did not show any noticeable depletion in the experienced skiers. In addition to the ST fibers, however, the group of excellent skiers had some 80% of the FTa fibers partially depleted after skiing.

DISCUSSION

Measurements of heart rate and total oxygen consumption during downhill skiing, together with determinations of lactate concentration and electromyography (EMG) recordings of working muscle suggest that downhill skiing is predominantly a dynamic type of exercise (Agnevik and Saltin, 1966; Ericksson et al., 1977; Nygaard et al., 1978). This description fits well with the results of this study on selective glycogen depletion, pointing to a predominant depletion of ST fibers and indicating a high degree of involvement of this muscle fiber in the skiing activity.

It has been shown that in dynamic work the total energy requirements have to be near or above maximal aerobic capacity before the fast twitch fibers are continuously involved (Gollnick, Piehl, and Saltin, 1974). The situation of excellent skiers with a partial depletion of FTa fibers indicates that they have a higher ability to ski at maximal aerobic capacity than do moderate-good skiers, who did not show any noticeable depletion of FT fibers.

From the results on total glycogen utilization during a day, it cannot be stated whether or not the group of excellent skiers economize on their glycogen utilization to a greater extent than the group of moderate-good skiers does, because measurements have not been made on the actual work performed or on total energy production. It should be mentioned, however, that both total distance covered and the speed of skiing varied significantly between the groups.

In laboratory experiments, a selective depletion of FTb fibers has been observed only in a type of voluntary work that involves maximal static contractions (Secher and Nygaard, 1976). Thus, the finding of a predominant depletion of FTb fibers in beginners confirms the common characterization of the beginner's skiing performance as involving more static contractions: the beginner tries to move the skis voluntarily by developing maximal static force in the leg muscles before the technique is properly learned.

CONCLUSIONS

No definite answers can be given to the question about the constituents of fatigue, but the results of this study indicate that glycogen as a substrate for muscular work during downhill skiing is of major importance. Because after a day of skiing recreational downhill skiers do not refill their leg muscle with glycogen overnight, it is strongly recommended that ski tourists pay more attention to the daily carbohydrate content of their diet during ski vacations.

Additionally, the fact that experienced skiers show oxidative fibers that are predominantly depleted of their glycogen suggests that recreational downhill skiing puts a high demand on the aerobic capacity of the skier. Thus it is recommended that skiers prepare well in advance for a downhill ski vacation by jogging, cross-country skiing, or engaging in other dynamic endurance activities that may improve the function of the oxygen transport system.

Of foremost importance, however, is that beginners in downhill skiing participate in ski school instruction to learn correct skiing techniques and to avoid uneconomic use of muscular engery. This would contribute to the prevention of ski injuries, which occur less frequently in skilled skiers than they do in unskilled skiers.

REFERENCES

Agnevik, G., and Saltin, B. 1966. *"Utforsåkning,"* Idrottsfysiologisk Rapport No. 2, Trygg-Hansa, Stockholm.

Bergström, J. 1962. Muscle electrolytes in man. Scand. J. Clin. and Laboratory Investments Suppl. 68.

Brooke, M. H., and Kaiser, K. 1970. Three myosin ATPase systems: The nature of their pH lability and sulphydryl dependence. J. Histochemistry and Cytochemistry 18:670–672.

Ericksson, A., Forsberg, A., Källberg, L., Tesch, P., and Karlsson, J. 1977. Alpint, Idrottsfysiologisk Rapport No. 17, Trygg-Hansa, Stockholm.

Eriksson, E. 1976. Sports injuries of the knee ligament: Their diagnosis, treatment, rehabilitation, and prevention. Med. and Sci. of Sports 8:133–144.

Gollnick, P. D., Piehl, K., and Saltin, B. 1974. Selective glycogen depletion pattern in human skeletal muscle fibres after exercise of varying intensity and at varying pedalling rates. (London) J. Physiol. 241:45–57.

Karlsson, J. 1971. Lactate and phosphagen concentrations in working muscle of man. Acta physiologica Scandinavica Suppl. 358.

Nygaard, E., Andersen, P., Nilsson, P., Eriksson, E., Kjessel, T. and Saltin, B. 1978. Glycogen depletion pattern and lactate accumulation in leg muscles during recreational downhill skiing. Eur. J. Appl. Physiol. 38.

Pearse, A. G. E. 1968. Histochemistry—Theoretical and Applied. 2nd Ed. Churchill, London.

Secher, N. and Nygaard, E. 1976. Glycogen depletion pattern in types I, IIA and IIB muscle fibres during maximal voluntary static and dynamic exercise. Acta physiologica Scandinavica. 96(Suppl. 440):287.

Fatigue During Downhill Skiing

A. Ericksson, P. Tesch, and J. Karlsson

Downhill skiing has been extensively studied as a risk factor in traumas, particularly to the lower limbs. Considerable interest has been devoted to reducing risk factors by designing types of safety bindings that release the skier quickly from the skis after a fall. Little or no interest has been devoted to the factors involved in the genesis of situations capable of causing a fall and subsequent injury. This paper will summarize some of the data on the physiology and biomechanics of downhill skiing. Data were obtained in studies involving both leisure and advanced skiers.

Muscular fatigue is probably caused by a number of factors that originate in events taking place in the muscle during intense muscular exercise. Three mutually similar factors have been shown to be directly or indirectly involved in the perception of muscular fatigue: depleted glycogen stores (Hermanson et al., 1967), pronounced accumulation of lactate in the muscle (Karlsson, 1971), and neuromuscular exhaustion (Stephens and Taylor, 1972). The two former factors result from increased muscle metabolism during muscular contractions; the last is induced by the firing pattern both in the motoneurons and in the muscle itself, according to electromyography (EMG).

A muscle contraction entails a transformation of chemically bound energy into mechanical work. The chemically bound energy for contraction is available in the form of ATP, either stored in the muscle or formed by metabolic processes. Most of the ATP formed originates from combustive processes in the mitochondria of the muscle fibers.

An adequate supply of molecular oxygen from the circulatory and respiratory systems is a prerequisite for this process. Another source for ATP regeneration is in the breakdown of glycogen in the muscle and the subsequent formation of ATP. The complete combustion of glucose is the most efficient form of ATP regeneration (approximately 39 ATP quanta are formed per unit of glucose residue metabolized in the muscle fibers). Only 3 ATP quanta are formed by glycolytic processes. This means that only a portion of the energy is transferred to ATP during glycolysis, in lieu of complete combustion (Figure 1). However, the formation of ATP by anaerobic glycolytic processes and subsequent lactate formation may be of great significance in situations similar to muscle anoxia.

Combustive processes utilize either carbohydrates or fats as fuels. In a subject at rest, the ratio between carbohydrate and fat is approximately unity, which means that approximately the same amounts of fats and carbohydrates are combusted (Saltin and Karlsson, 1971). As exercise intensity increases, however, more carbohydrate is combusted provided that dietary regimen is normal. At maximal or near-maximal

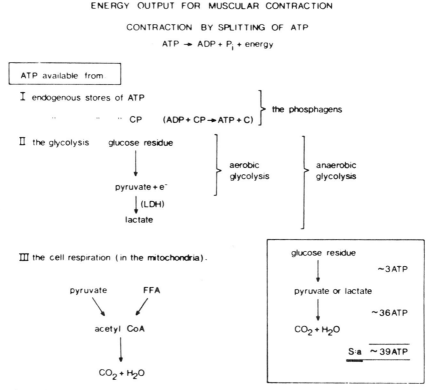

Figure 1.   Metabolic scheme of the ATP resynthetizing process in skeletal muscle.

exercise intensities (i.e., 100% of individual maximal oxygen intake, $\dot{V}_{O_2max}$), combustion is almost completely of carbohydrates. Clearly, the risk of a shortage of molecular oxygen in the contracting muscle is increased at such high exercise intensities. As noted above, this could lead to increased anaerobic glycolysis and concomitant lactate formation in the contracting muscle fibers. Muscle glycogen stores are the main precursor in the two metabolic processes of carbohydrate combustion and lactate formation in the skeletal muscle.

Since downhill skiing by both leisure and advanced skiers may be similar to intense muscular exercise, the inclusion of muscle metabolism in the physiological and biochemical studies of downhill skiing is considered of interest. These data have been presented more extensively in a recent paper by Tesch et al. (1977).

METHODS AND MATERIAL

Seven subjects participated in the study. Three were designated as leisure skiers and four as advanced skiers, either skilled instructors or elite skiers. The leisure skiers were all physical education students, so they were accustomed to physical exercise and fairly well conditioned in terms of muscular strength and endurance capacity. All the subjects were of normal height and weight.

Skeletal muscle metabolism was studied in muscle specimens obtained by means of the needle muscle biopsy technique (Bergström, 1962). The specimens were obtained before and immediately after skiing (within 15 sec after termination of active skiing). The specimens were immediately frozen in liquid nitrogen and stored in dry ice or in a freezer at $-80\,°C$ pending further analysis. The specimens were analyzed for their content of glycogen and lactate according to Karlsson (1971). Portions of the specimens were used for histological analyses such as muscle fiber typing (staining for myofibrillar ATPase-Gollnick et al., 1972) and the relative content of glycogen, according to periodic acid Schiff (PAS) staining in individual fibers (Gollnick et al., 1973).

Downhill skiing was performed either as ski-school practice or as intense skiing in a giant slalom pist or in moguls. This schedule was designed to achieve both "submaximal" and "maximal" skiing.

RESULTS

Submaximal and maximal skiing in both leisure and advanced skiers elevated muscle lactate concentrations above resting values. The highest value for each individual was obtained after maximal skiing. The mean values after maximal skiing amounted to 12.8 (4.1-24.1), compared to

7.9 (4.8-13.7)) mmoles × kg $^{-1}$ wet muscle obtained after submaximal skiing. There were, of course, wide individual variations in the values for lactate accumulation after both submaximal and maximal skiing. When individual data for lactate concentration in the skeletal muscle after maximal skiing were related to the individual muscle fiber composition and expressed as percentage of fast twitch (FT) or type II muscle fibers, it was found that the subjects with a relatively high percentage of FT fibers had the highest muscle lactate values (Figure 2). Similar patterns for muscle lactate concentration have been found after intense bicycle exercise corresponding to 90% of $\dot{V}_{O_2max}$; this could lead to exhaustion of some subjects after approximately 15-20 min, but it could be sustained in some subjects for 20-30 min. Exhaustion was the case for subjects rich in fast twitch (FT, type II) fibers, while the ability to sustain activity was seen in subjects rich in slow twitch (ST, type I) muscle fibers (Karlsson, to be published).

Muscle glycogen content was found to decrease in the course of a day of downhill skiing. This was true for both advanced and leisure skiers. The magnitude of the breakdown of muscle glycogen during a day of skiing was on the order of 20-35 mmoles of glucose units × kg $^{-1}$ wet muscle, in both subject groups. This value is about equivalent to normal overnight glycogen replenishment, providing the dietary regimen is adequate (Piehl, 1974). Therefore, glycogen stores were found to

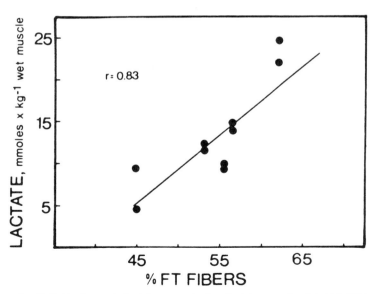

Figure 2.   Individual muscle lactate concentration in leisure and advanced skiers after intense downhill skiing.

decrease gradually during 2–3 days of ski-school or training activities in the subjects with pronounced glycogen depletion during skiing. (Figure 3) This gradual decrease in muscle glycogen content over a period of 4–7 days of downhill skiing has been reported elsewhere (Nygaard-Jensen et al., 1977).

On the basis of PAS staining for identification of the selective glycogen depletion pattern, it was found that predominantly ST fibers were depleted of glycogen in the advanced skiers. This contrasted with the state of the casual skiers in whom predominantly FT fibers were depleted of their glycogen content. As has been suggested earlier (Gollnick et al., 1974), the selective glycogen depletion pattern could be used to interpret the recruitment pattern of different motor units (phasic or tonic motor units). Accordingly, the casual skiers recruited their fast (phasic) motor units, whereas the advanced skiers recruit their slow (tonic) motor units.

DISCUSSION

The major finding in these studies has been the discovery that the pattern of lactate accumulation was governed by the individual muscle fiber composition. Thus, the same downhill skiing activity leads to higher lactate accumulation in individuals rich in FT fibers. Moreover, the advanced skiers apparently recruited mainly tonic motor units, while the leisure skiers mainly recruited phasic fibers. These findings

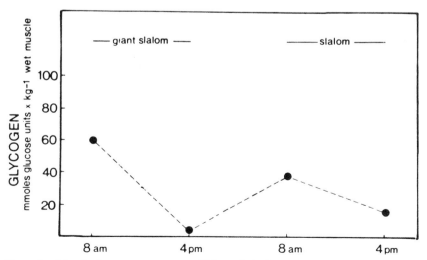

Figure 3. Muscle glycogen stores over a 32-hr period of advanced skiing during a 6-day training course.

must be compared to other findings (Eriksson et al., 1975) in which elite downhill skiers were not found to represent any selective group in terms of muscle fiber composition (mean value 48, range 30-64% ST) as has been found in cross-country skiers or long distance runners (Forsberg et al., 1976).

It might be argued that subjects with the most pronounced accumulation of lactate in their skeletal muscles and the most subsequent anaerobic glycolysis would be representative of the group of subjects with the most pronounced glycogen depletion. But no such pattern was found either in the absolute terms of total glycogen depletion expressed as mmoles of glucose units per kg of muscle, or in the relative terms of the selective glycogen depletion pattern according to PAS staining procedures. There is presently no explanation for this finding.

However, it seems reasonable to suggest that high muscle lactate levels, as were found in subjects rich in FT fibers, would reduce the ability to perform intensive skiing for long periods of time. Conversely, subjects with this ability would then breakdown and combust relatively more glycogen because of the longer duration of muscular activity. The advanced downhill skiers with a relatively high percentage of FT fibers might, by means of physical training, achieve a metabolic potential in their skeletal muscles yielding a relative increase in aerobic power as indicated by Sjödin (1976). They would subsequently enhance their potential for carbohydrate combustion when compared with physically untrained leisure skiers with similar fiber composition.

As was demonstrated by Thorstensson (1976), a high proportion of FT fibers appears to be a prerequisite to the performance of fast contractions with a relatively high tension output and to maximal contraction velocity capacity. Preliminary studies using film or videotape recordings suggest that angular movements in the advanced downhill skier may exceed 1000 degrees per sec in some cases (Ericksson, to be published). It then seems reasonable to suggest that a high percentage of FT fibers might be of value to the downhill skier in situations in which a correction of body position must be performed to avoid a fall. This would apply to both the advanced and the casual skier.

Thorstensson also showed that subjects with a high percentage of FT fibers demonstrated relatively greater fatiguability than subjects rich in ST fibers. In recent studies, this fatiguability pattern has been related to lactate accumulation in FT versus ST muscle fibers (Tesch et al., 1977). This fatiguability was partially counteracted by the circumstance that subjects rich in FT fibers were stronger than the subjects rich in ST fibers; this finding is in agreement with Thorstensson. On the basis of the present and quoted data, it then seems relevant to suggest that the FT fibers have both positive and negative effects on the performance capacity of the individual downhill skier. This circumstance would provide one possible explanation for the fact that downhill skiers, as noted above, do not represent a selected group of subjects in terms of muscle fiber composition, as has been shown for endurance athletes.

It also seems reasonable to suggest that pronounced susceptibility to fatigue might be one of the more significant risk factors incurred in downhill skiing by all types of skiers. Elevated muscle lactate levels have been clearly shown to govern the exercise intensity level selected for voluntary work performed with no perception of muscle fatigue (Karlsson, 1971; Juhlin-Dannfelt, 1976). Whether this also applies to the downhill skier, and especially the leisure skier, has not been determined, but seems likely. Accordingly, subjects rich in ST fibers should be capable of performing more intense downhill skiing at the casual level than skiers with a greater percentage of FT fibers in their skeletal muscles. However, it should be pointed out that the individual level of physical conditioning could modify this pattern and make a skier rich in FT fibers as resistant to fatigue as an individual with a high percentage of ST fibers. In addition to the individual percentage of muscle fibers and the individual level of physical conditioning, it should be noted that proficiency, expressed as neuromotor control, is of great significance to individual capacity.

CONCLUSIONS

To summarize, the metabolic pattern of muscle during downhill skiing displays the same pattern as has been previously described for other types of muscular exercise. Thus, muscle fiber composition, in addition to the level of physical conditioning and neuromotor control capacity, appears to be of great significance. Both high lactate levels and glycogen depletion in either muscle fiber type must be regarded as risk factors during downhill skiing. High muscle lactate concentrations appear to be more closely related to muscle fiber type than to the glycogen depletion pattern; high muscle lactate levels coincide with a high percentage of FT fibers, while the glycogen depletion pattern seems to be more closely related to the individual skier's technique and level of proficiency.

REFERENCES

Bergström, J. 1962. Muscle electrolytes in man. Scand. J. Clin. Lab. Invest. Suppl. 68.
Eriksson, A., J. Ekholm, G. Hulten, E. Karlsson, and J. Karlsson. 1976.

Anatomical, histological, and physiological factors in experienced downhill skiers. Orthop. Clin. North Amer. 7:159–165.

Forsberg, A., P. Tesch, B. Sjödin, A. Thorstensson, and J. Karlsson. 1976. Skeletal muscle fibers and athletic performance. In: P. V. Komi (ed.), Int. Ser. Biomech., Vol. 1A: Biomechanics V-A, pp. 112–117. University Park Press, Baltimore.

Gollnick, P. D., R. B. Armstrong, C. W. Saubert IV, K. Piehl, and B. Saltin. 1972. Enzyme activity and fiber composition in skeletal muscle of untrained and trained men. J. Appl. Physiol. 33:312–319.

Gollnick, P. D., R. B. Armstrong, C. W. Saubert IV, W. L. Sembrowich, R. E. Shepherd, and B. Saltin. 1973. Glycogen depletion patterns in human skeletal muscle fibers during prolonged work. Pfluegers Arch. 344:1–12.

Gollnick, P. D., B. Sjödin, J. Karlsson, E. Jansson, and B. Saltin. 1974. Human soleus muscle: a comparison of fiber composition and enzyme activities with other leg muscles. Pfluegers Arch. 348:247–255.

Hermansen, L., E. Hultman, and B. Saltin. 1967. Muscle glycogen during prolonged severe exercise. Acta Physiol. Scand. 71:129–139.

Juhlin-Dannfelt, A. 1976. Effect of ethanol on substrate turnover in man. (Thesis). Dept. of Clinical Physiology, Karolinska Institute, Huddinge Hospital, Stockholm, Sweden.

Karlsson, J. 1971. Lactate and phosphagen concentrations in working muscle of man. Acta Physiol. Scand. Suppl. 358.

Piehl, K. 1974. Glycogen storage and depletion in human skeletal muscle fibres. Acta Physiol. Scand. Suppl. 402.

Saltin, B., and J. Karlsson. 1971. Muscle ATP, CP, and lactate during exercise after physical conditioning. In: B. Pernow and B. Saltin (eds.), Muscle Metabolism During Exercise, pp. 395–399. Plenum Press, New York.

Sjödin, B. 1976. Lactate dehydrogenase in human skeletal muscle. Acta Physiol. Scand. Suppl. 436.

Stephens, J. A., and A. Taylor. 1972. Fatigue of maintained voluntary muscle contraction in man. J. Physiol. 220:1–18.

Tesch, P. 1977. Muscle fatigue and muscle lactate concentration. In: Jörgensen (ed.), Biomechanics VI. Copenhagen, Denmark (to be published).

Tesch, P., L. Larsson, A. Eriksson, and J. Karlsson. 1977. Muscle glycogen depletion and lactate concentration during downhill skiing. Med. Sci. Sports. In press.

Thorstensson, A. 1976. Muscle strength, fiber types and enzyme activities in man. Acta Physiol. Scand. Suppl. 443.

The Effects of Hypoxia on the Endurance and Coordination of Skiers

J. J. Stanley

It is suspected that hypoxia is a contributing factor in injuries sustained by Australian skiers when skiing overseas at altitudes greater than the 1800 m of the highest peaks in Australia.

EFFECTS OF HYPOXIA ON SKIERS

Effects of hypoxia were noted in the Australian Winter Olympic Team during the first two weeks of their pre-Olympic training in Europe, despite their extensive physical and technical training in Australia before travelling overseas. This was one of the reasons for their lengthy pre-Olympic training at those altitudes. Recreational skiers, with less preparation and knowledge, expose themselves to even greater risks of ski trauma.

When an individual travels from sea level to 3,000 m in a short time, some degree of mountain sickness will often occur. Although the effects of lowered O_2 pressure vary with individuals, most persons experience some breathlessness, palpitations, headache, nausea, fatigue, and/or impairment of most mental processes. Over a course of several days, the symptoms diminish and ultimately disappear, although maximum physical capacity remains reduced until acclimatization is complete. This takes approximately two weeks, depending on the altitude.

During their acclimatization period, some members of this Olympic team felt that they had lost fitness, and they therefore lost confidence; some even became depressed. It should be explained to skiers and to the officials that this passing phase will disappear with acclimatization. As the effect of low O_2 pressure is not great for the first minute, skiers should initially limit their runs to this short time, because it is when the muscles' demand for oxygen increases that trouble begins. The skier should also be given emotional support.

During this period, the coach may arrange soccer matches or swimming at the lower altitude to maintain the endurance capacity that the skiers had acquired at home; however, visits to lower altitudes must be brief if acclimatization is to be achieved.

Does lowered O_2 pressure contribute significantly to ski trauma? The effects of hypoxia on the unacclimatized skier should be considered. Two of the most important factors are decreased mental proficiency for achieving discrete motor movements and memory. At approximately 3,000 m, a skier's mental proficiency may decrease to 20% below normal.

Very active muscles may extract almost all the oxygen brought to them in the arterial blood, hence hypoxia. The fundamental purpose of respiration is to supply the cells of the body with the oxygen they require and to remove the carbon dioxide they produce. Failure to do these two things will contribute to muscle fatigue, both in the muscles themselves and through the nervous system controlling the muscles. The lactic acid concentration in the muscles will increase. It is reasonable to assume that these factors will contribute to accidents.

Of course, the effects of hypoxia vary with individuals. Despite these variations, the unacclimatized skier or mountain climber who remains at an altitude of 4,500 m for one hour will find his mental proficiency has fallen approximately 50% below normal, and his ability to perform feats of physical endurance will be greatly impaired.

Figure 1 applies this physiological data to the mountains around Aspen, Colorado. Even in the town of Aspen with an altitude of approximately 2,400 m, pulmonary ventilation increases. At Buttermilk Mountain, 3,000 m, the barometric pressure has fallen to 563 mm Hg. The O_2 pressure remains approximately 20% of the barometric pressure, regardless of altitude. When the O_2 pressure in the atmosphere decreases at higher elevations, a decrease in alveolar O_2 pressure (i.e., in the lungs) occurs. At lower elevations, the O_2 pressure of the alveoli and of the blood can decrease, but, by hyperventilation, the body can keep up the O_2 supply to the tissues, despite the lower O_2 pressure. In addition, the S shape of the association-dissociation curve for hemoglobin is such that small changes in Po_2 do not greatly affect the amount of O_2 bound to hemoglobin. When the arterial oxygen saturation has fallen to approximately 93%, this also induces changes in the CO_2 pressure in the blood.

In the Aspen Highlands and Aspen Mountain area (3,600 m), the

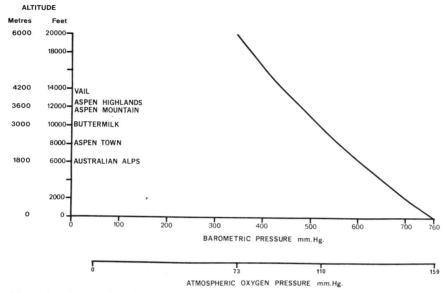

Figure 1. Barometric and atmospheric oxygen pressures in the Australian Alps and in the vicinity of Aspen, Colorado.

unacclimatized skier encounters drowsiness, lassitude, mental fatigue, occasional nausea, occasional headache, euphoria, sleeplessness, and lack of appetite. Mental proficiency may decrease to 20% below its normal level, if the skier is exposed for a lengthy period, and maximum physical capacity remains reduced for several days. If the barometric pressure drops to 483 mm Hg, as when the unacclimatized athlete is skiing Vail (4,500 m), mental proficiency may drop 50% within an hour.

ACCLIMATIZATION

Five principal means by which acclimatization comes about are:

1. Increased pulmonary ventilation
2. Increased hemoglobin in the blood
3. Increased diffused capacity of the lungs
4. Increased vascularity of the tissues
5. Increased ability of the cells to ultilize oxygen, despite the low O_2 pressure

Increased pulmonary ventilation results directly from the lowered O_2 pressure. One important feature of increased ventilation is that the

Table 1. Ski areas at different altitudes and the effects of hypoxia on unacclimatized skiers

4,500 m (15,000 ft)	VAIL			
	The unacclimatized skier should exercise extreme care at this altitude—mental proficiency may have fallen 50% below normal within 1 hour.			
3,600 m (12,000 ft)	ASPEN HIGHLANDS			
	Vertical decent	1,158 m	Advanced	25%
			Intermediate	50%
	Longest Run	5.64 km	Beginners	25%
	ASPEN MOUNTAIN			
	Vertical Descent	1,005 m	Advanced	75%
			Intermediate	25%
	Longest Run	4.83 km	Beginners	00%
	The unacclimatized skier encounters drowsiness, lassitude, and mental fatigue. Mental proficiency may decrease 20% if the skier is exposed for a lengthy period. Maximum physical capacity remains reduced for several days.			
3,000 m (10,000 ft)	BUTTERMILK			
	Vertical Descent	610 m	Advanced	18%
			Intermediate	44%
	Longest Run	3.2 km	Beginners	38%
	Although the effects of lowered oxygen pressure vary with individuals, most will experience some symptoms at this altitude—particularly increased pulmonary ventilation.			

pH of the body changes as a result of the hyperventilation blowing off carbon dioxide. During acclimatization this effect disappears and, although ventilation remains high, the pH returns to normal.

Hypoxia is the principal stimulus to an increase in red blood cell production and thereby an increase in O_2-carrying capacity of blood above what it would otherwise be at a given altitude. The amount of oxygen that is physically dissolved in the blood is directly proportional to the O_2 pressure of the blood, as is the amount of O_2 combined to hemoglobin in the blood. Therefore, lowering the O_2 pressure of the blood decreases the combination of oxygen and hemoglobin and, thereby, the total amount of O_2 carried in the blood.

Another feature of acclimatization is an increase in myoglobin, another O_2-carrying protein in muscle that gives up its O_2 at lower O_2 pressure levels. Myoglobin is therefore important in sustained muscular work. The increase in hemoglobin and myoglobin is slow, however, having little or no effect for the first two weeks of acclimatization. Increased vascularity occurs only with months of exposure to low O_2 pressure.

CONCLUSIONS

The skier should arrive at the mountain physically fit, should avoid excessive activity, excessive fatigue, and excessive alcohol, and, if experiencing the effects of mountain sickness, should begin by skiing the slopes below 2,438 m, and gradually increase altitude and duration of skiing periods.

Table 1 will help the unacclimatized skier select the slope most suitable for his state of fitness and skiing ability.

Results of Experimental
Heart Blunt Injury Studies

N. Dekleva

The concept of modern traumatology can be considered within the growing reference frame of interdisciplinary science. The types of trauma observed become more bizarre, the medical treatment required more complicated. Intensive experimental work is needed to explain biological phenomena that originate as consequences of physical force.

This study seeks solutions for the treatment of extensive and complicated injuries to the thorax caused by impact. Myocardiopathic stress becomes an important and often occurring consequence of trauma. After blunt and closed thoracic trauma, the injured person becomes a cardiac patient within a year or so. After treatment of the injury, the patient doesn't seem to be a coronary case because, except for subjective sensations, there are no visible clinical signs of distress. The ECG exhibits no outstanding changes, yet the seemingly inexplicable deaths of these patients have many real causes.

A number of research studies have shown that physiological and biochemical changes in the mammalian heart occurring during acceleration stress are localized in the cardiac cells. Animals of the *Macaccus circopitecus* species were used for the experimental work. They weighed from five to six kilograms, and were anesthetized with Nembuthal injected interperitoneally in standard dosages. All the animals were of the same sex and approximately the same age, and none were given special food while the experiment was being prepared. Ingestion of water was not limited.

The acceleration was accomplished on a ramp that was so constructed that the time unit and the acceleration value were equal.

Acceleration was measured using an accelerometer. Measurements of impact were taken by accelerometers fixed to the ramp chair and to the animal's thorax, pelvis, and lower extremities. An electromeasuring system was also used.

The impact values ranged from 10–20 G/sec. The ECG was taken during the interval between anesthetization and impact. Radiographic procedures were conducted to determine changes in the bones of the thorax, spine, and skull. Then an autopsy was performed. If the animal had sustained a fractured bone, it was not used for the thoracic blunt trauma analysis.

Macroscopic changes in organs were observed for 3 hours at 2-minute intervals after the experimentally caused trauma. Some of the observed macroscopic changes were that positive accelerations led to displacement of the heart similar to caudal dislocation, while deceleration resulted in cranial dislocations. In previous observations of these phenomena, the former were found to cause arrythmia more often than the latter. The rhythmic changes are the results of cardiac hypoxidoses, hypoxia, or ischemia. The cardiac lesion is the result of an oxygen deficit and mechanical lesions. This is not the case if multiaxial or uniaxial forces are concerned and if the multiaxial differential acceleration occurs unexpectedly. Special care has been taken in the study to detect the type of stressful situation the animal has been exposed to at impact.

The purpose of the investigation was to study injuries of cardiac muscle that resulted from impact. When impact did not cause bone fracture, this was accomplished through the use of the accelerating ramp that could direct the force to the thorax. A correlation was found between the microscopic sections and the pathological findings on the ECG record when an autopsy was performed immediately after trauma.

Morphological analysis of the ECG record showed no changes except for the bradycardia observed after each impact exceeding 10 G/sec. In records exhibiting a high value, and in cases in which moment of impact coincided with ventricular systole, the anemysied, bleak areas of the left ventricular walls could be observed macroscopically. Since the animals were sacrificed, these bleak areas could be examined in situ as they slowly contracted. Contraction was not completed, however, because minimal anemised parts remained that separated the hearts from the surrounding areas. This is presumed to have been the punctum maximum of the effect of the physical force.

Bradycardia persisted on the ECG record during the toracotomy and pericardiectomy. Longitudinal and transverse tissue samples, to be studied under light and electron microscopes, were taken from the anemised zone on which the force had been directed.

No histological changes were observed in transections studied with light microscopy. Localized changes characterized by discontinuities of the Purkinje cells in the endocardium were observed in some transections. Occasionally, myocitic necrosis was observed. The literature indicates that myofibrillar degeneration, characterized by the hypercontraction of a given region with simultaneous loss of normal striated myocardial cells, can be found in addition to the formation of dense fuksifibril bands of condensed contractile proteins. These have not been observed in this experiment.

Larger lesions were observed in the ultrastructures of the myofibrils. Changes have been related to the nuclear chromatin distribution, to changes of the mitochondria, to the thinning of the Z disc, and to the concentration and precipitation of contractile proteins. Irregular distensions of the sarcoplasmic reticulum were evident from electron microscope analysis.

In addition to the aforementioned changes, morphological changes of the mitochondria were observed. Crystalline structure of the mitochondria of necrotic cells was not observed in the transections taken 30 minutes after trauma.

The transverse transections used in the electron microscope analyses are characterized by changes in the Z zone, the transversal portion, and the intercolating disc that show that detached actin filaments of dense material can be found near the cell membrane. Mitochondrial changes involved a discontinuity of the number of sarcomere fibrils. Some sarcomeres contain groups of mitochondria. The mitochondria occupy 35% of the total volume of the cardiac muscle cells and are the primary source of energy (ATP) under normal conditions. Specific functional changes within the mitochondria are reflected in changes connected with the oxygen deficit.

From a morphological point of view, ultrastructural changes are somewhat similar to catecholamin toxicity and to a certain degree unlike ischemia. Mitochondrial respiration and calcium transport activity increase significantly within 1–2 hours after trauma (the acceleration stress) and are possibly the result of some humoral factor or substance that changes the active intercellular processes. Perhaps the increased mitochondrial activity was caused autonomically, by catecholamine. The speed of the cyclic (AMP) activation changes the course of the intercellular calcium transport. The literature claims that there is an increase of adenosine-nucleotide synthesis during the beta-adrenergic stimulation of the heart, and that there is a decrease in the concentration of adenosine-nucleotides during adrenergic stimulation of the heart. Furthermore, these changes in the intracellular concentration of adenosine-nucleotide affect mitochondrial processes.

The functional importance of the increase in intracellular energy output and its role in the calcium transport mechanisms in response to acceleration stress is not clear at this time. It is difficult to determine the causative factors of changes in mitochondrial behavior. Perhaps the acceleration of the mechanical damage to the heart wall, the compression, and the comparatively high hydrostatic pressure occurring in these situations (measured during the actual experiment) are causative factors because nuclear fragmentations and mitochondrial conglutination in the Z zone are observed. Nevertheless, it can be said that the cause of these changes remains unknown.

The heart is extremely vulnerable to constant acceleration, as well as to acceleration stress. It is very difficult to find an adequate model to study pathology of this kind. Experiments using the *Macaccus circopitecus* monkeys indicate that the ultrastructural changes are a result of anoxia, an effect of the applied force. One consequence of this force is endocardial microhemorrhage that worsens in relation to the strength of the cardiac contraction and the ventricular volume of systole. Subendocardial hemorrhage is direct and is detected with difficulty. When detected, it begins in the endocardium and deepens: this depicts traumatic etiology. Bradycardia has been found in all cases clinically and on the ECG. Myocardiopathic stress or myocardiopathia traumatica is related to hemorrhage quantitatively and qualitatively; it represents a lesion with a different and complex etiology, and it has many causes, including hypoxia and ischemia.

The importance of these changes in humans has not been examined nor identified. However, experimental evidence collected on animals has shown that stress can cause fatal cardiopathologies. In fact, the point of origin and the evolution of the syndrome remain a mystery. Fatalities occurring well after the accident can be attributed to this syndrome. At first, the fatalities seem to have no explanation, but if more were known, these deaths could be qualified in cardiological terms and attributed to this group of injuries. These deaths, then, represent the evolution of pathological changes that have been allowed to develop over time. The deaths are really the result of the mystery that enshrouds these types of injuries.

Behavior of Blood Flow in Accidental Hypothermia and Trauma

P. Krueger, G. W. Prokscha, T. Wagner, and G. Blümel

Blood differs from normal "Newtonian fluids," whose viscosity is a linear function of sheer stress and rate. The causes of this pseudoplastic (nonideal plastic) flow behavior are referred to as "abnormal flow behavior" by Schmid-Schönbein et al. (1973). They include:

1. Blood viscosity
2. Plasma viscosity
3. Aggregation of red blood cells
4. Deformability of red blood cells

These four parameters are influenced by several factors, including:

1. Hematocrit
2. Fibrinogen content
3. State of blood vessels
4. Environmental influences (e.g., temperature)
5. Chemical influences (e.g., acidose)

These factors are correlated to accidental hypothermia and concomitant trauma. Several authors (e.g., Rand et al., 1962; Merrill et al., 1963) have shown that, rheologically, blood is altered the most at low sheer rates. It seems therefore that microcirculation is involved and is influenced by perfusion pressure and flow resistance. The viscosity of the blood and the plasma is directly proportional to the resistance of flow.

How can the viscosity of blood be determined? In rabbits and rats, in vivo determinations of the flow rate by means of intravital microscopy at the mesentery are possible. The present study includes an investigation of this type using laboratory animals. The results, however, are not conclusive because the surgical procedure may falsify the effects. The isolated cooling of several portions of blood vessels, proposed by Hess, does not necessarily lead to the alterations seen under general hypothermia; therefore, only in vitro methods were used.

Rabbits were used in the experiments. Hypothermia was achieved in a cooling box with a temperature of 4°C. Trauma was caused by a multiple fracture of the femur. Arterial blood was withdrawn, and either heparinized or diluted (with sodium citrate) in order to avoid in vitro coagulation. Blood was measured using the Brookfield-Viscosimeter LTV that was modified by Schobein. The box was kept at the core temperature during the experiment.

Under normo-thermic circumstances, the viscosity of whole blood of victims in shock was reduced by approximately 10%. As the hematocrit (HK) was decreased by 11% following trauma, viscosity in vivo decreased even more (Figure 1).

The blood viscosity during hypothermia tends to increase. Under the environmental condition, the viscosity of whole blood at low sheer rate increases by more than 50%. At higher flow rates the viscosity increases by at least 30%. The viscosity also increased in the control animals (Figure 2). The difference observed in the injured animals is always significantly lower.

BLOOD – VISCOSITY

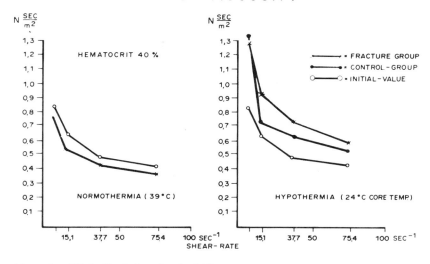

Figure 1.   Whole blood viscosity of rabbits.

BLOOD- VISCOSITY

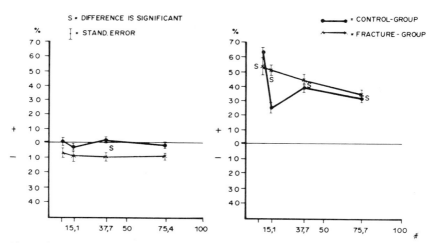

Figure 2. Whole blood viscosity of rabbits. *Left*, normothermia; *right*, hypothermia. Variation in percent.

What are the causes of this increase in viscosity? Apparent viscosity, which is the ratio of the viscosity of whole blood to the viscosity of plasma, was found to increase significantly in hypothermia and especially in traumatized animals. This increase in the apparent viscosity can be partly explained by the simultaneous increase of plasma viscosity.

According to Chien (1970), increase of apparent viscosity, especially low flow rates, causes an augmented aggregation of red blood cells. The problem, however, is more complex. Under normal thermal conditions, viscosity decreases in traumatized animals at an HK of 40%. In these cases, both the trauma and the control groups behaved alike in terms of the apparent viscosity. Under hypothermic conditions, all animals showed an increase of viscosity that was caused by an augmented aggregation of red blood cells and was enlarged with three-dimensional structures. The in vivo findings included the following: the HK in control animals increases by 6% under hypothermal conditions, and the viscosity must increase also. Rand et al. (1962) state that this increase is approximately 2 centipoise, a finding that corresponds to that in traumatized animals.

Traumatized and cooled animals show a decrease in HK of 11%. In comparison with the control animals, this decrease is 17% because of a prolonged bleeding that is documented in the thrombelastrogram (TEG). The constant of thromboplastin and the constant of thrombin are significantly prolonged because of hypocoagulability (Figure 3). In traumas under hypothermia conditions, more blood is lost and HK is decreasing.

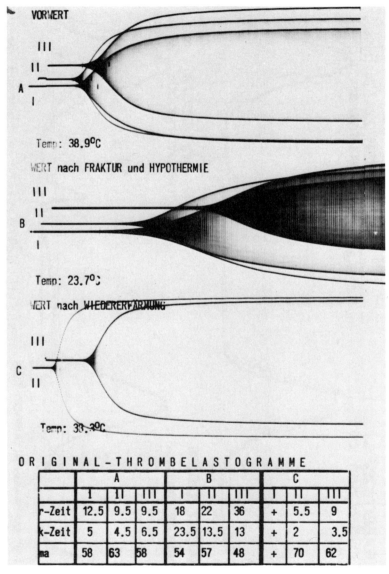

	A			B			C		
	I	II	III	I	II	III	I	II	III
r-Zeit	12.5	9.5	9.5	18	22	36	+	5.5	9
k-Zeit	5	4.5	6.5	23.5	13.5	13	+	2	3.5
ma	58	63	58	54	57	48	+	70	62

Figure 3.   Thrombelastrogram (TEG) of rabbits. A = initial value, B = hypothermia and trauma, C = rewarming. I-III = 3 different animals measured at the same time.

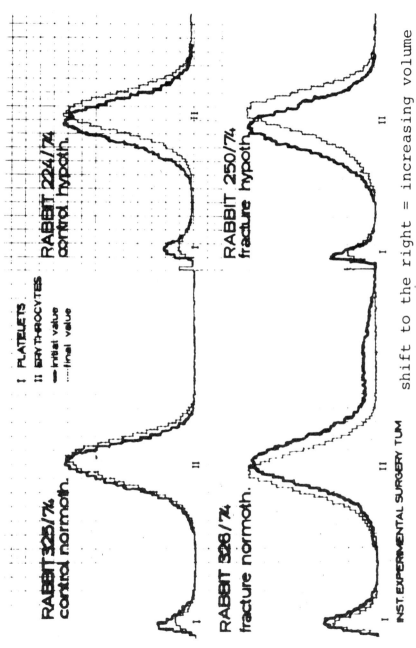

Figure 4.   Erythrocyte volume of rabbits, measured with a particle-volume analysator.

The increase of viscosity is not caused by augmented aggregation alone, because each red blood cell and its flow pattern is altered. The volume of red blood cells was measured and found to increase in traumatized animals (Figure 4). This increase causes a change of cell surface in relation to cell volume, which means that the erythrocytes become larger.

These experiments under hypothermic conditions were not pure in vitro experiments as were those of Schmid-Schönbein and coworkers (1973), Merrill et al. (1963), Bergentz et al. (1963), and Rand et al. (1962); hence, additional factors were determined. Blood gases were analyzed and a pH decrease from 7.9 to 7.2 was observed in the traumatized animals under conditions of hypothermia. This increased H^+ ion concentration most likely causes the decrease of deformability. In his experiments, Schmid-Schönbein et al. (1973) reported a significant increase in viscosity of rigid red blood cells. The process of passing red blood cells through micropore filters in order to measure deformability is not sufficiently reproducable, and probably of little value.

How can the increase of viscosity and the microcirculation be influenced by therapeutic methods?

1. Dilution of plasma in order to impede aggregation
2. Restoration of normal body temperature, because it has been shown that the viscosity normalizes following rewarming
3. Buffering acidose with sodium bicarbonate and Tris.
4. Substitute lost electrolytes, especially potassium, in order to balance intra- and extracellular fluid.

REFERENCES

Bergentz, S. E., Gelm, L. E., Rudenstam, C. M., and Zederfeldt, B. 1963. The viscosity of whole blood in trauma. Acta Chir. Scand. 126:289–293.

Hess, H. 1977. Veranderungen an der Gefäss-iunen Wand aus de Serie Alpinmedizin. (Variations in the inner walls of the Vascular muscles from the series on Alpine medicine.) Arztliche Praxis 16:753.

Chien, S. 1970. Shear dependence of effective overall volume as a determinant of blood viscosity. Science 168:977–989.

Krueger, P. 1975. Trauma und hypothermie. Habilitationsschrift. Technische Universität, München.

Merrill, E., Gilliland, E. R., Cokelet, G., Shin, H., Britten, A., and Wells, R. E. 1963. Rheology of human blood, near and at zero flow. Biophysical J. 3:199–213.

Rand, W. P., Lacombe, E., Hunt, E. H., and Austin, W. H. 1962. Viscosity of normal blood under normothermic and hypothermic conditions. I. Appl. Physiol. 19(1):117–122.

Schmid-Schönbein, H., Klose, H. J., Volger, E., and Weiss, I. 1973. Hypothermia and blood flow behaviour. Res. Exp. Med. 161:58–68.

Telemetry in Alpine Skiing

C-M. Grimm, H. Krexa, and E. Asang

Sports traumatology is faced with an increasing number of skiing injuries. The interpretation of these traumas and their injury mechanisms requires biomechanic research on the injury limits of the leg. It also requires basic biomechanics research in Alpine skiing itself, uphill and downhill.

To measure action, reaction, force, and torque, electromyography (EMG) and electrodynamography were used. In preparation for field tests, laboratory methods were developed for recording these data continuously and simultaneously, static-free and reproducable, transmitted by a telemetric set. For the electrodynamogram, use was made of the technique and the results reported by Wittmann, a member of the research team in Munich. The dynamograms were gathered using five strain gauge force transducers placed between ski and binding elements for the boot top, the ball of the foot, and the heel. These gauges measured force and torque in horizontal and vertical directions.

Analysis of the dynamograms gathered in Alpine skiing revealed the following:

1. Steering forces as slow spikes ranging up to a maximum of 0.1 sec
2. Disturbing forces as high, frequently occurring spikes ranging up to a maximum of 0.1 sec—they added themselves to the steering forces. (Figure 1).

The steering forces depend on the individual way of skiing, on the temperature and consistency of the snow, and on the terrain. The disturbing forces are primarily caused by the slope condition and were, therefore, exceptionally high when slopes were icy and at high speeds.

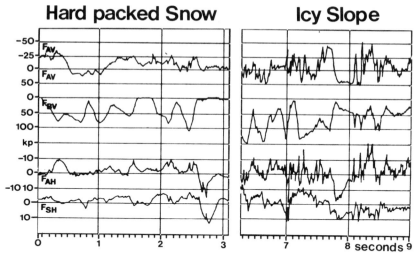

Figure 1. Dynamograms of downhill skiing in smooth snow (*left*) and on an icy slope (*right*).

The statistical evaluation was achieved by the principle of cumulative frequency analysis, which in certain terrain and snow conditions shows a typical curve pattern of the measured forces. It is this recognizable pattern that permits display of the influence of various ground and snow conditions, skiing styles, and test persons.

For practical protection in Alpine skiing, the retention forces that help to avoid inadvertent release of bindings were established. The upper release limit depends on the loading capacity of the bone—the injury threshold. Any safe binding adjustment has to be between these two limits.

For the electromyogram, a series of preliminary laboratory tests had to be done. First, a new method of registering EMG's had to be developed because the commonly used needle or wire electrodes did not fit our purpose.

Bipolar integral action potentials of each investigated muscle group were achieved by using skin electrodes. For this research four muscle groups that are important in Alpine skiing were chosen:

> —adductor muscle groups
> —quadriceps femoris muscle
> —tricep surae muscle
> —tibialis anterior muscle

The action potentials of these muscle groups recorded with various electrode positions had to be determined and analyzed systematically.

EMG amplitudes were found to be dependent on the electrode positions relating to topography, muscle fiber and distance. In general good results could be achieved when:

—the electrodes were placed parallel or transverse to the muscle fiber
—the electrode's distance lies between 3 cm and 9 cm, depending on the muscle's dimension
—the electrodes were placed at the distal transition of muscle to tendon

Under the same test conditions and with identical electrode positions, individual characteristics were found in the EMG of each tested muscle. Based on these individual characteristics even a quantitative analysis of electromyographic data could be done, as this chapter shows.

For comparison of the active torsional and heel-tension forces of the human leg, those movements typical for Alpine skiing were recorded and analyzed in laboratory tests. The following relationships were found between muscle force and the characteristics of an individual. There is:

—a direct relation between stature and maximal developed muscle-force (MDF)
—a direct relation of weight to MDF up to 75–80 kg. (beyond that weight, it was inversely proportional)
—a direct relation of age to MDF, but beyond the age of 30, a significant decrease of the MDF was found.
—a direct relation between the circumferences of thigh and calf and the MDF.
—a direct relation of the diameter of the tibia head and the ankle to MDF
—no relation between leg length and MDF

Analysis of the electromyograms of the investigated leg's muscle, and the dynamograms of the tension forces, achieved the following results:

—the mean tension forces were four times greater than the rotational forces
—in dynamic tests showed a higher rate of rotation and tension forces than in quasistatic tests: within the 0.1-sec range, there was an increase of the developed forces of 10.5 to 33.5%; and within the 0.01-sec range, there was an increase of 28.1 to 63.9% (comparing dynamic and quasistatic conducted tests)
—the ratio derived from heel-tension force to rotation force, and the rating of EMG amplitudes of corresponding muscles, allows a

conclusion to be drawn about the training condition of the test person
—during analysis of the EMGs and dynamograms by cumulative frequency analysis, the following relationships were discovered:

1. A linear relationship between EMG amplitude of a tested muscle and its corresponding force
2. An exponential dependence between irritation frequency of the tested muscle and its corresponding force

Based on these laboratory findings, it was possible to record the following in field tests while skiing:

—active and passive forces between ski and binding
—action potentials of the leg's most important muscle groups
—mutual effects between muscle actions and reactions

For the electromyogram, a method had to be found permitting a statistical analysis. One approach was to make a summary of statements regarding muscle activities and forces during downhill skiing, which contains various movements. For the following investigations, six different skiing styles were selected and evaluated in a total of 122 skiing tests. The six ski styles analyzed were the herringbone step, side step, snow plow turn, stem turn, stem swing, and parallel swing.

Significant differences in the EMG diagrams can occur in the activity of one muscle in different skiing styles or in the activity of different muscles in one skiing style. The activity of the tibialis ant. muscle is great in comparison with the amplitude of the quadriceps femoris muscle, whose performance capacity is much higher. It is therefore wrong to assume that a comparison of the amplitudes of two different muscles can determine their capacities.

The adductor muscle group closes the skis and keeps them closed. This explains the high activity of this muscle group at the end of snow plow turns with a final swing, while the steadily high activity during the parallel swing is the result of the closed skiing style being emphasized.

The reason for the minor electric activity of the triceps surae muscle in all styles is the lack of use of this muscle during skiing. It usually becomes passively strained by a tensile stretch. Action potentials are therefore mainly expressions of isometric contractions (Figure 2).

To make use of these numerous investigations, a new method of evaluation was needed, one that permits statistically developed statements. For analysis of the EMG, the technique of cumulative frequency analysis was chosen.

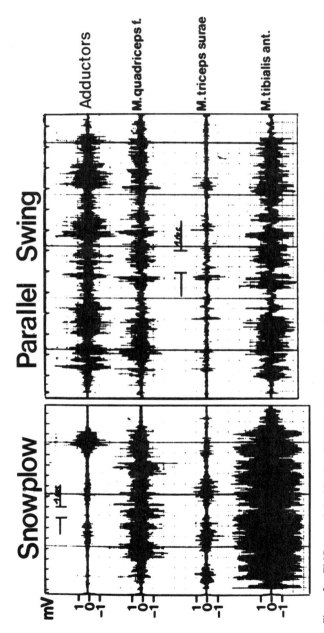

Figure 2.   EMGs recorded while downhill skiing. *Left:* Four snow plow turns. *Right:* Five parallel swings.

Two parameters derived from the muscle physiology determine the diagram of the integral action potentials exactly: the amplitude, representing the number of stimulated motor units, and the frequency, representing incoming neural impulses. With this technique, the amplitudes of the respective integral action potentials are classified according to amplitude and frequency. From a semilogarithmic plot of the test results, statements can be made regarding medium stimulation frequency as well as amplitude characteristics.

The summit of the curve gives the medium stimulation frequency of the investigated muscle. The opening angle of the curve is a scale of comparison for the amplitude characteristic, i.e., for the numerical relation of small to large spikes that are recorded during the test (Figure 3).

As expected, under the same test conditions the same cumulative frequency distribution curve appears. The many types of evaluations can therefore be illustrated by one represetative curve if the following conditions prevail:

—the test conditions must be identical
—the electromyogram must not show any major artifacts
—the difference between the opening angle and the frequency values
    of each test must not be greater than 10%

It should be noted that by consolidation of the vertex in one point an average frequency results. This frequency must not be accepted unconditionally because the stimulation frequency also represents a possibility of the muscle changing its capacity.

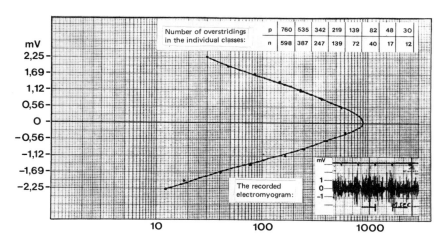

| Number of overstridings in the individual classes: | p | 760 | 535 | 342 | 219 | 139 | 82 | 48 | 30 |
| | n | 598 | 387 | 247 | 139 | 72 | 40 | 17 | 12 |

Figure 3.   Example of a cumulative frequency curve of an EMG.

With this developed method, representative cumulative frequency distribution curves were established with special dependence on proband, muscle group, and style of skiing. An investigation of relationships between the established cumulative frequency analysis and the respectively used muscle energy is not available. An analysis of the existing results can therefore include only comparisons of the recorded data, such as amplitude and frequency.

For all six skiing styles, the opening angles of the representative cumulative frequency distribution curves are compiled in a graph along with the medium frequency values of the four investigated muscle groups. The results confirm the relationships that are based on biomechanical analysis (Figure 4).

The adductor muscle group showed increasing amplitudes and frequencies going from the herringbone step to the parallel swing. This is evidently because the latter style requires keeping the skis close together.

Although the opening angle of the quadriceps femoris muscle is the same for both snow plow turn and parallel swing, it is established that the snow plow turn is the more strenuous style for this muscle because the frequency value when compared with the parallel swing is increased by 25%.

In Alpine skiing, the triceps surae muscle is strained passively only. Through stretching, a tensile force is created that in this case is the greatest in the snow plow swing. The electric activity of the tibialis ant. muscle where it reaches its maximum is very clearly expressed during the snow plow turn.

It must not be assumed from these evaluations that the strain of the muscles will be the same for every skiing style. For equal body constructions, it will be possible to define muscular activity that will be the same for the advanced skier when extended to his extreme as for the beginner who is struggling with the stem turn.

Furthermore, with knowledge of the individual characteristics of the electromyographic signals of a muscle, this method of analysis permits quantification of the integral action potential of single muscle groups by means of skin electrodes. Hence the relationship between muscle activity and the resulting forces is based on a specific scale of measurement even in dynamic sequences of movements.

To check the reliability and validity of the developed analyzing method, dynamographic and electromyographic data were transmitted simultaneously and recorded. Therefore, the relationship between activity of a certain group of muscles and the resulting energy can be established immediately (Figure 5).

The single analysis permits a detailed breakdown of the sequence

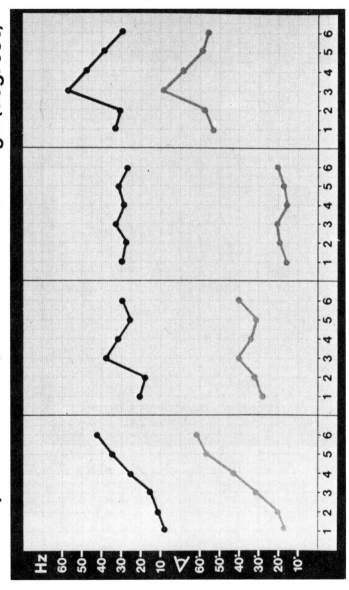

Frequencies(Hertz) and Total Vertex Angle(degrees)

Adductors   M.quadriceps   M. triceps surae   M. tibialis
femoris   anterior

Figure 4.   The graph shows the opening angle and the medium frequency of the four investigated muscles in six different skiing styles. 1: Herring bone step; 2: Side step; 3: Snow plow turn; 4: Stem turn; 5: Stem turn swing; 6: Parallel swing.

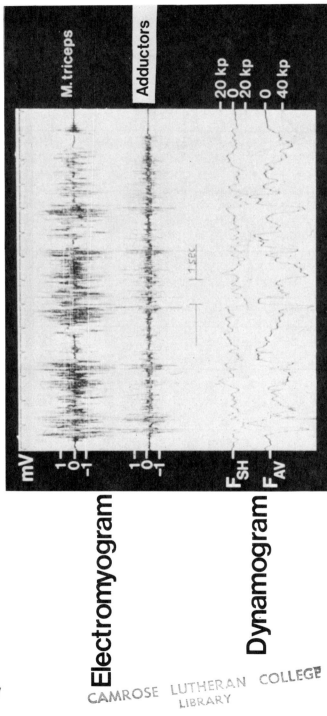

Figure 5.   Synchronized EMG and dynamogram of downhill skiing in parallel swing. F$_{SH}$: Forces in vertical direction at the boot top; F$_{AV}$: Forces in vertical direction at the heel.

of movements. In this way it is possible to determine the latent period, which is the time between commencing muscle activity and commencing movement. The action of the quadriceps femoris muscle results in a latent period of less than 0.2 sec. The muscle's reaction can also be determined under the influence of forces and thrusts. Statistical evaluation of the simultaneously recorded EMGs and dynamograms shows, as expected, a direct relationship between the activity of a muscle and the size of its respective force.

This method, developed for simultaneous recording and analysis of surface electromyography and dynamography, may also be applied to other sports. It could be of special interest for those disciplines not allowing direct mechanical control of training conditions and effects.